A Political Sociology
of Educational Reform
Power/Knowledge in
Teaching, Teacher Education, and Research

A Political Sociology of Educational Reform

*Power/Knowledge in
Teaching, Teacher Education, and Research*

THOMAS S. POPKEWITZ

Teachers College, Columbia University
New York and London

Published by Teachers College Press, 1234 Amsterdam Avenue
New York, NY 10027

Library of Congress Cataloging-in-Publication Data

Popkewitz, Thomas S.
    A political sociology of educational reform : power/knowledge in
teaching, teacher education, and research / Thomas S. Popkewitz.
        p.   cm.
    Includes bibliographical references and index.
    ISBN 0-8077-3091-2.—ISBN 0-8077-3090-4 (pbk.)
    1. Education—Social aspects—United States.   2. Educational
change—United States.   3. Educational change—United States
—History.   4. Higher education and state—United States—History.
5. Teachers—Training of—United States.   I. Title.
LC191.4.P66   1991
370.19—dc20   91-11444
                                                                              CIP

ISBN 0–8077–3091–2
ISBN 0–8077–3090–4 (pbk).

Printed on acid-free paper
Manufactured in the United States of America

98 97 96 95 94 93 92 91   8 7 6 5 4 3 2 1

To Adam and Ian,
who knew to look for me in the study
as I struggled with the writing of this book,

and to Marilyn, my dear sister

Contents

vii

Acknowledgments

As I have worked on these chapters, a number of people have reacted to different parts of the manuscript and have challenged me on a number of issues. Without correcting all that they noticed or responding to all that they challenged, I wish to thank them: Berit Askling, Marie Brennan, Donald Broady, Pat Burdell, Catherine Cornbleth, Jay Cradle, Tomas Englund, Sigbrit Franke-Wikberg, Barry Franklin, Kerry Freedman, Jennifer Gore, Jody Hall, David Hamilton, Ingólfur Jóhannesson, Markay Kerr, David Labaree, Jim Ladwig, Sverker Lindblad, Henry St. Maurice, Jim Middleton, Evanthia Milingou, Sigurjón Mýrdal, B. F. Nel, Fazil Rizvi, Wendy Sterne, Lynda Stone, Ahmad Sultan, Carlos Torres, Geoff Whitty, colleagues who spent the semester with me at the Swedish Collegium for Advanced Study in the Social Sciences, members of the Cultural Production and Reproduction Research Group at the Stockholm Institute of Education, and members of the Department of Educational Research at Uppsala University. The conversations I had with Cleo Cherryholmes as he was writing his book subsequently helped me in pursuing certain issues of post-structural thought. I appreciate talks with Miguel Pereyra, whose library on social theory and history I worked through as I was writing the final revision. The discussions with these various people and in various contexts are important to the construction of this text. I also wish to thank the University of Wisconsin Graduate School Research Committee for a summer grant that enabled me to pursue issues raised in Chapter 7. Finally, I need to acknowledge the patience, support, and help provided by Sally Lesher and Carol Newland as this manuscript was prepared.

Chapter 5 is a revision of an article originally published in the *Journal of Curriculum Studies* (1986, *18*(3), 267–284, ''Educational Reform and Its Millennial Quality: The 1980s,'' with A. Pitman and A. Barry). I appreciate the publisher's and co-authors' permissions to include this work. A section of Chapter 6 is drawn from discussions found in my article ''Institutional Issues in the Study of School Mathematics: Curriculum Research,'' in *Educational Studies in Mathematics Education* (1988, *19*, 221–249).

A Political Sociology of Educational Reform

Power/Knowledge in
Teaching, Teacher Education, and Research

Introduction

Much of contemporary analysis ignores the history of reform and takes as its rhetoric the definition of change. The "common sense" of reform is to assume that intervention is progress. A better world is to evolve as the result of new programs, new technologies, and new organizations that increase efficiency, economy, and effectiveness. Change is thought of as the introduction of some program or technology into a school district or classroom, as evidenced by use and/or people's feelings of satisfaction. The literature is replete with studies that identify the traits of the "successful" teacher or principal as a source of developing programs or as a model for the conversion of "others." In some instances, the program developers' perspectives are adopted to assess the degree to which reforms are accepted. At other times, theories of change give value to the perceptions and behavior of people who work in schools, assuming that the reasons, intent, and practices of those involved in reform determine the objective outcomes of reform and change. The focus is on the dramatic event, or the person and the technical notions of change.

While *reform* and *change* are used interchangeably in U.S. education, the words can be distinguished for analytic purposes. *Reform* is a word concerned with the mobilization of publics and with power relations in defining public space. *Change* has a meaning that is, at first glance, less normative and more "scientific" in outlook. The study of social change represents an effort to understand how tradition and transformations interact through processes of social production and reproduction. It is concerned with a confrontation between rupture from the past and what seems stable and "natural" in our social life. Further, and for the purposes of the discussion that follows, the confrontation between breaks and continuity of social change entails systematic attention to the relation of knowledge and power that structures our perceptions and organizes our social practices.

My notion of "scientific" should not be confused with certain posi-

1

tivist concerns with abstract rules and standards that are unrelated to social and historical conditions. My interest in a science of change involves a concern to give attention to systematic questions about our social affairs and to disciplined methods for deriving answers. To assert that *change* is a scientific term, in the broad sense of the meaning of scientific, is not to assume that it is value-free. Science cannot be assumed to be a suprahuman endeavor, separate from the affairs and social location of the scientists. As the discussion continually suggests, our conceptions of change are practices that establish priorities and positions for individuals in social relations. Further, theories in their nonpositivist sense embody the social forms of regulation and the production of social capabilities in the worlds that we inhabit. While I believe that the point of a social science of schooling is to provide theoretical statements about its social context and effect, these statements are historical rather than predictive and positive.

A QUESTION ABOUT SOCIAL REGULATION AND SOCIAL THEORY

The discussion of this book places reform in the social field of schooling and its ecology. It asks: What constitutes reform? What are its changing meanings over time? How are those meanings produced? The consideration of reform as an ecological phenomenon enables me to consider the arenas in which reform occurs and, at the same time, to pursue questions about the different relations of schooling and society over time. *Reform* is a word whose meaning changes as it is positioned within the transformations that have occurred in teaching, teacher education, education sciences, and curriculum theory since the late 19th century. It has no essential meaning or definition. Nor does reform signify progress, in any absolute sense, but it does entail a consideration of social and power relations.

My central thesis is that reform is best understood as a part of the process of social regulation. While it is not in vogue in many circles (as one historian said to me, "social control is a residue of the sociology of educational knowledge of the early 1970s"), the issue of control as a more general problem of power is still with us in theory as well as in the daily practices of institutional life. In contrast to the 1970s sociology of educational knowledge, which assumed global mechanisms of control, my concern is with how reform relates to the multiple layers of social affairs—from the organization of institutions to the self-discipline and organization of perception and experience by which individuals act.

must look at the power origins of power

I use the concept of social regulation rather than control to emphasize the active elements of power in socially producing and disciplining the capabilities of individuals. Further, I am interested in the specific and regional ways in which power affects and produces social relations, making less central questions about the ultimate origin of power, such as capitalism or industrialization.

even first

While I will deal further with this in the narrative of the book, here I want to note that most attention to power is concerned with how it limits and represses social practices. My concern is with how power is related to the knowledge that enables us to express personal desires, wants, bodily needs, and cognitive interests. It is the power by which we judge what is reasonable and good, what is irrational and bad; which practices to feel guilty about, and which are normal, or which are to be transgressed. By focusing on this notion of power, I incorporate current interest in discourse theories in order to consider the rules and standards of texts as a social practice. But I am also interested in the historical conditions in which certain speech prevails. The study of contemporary school reform practices entails placing particular events in schooling within a historical formation that presupposes relations of power/knowledge. Thus the focus is on historical conditions, institutional practices, and epistemologies, rather than on speech and the texts themselves.

The integration and relation of questions of power and its effects on school reform follow. The first chapter of the book provides a theoretical examination of some of the issues and problems associated with developing an adequate theory of school change. I focus on some of the issues that have engaged a strand of sociology in Europe and the United States about history, social structure, and particular events, but at the same time I conceptually focus the argument to respond to the practices of schooling as organizing and thereby regulating the production of knowledge.

In the historical analysis in Chapters 2 and 3, I focus on epistemology and institutional patterns—the general themes are drawn from studies that give attention to those in authority who defined the occupation. This perspective is dictated by the availability of sources that depict the way in which school leaders perceived the issues at hand. Until the organization of teachers into unions at the turn of the 20th century, there were few writings by teachers about their daily conduct in school and even fewer about issues of conflict and confrontation in their work. The discussion is documented through references to books and articles by historians. My contribution, in this instance, is conceptually organizing these findings to respond to the issues raised in this text. The history is not intended to provide a chronological history of events and people. In the later chapters (4–7) the period after World War II is considered, with major attention to the 1980s. The data shift to how social regulation is manifested at the various layers of school life as they interrelate with the state, drawing on the events and documents as monuments that stand to be interrogated.

I interpret school reform as concerning the relation of knowledge (epistemology), institutions, and power. At the same time, the focus concerns breaks and ruptures in social relations produced in epistemology and institutions. I am not concerned directly with individual actions or purpose, except as they relate to understanding collective patterns. I make this point in anticipation of the fact that some readers may be inclined to insert conceptions of progress and a teleology into the discussion. That is not my intent. I recognize my sense of play here, and its irony. The discussion should not be read as a theory about conspiracy. The analysis suggests that our factual descriptions are not the source of meaning but presuppose meaning. The problem of analysis is one of moving away from the search for a heroic figure (the great leader or the expert teacher), away from the influence of the instant and the dramatic in peoples' lives, and away from intent (the thought or volition of person[s]) as explanation. Following Durkheim's focus on the importance of the social, the collective, and the historical in forming communities, I believe the point of studying change is to bring the past into contact with the present in order to consider the relation of continuity, recurrence, and breaks in our social conditions.

LOCATING "ONE'S" LANGUAGE OF INTERPRETATION: THE RECEPTION OF TRADITIONS AND THE PRODUCTION OF IDEAS

The consideration of knowledge as located within institutional relations involves an elaboration and shift in my own work. I have become more concerned with the historical issues of structural relations that influence the everyday practices of schooling. My interest is to find a more historically bounded social science that can understand the intersection of multiple elements of time and space in studying problems of power. This interest has also required that I try to find more adequate ways of understanding the production of knowledge in schools.

In many ways, this study is indebted to Durkheimian sociology and the philosophical traditions of social epistemology developed primarily in French intellectual circles.[1] This French scholarship has helped me think about a number of important theoretical issues: social change that does not entail conceptions of progressive practices; the importance of epistemology as a method to consider social life; a method for study that moves the individual from the center of analysis and challenges the primacy given to the here and now; and strategies to focus on the relation of power and knowledge. The French historical tradition of the *Annales*, for example, considers patterns of thought as they intertwine with long-term changes in patterns of production and reproduction. The *Annales* tradition offered me entry into a way of thinking about the historical phenomena of schooling as interweaving epistemologies and material conditions. This historical tradition also provides an approach for considering "change" as social ruptures in ongoing patterns, rather than as an evolution or a chronology of events that seems inevitably or potentially progressive.

The work of Michel Foucault is important here when viewed in relation to the *Annales* tradition. A French historian, philosopher, and social theorist whose work is taken up in more detail in Chapter 1, Foucault explores historically the structural relations that are part of the organization of social life and of conceptions of self so that individuals engage in their own self-regulation. He visualizes change as ruptures, as does the *Annales* tradition, but differs in identifying the locus of its investigation. Whereas the *Annales* tradition is concerned with global changes across continents, Foucault focuses on regional, localized sites or spaces, such as prisons and asylums. He introduces the notion of power into the social-historical analysis, drawing upon Nietzsche as a way to overcome the conceptions of progress embedded in much contemporary scholarship. Foucault's studies of the relation of macro-patterns and micropatterns of governing also provide a way of introducing a notion of state into the arena of schooling. He does this without resorting to global explanations and theories but provides a way of maintaining an interest in particular institutional and social patterns. His work, I believe, supplies a central motif for historically considering school pedagogy: His historical conception of change (as regional, and breaks in epistemology) serves as an "anchor" to interpret the formations of mass schooling and pedagogy in the 19th century and reformulations that occur in current educational reforms.

The French sociologist Pierre Bourdieu complements and extends the previous scholarship by providing methods for the study of the social space in which epistemologies operate and of the patterns of social relations that constitute the field of social power—again, conceiving of power as relational. Whereas Foucault enables us to consider the relation of knowledge and power, Bourdieu offers conceptual strategies for focusing on social relations at a given time and on the manner in which sets of institutional relations coalesce to produce social distinctions and differences.

In thinking about the intersection and diversity of the different intellectual projects of others, I have continually confronted the problem of finding a language (or more correctly, an intellectual discourse) of my "own." That is, my long-term interest in problems of knowledge and power has been enriched, I believe, by recent translations of French social theory, history, and philosophy, which I introduce in Chapter 1 as a method of social epistemology. This corpus, while not singular, provides the theoretical potential for interpreting the ways in which reform is historically and sociologically constituted in contemporary practices of schooling. My intent, however, is not to look at these French scholars as authorities for my inquiries but to engage in a dialogue with them; to use them to provoke further questions about the organization of social affairs that respond to the themes underlying this work.

The finding of a language to respond to the phenomena scrutinized in this study, while taking into account the profound insights of the French social theorists, has not been easy. Let me briefly explore some of these difficulties through examples that are taken up more systematically in the discussion of the following chapters.

First, I recognize that there are different traditions within French sociology, philosophy, history, feminist analysis, and linguistic theory. They represent a variety of nuances in their epistemology as well as offering different concepts. To view Foucault's work in relation to the historical school of the *Annales* is to recognize that there is much debate and diversity in that historical school. There is also a need to recognize that French intellectual life is located in Paris—tied to an essayist tradition that is reinforced through the licensing of secondary schools—and that it exists in a highly selective, competitive, and structured system.

Second, the focus, assumptions, and concepts within a corpus of any author change over time. Foucault's notion of power shifts as he moves further away from the orientation to literary tradition in his earlier writing. Bourdieu's work is continually evolving; his analysis moves from earlier discussions about class to later arguments about social grouping, since he finds the former an inadequate concept for the changing relations that he empirically explores.

Third, these different traditions and their interrelation impose hazards to someone who "borrows" them. Much of the work that I find useful for the development of this study is contained in intellectual communities that exist in France and to some extent in Germany. Here I would mention the work of Jürgen Habermas, a German philosopher who is part of the Frankfurt School. Habermas has reworked Marxian social theory to provide insight into some of the pragmatic problems of change. These are most directly taken up in the last chapter. These continental traditions focus on the interplay of philosophy, history, and social theory, something that I find lacking in most U.S. social science.

But to draw upon these literatures is also to recognize that they exist within social fields that have power relations, internal dynamics, and self-checking mechanisms that are not always available to the outsider. Sometimes they fight among themselves about who has the most authoritative version of social theory; sometimes their work coheres. In reading the *Annales* literature, Bourdieu, or Foucault, one is aware that there are always the hidden audiences to which they respond as they write (see Bourdieu, 1988). The rules and invisible actors in the styles of arguing, including what is assumed by the scholars themselves, are not easily accessible to the outsider. For example, Foucault's claim that he is not a structuralist is, I believe, related to the French literary notion of structuralism found in his earlier work and to the French debates about Marxist analysis. Further, it is interesting that Foucault's work is indebted to the *Annales* tradition and to the French epistemological tradition in philosophy, but these are associations ignored in the context in which his work is received in the United States. He is located as part of a criticism associated with the literary tradition of post-structuralism, rather than in the more extended and elaborated French academic community of Durkheimian sociology and philosophy of science.

Fourth, I must mention the problem of language, that is, the ability to converse in the language in which the scholarship is written. I have sought to compensate for my lack of fluency in French, as best as possible, through seeking, wherever possible, to interact, in English, with members of the communities of scholars that I am reading and by exploring the traditions in which they work.

These examples point, I believe, to the difficulty encountered upon the reception of intellectual traditions that have been developed elsewhere. I hope that I have been sufficiently sensitive to these subtleties so as not to misappropriate ideas or concepts. But in seeking to understand the metatexts or paradigmatic relations of those whom I have found helpful in my work, my concern has not been with translations that assume fidelity. While I seek to understand the differences, at the same time I do not believe that written words have an independent life. My intent is to draw upon, integrate, and rework the epistemological questions and social theory *with* the phenomena under scrutiny. It is in this context that I referred earlier to "a language of my own."

In trying to conceptualize this study of change, I have also come to view efforts to tie science directly to social movements with greater skepticism than previously. This is important because both mainstream and critical traditions in education relate the production of knowledge to conceptions of progress that place research and the researcher in an authoritative social and cultural position. As I will discuss in the last chapter, it is a position of which I am leery, arguing for commitment yet also for some autonomy from social movements.

My contention here is that intellectual work always faces the problem of the relation of power and knowledge, but that the researchers must decenter the problem of social science from immediate social movements in order to regain a sense of themselves as critical historical actors. This stance is not to envision the researcher as a free-floating intellectual, unattached to social commitments and politics. Rather, I am taking a position that the politics of intellectual life lies in the distinction, categories, and visions that structure and are structuring social life. In fact, my purpose in focusing on knowledge as material practices is to decenter progress as an epistemology of educational research and therefore to enlarge the arenas of democratic practice and make it less likely that the researcher will consider himself or herself as a bearer of progress.

MULTIPLE "ORIGINS" OF THIS BOOK

Writing this book has been one of the most difficult intellectual tasks that I have ever confronted, but, at the same time, I have to say that I have enjoyed the three to four years that I have spent on it. The difficulty lies in my trying to work across the multiple disciplines and intersecting arguments that are fundamental to what I see as major intellectual issues of social theory and the understanding of change. Among these are current conceptions of history and its notions of time and space in social theory; the relation of society and individuality in modern thought; the productive as well as the repressive elements of power; and the dialectics of schooling in a social and historical context. At a different but interrelated layer is my rethinking of the location of the intellectual in social change and my rejection of an epistemology that places the educational researcher in a privileged position in producing change. The assumption of progress embedded in a research epistemology, I believe, is politically dangerous in a democratic society, no matter how much researchers speak of helping people find more progressive and democratic solutions to their situations.

An origin of this book, then, is my engagement with a concept of change and the politics of the conceptions of change that are embodied in educational research. This engagement has been energized by a wealth of discussions concerning social theory that has a "linguistic turn." For historical reasons that are not always as clear as I would like, traditions of philosophy, social theory, feminism, history, and literary theory have come "to speak" to each other more often, breaking down certain disciplinary boundaries. This process has been facilitated by the translation of continental European scholarship, which has been more philosophical in its arguments about social science than that of the United States. At the same time, a resurgence of pragmatism, a unique U.S. contribution to philosophy, has sharpened my own interests and provoked me to think about the phenomena of schooling in ways that I had not previously been able to articulate.

I am reminded of a conversation that I had in 1978 with Daniel Kallios, a Swedish Marxist educational researcher. We were riding back to Madison from a conference at Wingspread in Racine, Wisconsin. I commented about the restriction of citations in his paper to Marxist writers. He reminded me that he was working in a tradition that he wanted to maintain through his historical ties to preceding work. But, as important, he challenged me to identify non-Marxist literature that was as theoretically interesting. My best shot was Peter Berger and Thomas Luckmann's book *The Social Construction of Reality*, published a decade earlier (1967). Such timidity is no longer the case. There is a host of literary works that emerge out of the Marxist debates of the time, uniting but reformulating and rethinking contemporary concerns with the work of Max Weber and Émile Durkheim. I have found the vistas created exciting.

While in the chapters ahead I focus on these literatures to work with the phenomena of schooling and reform, I know that I have not resolved the issues that have consumed me. At best, I can say I have been engaged in ways that have stimulated my own thinking about the conceptual and political implications of educational research. I can say that I have come to recognize more adequately than before the interrelation of social study and the politics of its work.

But the impetus for this work also involved other multiple contexts that became interwoven in the production of this book.

The study takes as one starting point the status and publicity given to education by the range of U.S. governmental, professional, and philanthropic organizations that have made education a priority in the 1980s. It is the questioning of this public rhetoric as social practice that I have struggled to think about and explore here.

The study emerges from my association in Wisconsin with Robert

Tabachnick and our work in the teacher education program there. We both taught elementary school social studies methods in the teacher education program and worked hard to introduce a "problem-solving" curriculum, an inquiry approach into elementary school teaching. But when we would visit the schools and observe our student teachers, it seemed a matter of hit and miss as to whether we were reproducing or altering teacher practices. As many who study schooling realize, inquiry is not a predominate force. While we did ask what were we doing wrong, an equally serious question arose about social conditions that intersect in schooling, teaching, and teacher education. Our conversations about this question have continued and broadened over the years.

I could also cite my doctoral studies as another source or impetus. With the help of Millard Clements at New York University, I began to wonder about epistemology as part of social relations. Millard introduced me to the sociology of knowledge and its relevance to curriculum. History, sociology, philosophy, and pedagogy are not "just" what they tell us about the world; they are also socially constructed and politically embedded disciplines of practice. This concern with the sociology of knowledge and power is still with me.

I also have to recognize the years that I have been on the University of Wisconsin campus in Madison. It is historically a place where research and scholarship are part of the infrastructure. My department has enabled me to deepen my intellectual interests through interaction with colleagues and graduate students, and through courses that I develop to respond to my changing intellectual interests. In the past three or four years, participation in the Wednesday Seminar has been a central stimulus to my thinking about the different strands of the current reexamination of social theory. The Wednesday Seminar meets whenever it can find a time; now on Tuesday. The group has continually focused on different paradigmatic concerns of contemporary scholarship in a way that compelled me to consider and confront the intersection of the arguments of pragmatism, feminism, new forms of structuralism, and modernism/postmodernism—as well as considering a literature arguing about interpretation, presentation, and politics of academic work. The points of debate, the struggles and dilemmas that emerged from our discussion were an important horizon as this book was written. I have profited from this ongoing dialogue.

With all this said, there is no origin to this discussion of reform, but, rather intersecting points that occur within historical contexts. Among these different weavings of biography, history, and social structure is my commitment to work for intellectual honesty and social integrity in schooling and society. It is also to be critically reflective of my own occupational positions and relations, for schooling and educational research are elements in the production of social regulation. It is these concerns that are the metathemes of this work.

HOW NOT TO READ THIS BOOK

This book begins and ends with chapters that focus on the conceptual issues of change and the political issues of the intellectual as a social actor in structural relations. Chapters 2 and 3 consider historical patterns that, I believe, are both brought forward into the present and are a background to the breaks in social relations that form contemporary educational reform. Central in these chapters, and in Chapters 4–7, dealing with the 1980s and early 1990s, is the problem of power and social regulation.

In many books, the reader is often urged, if inclined, to skip the theoretical material and go on to the narrative. I want to warn against that. In part, the narrative about reform in subsequent chapters is dependent upon the discussion in Chapter 1. I make continued reference to the discussion of power and social regulation framed in the first chapter. The last chapter rejoins the conceptual argument of the beginning, recasts it, and explores an important problem: What are the political obligations, responsibilities, and implications of the social organization of research? It is this layer of theory as it interrelates with the narrative about reform that I hope engages the main themes of the various chapters.

My uneasiness about separating the theoretical and narrative arguments is that the formulation of the narrative is always a theoretical enterprise. There is no datum or fact without theory. To deny that theory is embedded in what we write is precisely what I want to struggle against as a social practice. We are compelled to interrogate our writing and that of others to understand that relation.

I am unwilling, therefore, to absolve myself and the reader from a commitment to confront the relation of theory to narrative and data. I am reminded of Feyerabend's *Science in a Free Society* (1978). He said that he used to go to meetings and talk to people who did not consider where the questions of the field came from and seemed not to have read the works that helped historically to define a field. At first, he believed that these were just incompetent professionals. Later, he realized that the educational organization of the field produced professionalized incompetence. My concern is that this professionalized incompetence is more widespread than we realize. It is in the formulas that are used to write dissertations, in the distinctions of statistics or qualitative methods as research courses rather than as procedures that are part of and understandable in relation to the projects of research. It is in our talk about descriptive research, qualitative versus quantitative, value-neutrality, and the separation of theory from practices, the textual from the social. To fight against these forms of institutionalized incompetence, I place the "theory" chapters as part of the narrative, not separate from it. Further, I sought to integrate a number of disciplinary perspectives to provide a comprehensive focus to a particular social phenomenon. While I do not know how able I am in these matters, I recognize the need of that struggle to relate theory and narrative.

A final comment: In writing these lines, I have wondered whether the debates and struggles that have engaged me should be a preface, introduction, or a postscript. Maybe it is all. The positioning of this work in a social field of educational research is raised as an initial problem here to provide an orientation to a first reading. Yet after working through the chapters, these comments can also be read as postscript documenting the tribulations and joys that engaged me as I struggled.

1

A Political Sociology
of Educational Reform

Power, Knowledge, and Schooling

The last decade has seen a resurgence of interest in the problem of educational change. School reform is viewed as a mechanism to achieve economic revival, cultural transformation, and national solidarity. The impetus for change in the United States has come from multiple sources: Federal and state governmental and philanthropic reports have focused on the quality of teaching, school curriculum, and student achievement. Legislation has increased the state's direct control over the policy and content of public school instruction and teacher education. A professional infrastructure has supported new programs and standards as ways to alter occupational practice, to increase teachers' remuneration, and to improve the quality of teaching. Central to the literature is a call for more educational research and professionalism among teachers.

Rather than as a formal process for describing events, the current discourse of reform should be viewed as an integral element of the events and structured arrangements of schooling. As a primary institution for establishing direction, purpose, and will in society, schooling ties polity, culture, economy, and the modern state to the cognitive and motivating patterns of the individual.[1] Educational reform does not merely transmit information on new practice. Defined as part of the social relations of schooling, reform can be considered a strategic site in which the modernization of institutions occurs.

But to understand contemporary educational reform as a social and political practice, conceptual issues about the study of reform need consideration. This chapter's focus on the ecology of reform provides a background for the subsequent narrative about school reform. These considerations about change relate to historically formed patterns of knowledge (epistemology), power, and institutions.

First, the word *reform* embodies different concepts over time in the context of historical developments and social relations. In the beginning of the 19th century, reform was concerned with helping sinners find salvation, but by the mid-20th century, reform referred to the application of scientific principles as the means to achieve social enlightenment and truth. In current practice, reform maintains a millennial cosmology but depends in part on particular ideologies of individualism and professional practice. In exploring the ecological context that gives rise to reform, this study assumes that there is no constant definition of the term but that its meaning shifts with a continually changing institutional environment.

Second, the ecology of reform is related to the patterns of social regulation found in schooling. Mass schooling was a major reform of modernity, institutionalized during the past 200 years as the modern state assumed the tasks of socialization and upbringing in response to ruptures in the patterns of production and reproduction (Lundgren, 1983). The significance of modern pedagogy is its tie to problems of social regulation; pedagogy links the administrative concerns of the state with the self-governance of the subject. The forms of knowledge in schooling frame and classify the world and the nature of work, which, in turn, have the potential to organize and shape individual identity. This focus on social regulation is different from the relation of power/knowledge identified in the sociology of knowledge in the early 1970s (see Young, 1971). For some of the recent movements in this literature, see Apple (1986), Ginsburg (1988), and Whitty (1985). The social control thesis contains a structural concept that includes a fundamental hypothesis about power; that is, one purpose of the study is to uncover the total mechanisms by which certain social actors dominate and are dominated by the workings of schooling. While I am sensitive to the structural relations presupposed in the social control literature, this current study is more concerned with the multiple productive elements of power. Fixed in the rhetoric of reform, the patterns of schooling and teacher education, and the sciences of pedagogy are multiple and regionally organized procedures, rules, and obligations that organize and discipline how the world is to be seen, acted on, felt, and talked about. Power, in this positive sense, rests in the complex sets of relations and practices by which individuals construct their subjective experiences and assume an identity in social affairs.

Third, history provides criteria about what has changed. But the history referred to here does not define a chronology of events or the purposes of individuals. The study of change considers the rules and standards that underlie the knowledge of schooling and how that knowledge is produced and made acceptable as social practices and within institutional arrangements. Historical method facilitates an exploration of how events in the present are related to other events, formed by and disconnected from the patterns of the past. Contemporary reform practices are related to problems of social and self-regulation that emerged in the face of transformations that became apparent after World War II but historically dominant in the 1980s and early 1990s. I use World War II and the Progressive Era as "markers" that signify uneven social, cultural, economic, and political changes that are related to schooling.

To study the past in the present is to locate breaks, discontinuities, and ruptures in the institutional life. There is no serial and sequential movement of events or institutions, nor can we ascribe change to the motives or beliefs of historical actors. Durkheim (1938/1977) argued in lectures given at the turn of the century that in all cases regardless of forethought or planning, there are significant modifications to social planning that include unforeseen developments and consequences.

Fourth, this study views change as a problem of social epistemology. *Epistemology* provides a context in which to consider the rules and standards by which knowledge about the world is formed, the distinctions and categorizations that organize perceptions, ways of responding to the world, and the conception of "self." Concurrently, *social* epistemology takes the objects constituted as the knowledge of schooling and defines them as elements of institutional practice, historically formed patterns of power relations that provide structure and coherence to the vagaries of everyday life. I consider, for example, the changing concepts of reform, professionalism, and educational science as components of a material context that the concepts both describe and embody. These words assume meaning in the context of a complicated set of relations that combine to produce schooling.

I use the phrase *social epistemology* as a means of making the knowledge of schooling as a social practice accessible to sociological inquiry; it is intended to emphasize the relational and social embeddedness of knowledge in the practices and issues of power. In this sense, I accept the pragmatic philosophical tradition and reject the notion of epistemology as concerned with universal knowledge claims about the nature, origin, and limits of knowledge (see Rorty, 1979).

The concern with a social epistemology is a political as well as conceptual practice. The "rules" of science embody visions of the social order as well as conceptual distinctions that define power relations. Various traditions in contemporary school research, for example, accept the role of the intellectual in organizing the future. The positivism of traditional research promises that efficiency and rationality will produce social progress. Critical sciences, with their Hegelian assumptions, are to identify the repressive functioning of the present in order to move social practices toward some universal purpose of good; that good is often signified by the label "progressive" practice. In both instances, although dependent on different ideological claims, the attempt to identify future significance from studies of the present establishes the social scientist as a legitimate and authoritative figure in designing social affairs. I consider the epistemological assumption of progress in social and educational sciences to be dangerous in a democracy.

In contrast, a focus on the historical breaks and ruptures is intended to redefine the purpose of intellectual work. Its goal is to investigate the relation of institutional practices and the regimes of truth as they change over time. Regarding regimes of truth, I draw on Michel Foucault's notion to make problematic the rules and standards by which individuals define what is good and bad; reasonable and unreasonable; rational, irrational, and nonrational. This stance poses the paradoxical task of placing the individual into history so that we, in the present, can more adequately understand the collective patterns that organize social life and, in the process, poke holes in the causality that organizes our behaviors. Thus it is the role of the science of human affairs in a democracy to locate discontinuities in the patterns structuring social life. Critique can open new systems of possibility for our collective and individual lives. Making visible the governing systems of order, appropriation, and exclusion makes those systems potentially resistable. The construction of new possibilities is left to the larger dynamics of public debate in which the intellectual participates, but not necessarily with an authoritative voice—a condition I return to more forcefully in discussing social ameliorative and critical intellectual work in the final chapter.

Focusing on social epistemology of schooling as a part of power relations, this study is one of political sociology. Conceptually, it makes visible the rules by which certain types of phenomena and social relations of schooling are made into "objects" of reform, the conditions of power contained in these constructions, and the continuities and discontinuities that are embodied in their construction. At the same time, the social epistemology has implications for the positioning of the intellectual in social movements. Denying a conception of progress in the structuring of intellectual work simultaneously denies that the intellectual is authoritative in social change.

This chapter considers the conceptual issues of epistemology, history, and power in the study of change. I stress the importance of understanding structural relations and history in the study of contemporary change, and pursue the centrality of epistemology in a conceptualization of how power operates in contemporary institutions. The analysis draws on recent scholarship interrelating the French philosophical tradition of social epistemology with social theory. In the subsequent chapters, the narrative attends to the patterns in which contemporary school reform occurs. Present reform movements are viewed as the product of breaks in the patterns of social regulation in which schools have formed. The discussion considers how educational research posits distinctions and visions of social regulation, and how those patterns have consequences for constricting the process of democracy.

EVENTS AS CHANGE:
THE INSTANCE, THE INDIVIDUAL, AND THE UNIVERSAL

A certain irony is apparent in contemporary U.S. studies of educational change in that none articulates what is to be considered "change." The criteria tend to be administrative: Are there more efficient attributes or skills to be developed that make teaching and learning more effective? Are people more or less satisfied by the introduction of some innovation? How can the researcher (administrator) find better ways to make educational actors accept and become involved in change? Change is viewed as intrinsic to movement or activity, but little attention is paid to change itself.

As I examined the conceptualizations of reform in educational research, I recognized a clear emphasis on stability, harmony, and the continuation of existing institutional arrangements—not on change (see Popkewitz, 1983b, 1984). In part, this emphasis is related to a series of functional foci that are historically embedded in social and educational research. Concern has long centered on how things work and how they can be made to work better; such an approach assumes that the goals of existing social relations are appropriate and need only to be made more effective.

That research creates universal models with particular and discrete strategies for regulating the acquisition of knowledge and school practice. In this context, one has only to apply the model to teaching situations in order to effect change; evidence of teachers' use of the model is presumed evidence of improved quality. For example, constructivist psychology has been considered a major revolution in educational research. The methodology involves the application of cognitive psychology to the ways in which knowledge is mediated, interpreted, and created through individuals' interaction with their environment (Clark & Peterson, 1986; Shulman, 1986, 1987). Expert teachers' activities have been studied to discover the governing rules of behavior. A "knowledge base" of teaching is to be identified, "base" signifying the assumption that there are essential "laws" or truths in teaching that are stable and independent of teachers and history. These rules are codified and organized as objects that have constancy. But as I will argue in a later chapter, the research to improve the effectiveness of existing forms of teaching makes the forms of social regulation in teaching less visible.

Another aspect of school change involves the sociology of school innovation. The study of reform illuminates the reasons why some people accept and others resist change, and it identifies efficient methods of organizing people and their environments. Participation in reform is viewed as valuable in that it helps people accept the scope, direction, and management of the planned change. These assumptions are emphasized in research that describes the school principal as the most "powerful influence on teachers" and identifies other "agents" of change that influence teachers' acceptance of reforms—such as consultants, community, and national, state, and local governments (see, e.g., Fullan, 1982). The purpose of change is to redesign social conditions to enable the individual to exhibit the specific attributes, skills, or effects that are the expected outcomes of the designated change. Research determines whether program materials have been implemented over the course of a year, whether teachers' attitudes toward the program have become more positive, and whether student achievement and dropout rates have varied within a specific period. If measurements suggest improvement, such as in achievement or satisfaction, or if the program is maintained after external funding is exhausted, then change has reportedly occurred and the reform has been successful. (See Berman & McLaughlin, 1978, for a study that has been cited often to illustrate this view of institutionalization.)

The school-organization and teacher-thinking approaches to reform, while apparently different on the surface, contain certain epistemological similarities. Current research accepts and validates the particular and discrete elements of social and cultural relations; change considers how individuals or discrete "variables" of organizations can become more efficient in achieving existing goals or purposes. Knowledge is removed from the situational considerations of time and space that are a part of social conditions. This is achieved through a positivist approach that focuses on the specific and on the individual and, as a result, loses sight of that which is social and historical about the present.

C. Wright Mills (1959) spoke of this science as a concern of those social actors who, by virtue of their positions, handle individual cases, such as judges and social workers. The perspective is limited to the framework established by existing standards and by professional practice that makes people incapable of rising above a series of limited "causes."

To limit curiosity solely to the present and the functional is anti-intellectual and even antiscientific. Here, change is treated as the organization of teachers' thought and behaviors into hierarchies that can be rationally sequenced but that are historically neutral. The criteria of knowledge and intervention are brought to bear to administer and control social organizations. Means and ends are united into unidimensional time and space: Talk centers on whether teachers are reflective or a school organization permits innovation, but reflection and organization have no philosophical reference or historical context to facilitate an understanding of how, why, or what is occurring. (See Fabian, 1983, for a discussion of the naturalization, secularization, and specialization of time.) Reports of change do not reflect that reasoning and practices are a part of historical processes, nor how perceptions, attitudes, and beliefs are socially constructed and cited in specific cultural milieus (for various interpretations of the historical in knowledge, see Berger, Berger, & Kellner, 1973; Braudel, 1980; and Foucault, 1973). When we talk about implementation and teachers' thought, our discussions are organized in relation to a particular institutional arrangement of schooling and, in certain ways, made plausible by our very participation in those arrangements. To make the problem of reform one of "managing social change," as Fullan (1982) suggests, is to accept the underlying social relations and power that shape and fashion institutional arrangements as natural, normal, and inevitable.

While research on change is part of a reform language that calls for a more benevolent social organization, different implications inhere in actual practice. As will be argued, the sciences of social change make possible finer methods of regulating and disciplining the individual. These premises emerge from 18th-century cosmologies that sought a universal set of rules about human evolution. Social development was considered cyclical and social regulation, administrative. In the 18th century, the cosmology was designed to control the colonies and discipline the individual in the nascent state. In the current reforms, it is intended to manage the teacher, who is typically female. To consider these implications more fully and to outline an alternative approach to the study of change, the following discussion will consider the relations of *structure, history,* and *epistemology.*

RELATIONS OF TIME AND STRUCTURE:
PROBLEMS OF SOCIAL CHANGE

Just as there is an inherent irony in contemporary research about change that centers on stability and social harmony, similar tension characterizes a discussion of social structures as an important element in a conception of change. Structure, at one level, is part of the set of hidden assumptions that underpin research in the sociology of organization and teacher thinking. That is, "things" are functional in relation to some notion of what is permanent and consistent in social affairs. But in traditional research about change, historical differentiations and distinctions in society are taken for granted and, where acknowledged, become the technical control of variables of stratification, such as race or sex.

I introduce the notion of structure to call into question the background assumptions, social values, and institutional forms that are endemic to current research practices. This concept of structure recognizes that many of our commonly accepted institutional patterns were in fact created as responses to complex social tensions but are now viewed as natural parts of everyday interactions, language, and practices. But I will conceptualize structure as a dynamic, historical concept in order to consider both points of continuity and discontinuity. Structures are not stable, but are constantly changing, when viewed in the appropriate context of the social fields in which human practice occurs.

Structure as an Object of Analysis

Structures are an unspoken element of schooling. The history of school reform is not only a history of its changing ideas of organizational practices but of the unacknowledged values and interests that are embedded in the ongoing practices of schooling.[2] For example, the everyday speech of schooling is not merely an expression of individual intent or purpose. Teacher talk or organizational characteristics are composite practices that transcend the lines of particular people and events. Lindblad (1986), for example, has studied how teachers' talk is related to class divisions in society. Englund (1986) has focused on the conceptions of citizenship education that came to the fore in Swedish school curricula during the 20th century. The analysis explores the long-term processes of pedagogy in a manner that takes into account the conditions of education and society. From these different studies, we come to understand more fully that to posit a curriculum, to define teacher reasoning, or to identify categories of student competence presupposes certain ordering procedures and selective mechanisms that structure the events under immediate scrutiny.

Initially, then, any concept of change needs to account for structuring patterns. We can consider structure as patterns that impose upon social life certain regularities, boundaries, and frames that facilitate understanding and practice in the world. In one sense, structure is analogous to the frame of a building: The framing provides a support that incorporates the dimensions of space and time for inhabitants of a building, although the boundaries are such that there are multiple possibilities and choices. (For a discussion of the notion of structure as object, see Blau, 1976). Among these frames are geography, modes of organizing production, cognitive frameworks, patriarchy, and spiritual beliefs.[3] A study of structures involves identification of presuppositions and rules that are unacknowledged and unspoken in everyday life but, nevertheless, shape practice. Attention is paid to how the major forms of collective life (economics, politics, and culture) have been formed and impinge on that which is taken for granted in schooling. Structures are global or universal ordering principles of the social world.

In much contemporary literature, words such as *class, race,* and *gender* denote principles of structures that are thought to provide background patterns that help to characterize actions, practices, and thought. To use these terms as structural concepts is to focus on the origins or "causes" of the ongoing events, suggesting that inequities, power relations, and domination occur as a result of one or multiple structural patterns that underlie daily life. Much critical educational research makes strong structural assumptions as it locates power in an understanding of the differentiations that relate to some oppressive pattern, such as that posed by capitalism or patriarchy. Structural analysis is also presupposed in words such as *individual voice, resistance,* and *agency,* with these concepts suggesting a hidden pattern that restrains and calls for opposition. Although there may be tensions and contradictions (gender relations may work in opposition to class interests), a fundamental understanding of the mechanisms of social life is thought to lie in tracing the origins of practice to the structural characteristics inherent in daily practices.

Structure, then, is a set of assumptions or principles by which social events become defined or opposition is expressed. Power as a structural category, for example, is one of sovereignty in the relations of the dominated and the dominating. The task of inquiry is to understand what particular social actors maintain their position of dominance and possess power, as well as to understand the mechanisms by which that sovereignty can be reversed, such as replacing the ruling elite with a different, but nonetheless socially acceptable, group.

To this point, I have talked briefly about structures as objects to be analyzed. The occurrences of schooling embody social forms that are inherited from historical social conditions. The past intrudes into the present as boundaries in which choice occurs and possibilities are made available. In this context, the concept of structure gives focus to the constraints and restraints placed on schooling. At the same time, however, attention to structure posits the production of innovations as the result of ruptures and modifications in existing routines, habits, and patterns. It is in this latter context that the paradox of the study of change is most clear.[4] I explore this paradox next through a consideration of structure as sets of relations rather than as an object with unyielding and stable qualities.

Structure as Institutional Relations

A perspective of structure that draws on the physical analogy of an object had initial didactic purposes, but this analogy obscures the historically constructed patterns of relations in institutions. To assume the validity of global categories of power is to lose sight of the complex social structuring in particular social formations; a repressive thesis about power is accepted that ignores its productive elements. To consider the dynamics of social life, we need to attend to a second meaning for structure: Changing boundaries and points of interaction among institutions and social systems define structural patterns. Perceiving structural patterns as sets of relations that are not linear but have breaks with the past provides the criteria for studying change.

The focus on the *structured relations* that pattern the events of schooling can be considered in the single word *curriculum*. Curriculum embodies sets of social and structural relations through the very patterns of communication on which it is premised. Many European countries have no word for curriculum; it is a term that appears in the 16th and 17th centuries to interrelate social philosophies and economy with management practices that were being established as part of the school day (Hamilton, 1989). Curriculum, methods, and school class were inventions to stress the rational coherence, internal sequencing, and, later, the Calvinist discipline, which collectively related to the forming of the social and economic organization.[5] Implicit in the social forms that developed around the word *curriculum* is a discipline for appropriate options and the scope of permissible action. To talk about curriculum, then, presupposes sets of assumptions and social values that are not readily apparent but that limit the range of available choices.

The pedagogical forms associated with curriculum, however, change over time as pedagogy relates to complex patterns within and external to schooling. To foreshadow a discussion in other chapters, a number of social transformations interrelate in the 19th-century United States to produce mass schooling. These changes are in the arenas of transportation, economy, and the family; in the reformation of government and culture; and in the demography and technology of rural and urban life.

The formation of the school entailed the coming together of a number of semiautonomous sets of practices whose outcome constituted a break with past practices. Teacher education, modern pedagogy, school organization, and educational sciences appeared and combined with these material developments to produce particular characteristics that came to be associated with mass schooling: textbooks, chalkboards, hierarchical staffing, and a gendered occupation. The creation of mass schooling was neither inevitable, natural, nor the product of a singular progressive development. The study of school reform must concern itself with the breaks in and reforming of relations between the various elements in schooling and the larger society, such as how curriculum and teacher education became associated with secular notions of moral education and labor socialization. In this sense, it is the relations among various elements in the field that lend reform its significance as a social practice.

Again, we can focus on an apparent commonplace in education and make it historically problematic: science as a guide for policy and practice. The development of educational sciences at the turn of the century, discussed in Chapter 3, occurred at the intersection of the university, the modern state, a secularization of Protestant assumptions about salvation, and a pragmatism that combined with the development of mass schooling. These relations produced constraints and restraints on what was to be disciplinary knowledge about schooling. Human sciences produced new technologies designed to organize, supervise, and evaluate teachers and children. By examining a number of developments occurring in various facets of social life, it becomes apparent that the paths followed were not predefined at the outset but were the outcome of intense debate and struggle. Further, the personal intent of the sociologists or the psychologists in the late 19th century becomes less important than the sets of assumptions, implications, and consequences that defined the social relations in which the social sciences were established. Globally defined concepts about structure would lose sight of the empirical complexity of the social practices of schooling and the ways in which change is produced.

The need to construct a conception of change as it occurs in the context of structural relations is illustrated in Pierre Bourdieu's (1988) study of power relations within the French academy during the 1968 student rebellion. To explain the significance of the events, the study explores a number of semiautonomous structural relations occurring in higher education. There was an increase in the number of students attending universities, an expansion of higher education lectureships, and a devaluing of certain educational credentials. The trajectories of these sets of practices, Bourdieu argues, traveled independently but intersected at a certain point to produce a break in the patterns that had existed. Meshing of these patterns was the result of a conjunction—not of evolution or necessity. Bourdieu explains that conjunction through exploring the power relations of the French academics, exploring the difference between academic and intellectual capital.

To summarize, my discussion has focused on a pragmatically formed ecology of reform. It rejects global concepts or essential standards of truth but acknowledges the historical contexts that illuminate particular social locations and cultural circumstances. For example, social relations defined by the state or by issues of gender are not categories whose stable characteristics can explain phenomena. Further, less attention is given to individuals and to the dualities of structure and the individual. Psychology is no longer a central domain, nor is individualism a central ideology. The following section explores structure as a historical and relational concept, by deemphasizing the individual as an object of study and by giving focus to power relations and their discontinuities in institutional practice and knowledge. A theory of change is a history of the objects that constitute our present, of the practices and discourses on which daily activities and individual thought are premised.

HISTORY, EPISTEMOLOGY, AND POWER

A consideration of structure as a relational problem helps to provide some rationale to a central methodological issue in the study of change. While there is general agreement that society embodies patterned ways of acting, there is less agreement about how structures should be viewed. To focus too heavily on structures as discrete objects produces a picture of a world that is consistent and without change. But to focus on actors as the initiators of change is to err in the opposite direction: to produce a volunteerist theory of change that, at one end, is highly individualist—posing actions as unique and significant in and of themselves—or, at the other end, characterizes change as a natural and evolutionary process produced through purposeful actions or forces. In both instances, structural relations are the hidden partner to the purposeful action.

A major alternative to this dualism—volunteerism and determinism—is found in a strand of theory called post-structural analysis that relates literary theory to the constructions of social analysis (see, e.g., Cherryholmes, 1988; Eagleton, 1983; Giddens, 1987). Social life is made analogous to the text that can be read in multiple ways and in which there is a dynamic relation among author, text, and audience, especially in that there is no final truth but a pragmatic search for knowledge.

The purpose of turning to a literary theory is to understand the intersection of language and the construction of practice. Emphasis is given to the constructive role of language, posed in a broader conceptualization of the rules and standards by which speech is expressed (discourse). Language is viewed not only as an expression of social affairs, but as one aspect of the mechanisms by which the world is produced and reproduced through the subjective elements of everyday life. Discourse, the rules and patterns of communication in which language is used, creates distinctions, differences, and categories that define and create the world. The linguistic approach moves from a consideration of the meaning of people to the rules and standards of social life that form the practices of daily life. These rules are not fixed and do not provide final truth but are continually changing in relation to shifting circumstances.

One Anglo-American point of departure to this discussion of social theory is the work of Anthony Giddens (e.g., 1987). For Giddens, structure involves sets of relations or interactions among actors, with specific attention given to the practices produced through emergent patterns; relations establish and are established by practices. Giddens is concerned with the diversity of social contexts by which structure functions not only as a constraint but as a medium of living in the world, which it recursively organizes. He recognizes, though, that social conduct is fundamentally complex and therefore different from the pages of a literary text, which depends on writing as a means of communication. In this context, Giddens focuses on the sets of rules and resources that act as a medium of social practice, and on the outcomes of such practices. He calls the dynamic quality of these relations "structuration."[6]

Giddens draws on literary theory to flesh out a meaning for structured relations as socially formed practices. He considers the recent literature on textual meaning, communication as process of interpretation, and the role of signification in the producing of worlds and individuality. These contributions, he argues, provide important and provocative avenues for a construction of social theory. He takes literary theory, combines it with a Durkheimian concern with collective patterns, and extends it to consider both the contextuality of action and practical consciousness. Giddens attempts to do away with the dichotomies of society and individuality, structure and agency, that underlie contemporary social theory and its attempts to explore change. The structuration principle that Giddens introduces involves a theory that focuses on the ways structures are contained in language and, at the same time, form and transform social institutions through action of human agency.

Yet in his reconstruction of social theory, Giddens is unable to transcend the limitations he recognizes in literary theory and the text metaphor that he applies to social phenomena. While Giddens argues that time and space are integral concepts to social theory, the discussion of structuration reduces temporal and spatial differences to specific practices of the present. There is a focus on practical reasoning to emphasize how members carry out their day-to-day activities by virtue of their ability to give reference to the structures in society. The greatest weight is assigned to a practical consciousness, to the individual as actor, and to the notion of time as bounded to particular events. (Also see Connell, Ashenden, Kessler, & Powsett, 1982, for a discussion of structure as it relates to problems of gender. Connell and colleagues, as well, tie the concept of historicity to the present and the event.) The relation of institutions and discourse in the formation of "self" tends to be lost. Institutions are reduced to standard and visible practices that have no history and no future. History is the involvement in the moment rather than a relational concept about institutions that ties the past to the present in various elements of time and space.

A more elaborate and, I believe, more fruitful theoretical discourse is provided by French sociologist Pierre Bourdieu. Bourdieu (1977, 1984) considers any series of events as having interlocking principles that produce a *habitus*: Structural relations provide the patterned relations and symbolic systems of classification and categorization that order the social spaces in which practices occur. At the same time, there are the perceptions, dispositions, activities, and awarenesses brought to social affairs that are both determined and determining of practice. It is in the interrelations of these structured and structuring principles that social relations can be assessed, power understood in its various dynamic qualities, and history reintroduced without a chronological or volitional quality. Bourdieu uses the notion of social space to consider how various actors as structural figures relate through the expression of different forms of power (cultural, social, and economic).

While this current study of school reform is not an application of Bourdieu's theory, it is sensitive to the sociological issues that he raises. What is central to the current study are concepts of change and power as aspects of the relations defined in a social space. This perspective allows an exploration of changes in the relations among groups and actors as problems of power. My particular concern with school change, however, combines a consideration of the social space within and among institutions, and an investigation of how that social space merges with the epistemologies of schooling and its programs of reform.

Structural Relations as History

I now turn to the epistemology of social practices to maintain this central focus on structural relations. As I mentioned earlier, my concern with epistemology is with the social rules and power relations in which knowledge about schooling is formed. An emphasis on the social construction and social relations embedded in knowledge is only partially related to the notion of discursive practices found in educational "poststructural" criticism (Cherryholmes, 1988). The rhetorical and ethical qualities of language give priority to textual constructions and their analytic qualities, thereby inserting social patterns into a multidimensional space but in a nondifferentiated time. My emphasis on social epistemology rather than discourse is related to a concern with a historically embedded social theory about change. Here the traditions of the French historical school of the *Annales* and Michel Foucault are helpful in tying the problem of structural relations to power and knowledge. At points in this book, however, I do use the word *discourse* to focus on the textual and language qualities of contemporary school reforms, though my larger conceptual purpose is to relate epistemological concerns in social and historical contexts.

The *Annales* is a French school of historical studies that takes its name from its journal *Annales d'historie economique et sociale* started in 1929 (see, Bloch, 1963; Braudel, 1980; Stoianovich, 1976). From the *Annales* comes a concern with institutional development and structures of knowledge (*mentalité*) emerging through an interplay of different historical times: At any one moment we can "see" the immediate events and perceptions of school reforms in relation to longer-term periods (*durée*), such as patterns of events and social changes that underlay the curriculum reforms of the 1960s. The public rhetoric from this era is bound in the symbolism of the Russian spacecraft *Sputnik,* in the debates about why Johnny can't read and the charges about schooling being an educational wasteland. The particular criticism, symbolic articulations, and curriculum development were part of changes in structural relations by which new forms of social regulation emerged. These changes were embodied in the professionalization of knowledge that became pronounced in the post–World War II United States.

Viewing the professionalization of curriculum as part of more lasting patterns *(durée)* in material and cultural life places the particular school reforms of the 1980s in relation to the reforms of the 1960s, and at the intersection of other social patterns. For example, in Chapter 4, I explore the idea that it may not be important that particular "new" science and math curricula were not used in the 1960s; the significance lay in the new distinctions, categories, and rules assigned to the knowledge brought into the school and the ways in which the rules of curriculum embodied new power relations. The production of a professional knowledge (teaching sociology, political science, and genetics) indicates a break with previous concepts of curriculum that need to be considered as part of larger ruptures in the social patterns of regulation produced by schooling. The movement toward standardization and control of outputs in the 1980s takes the distinction and categories of the 1960s and redirects them in relation to a particular conjuncture.

Such a historical focus can enable us to consider structural relations as accumulated practices that are not unidimensional or linear. The patterns maintain certain continuities but, at the same time, embody varying rates of movement and the crossing of several destinies. In schooling, for example, there are multiple issues related to change: how teacher education interrelates with school patterns of teaching and administration, how it is brought into higher education, and the work of philanthropy and the university in defining pedagogical practices, to name a few. The histories of how these practices developed is not a chronological one of progressive advancements, or of a serial progression, but of a time that "goes at a thousand different paces, swift and slow, which bear almost no relation to the day-to-day rhythm of a chronicle or of traditional history" (Braudel, 1980, p. 10).

The Spanish historian Maravall (1986), for example, a student of the *Annales,* describes multiple interwoven patterns of relations over time that are elements to a study of change. Maravall focuses on the issue of continuity and change in the 16th- and 17th-century patterns called "the Baroque." He argues that the Baroque contains certain ways of "seeing," talking, acting, and thinking about the world that emerge over a particularly long period and that retain common characteristics over time. Maravall weaves together social values, aspirations, beliefs, myths, lifestyles, and behaviors as elements of a cohesive collective mentality. These mentalities do not stand alone; the thought and reason of the day are situated in a complex relation with institutions, social interests and power.

The structural relations of the Baroque are residues in the patterns of schooling. The images of the period, as represented in the plastic arts of the church and politics, were to drive the populace toward particular types of actions defined by an emerging relation between the church and the ruling sovereigns. Schooling included rhetoric, grammar, and dialectics that enabled students to interpret the laws of the sovereignty of the church and state. Yet the curriculum itself was to foster an inquisitiveness that would later challenge the very relations that the curriculum was to legitimate (Durkheim, 1938/1977).

The Baroque period did not span an easily identifiable time frame or era; there was not a singular or specific shift in the political, economic, or cultural elements of the society. What has come to be recognized as Baroque developed at differing rates across Europe and, with some autonomy, within different institutions. What occurred was the result of multiple actions and events; it is in the common exchanges of these semiautonomous institutions that there arises something that we call Baroque. Change was found in the meshing of structured relations that occurred at varying rates of movement within different institutions.

In this sense, we can think of structural relations as a complicated network of similarities that overlap over time. To borrow from Ludwig Wittgenstein (1953/1966), structural relations are like a thread made up of fibers. The strength of the thread does not reside in the fact that some fiber runs its entire length, but in the overlapping of many fibers. Instead of viewing change as a singular monolithic entity, we can study the patterns in which school reform occur as plural and unstable. There are different layers of institutional conduct that interact in a manner in which conflict, tensions, and contradictions inhere. The sets of relations that become schooling, therefore, exist across different dimensions of time and provide examples for organizing cases and recognizing shifts in what had seemed continuous (Dreyfus & Rabinow, 1983).

Institutional Formations and Epistemology

To pursue further the role of history in a conception of change, I want to combine the concern of the *Annales* with structural history and the French philosophical tradition of science to form a *social epistemology*.

It is a tradition exemplified in the work of French philosophers Gaston Bachelard and Georges Canguilhem and the American, Thomas Kuhn, and given a material focus in the social studies of Foucault. (See Foucault, 1978, 1979a, 1979b, 1980; Lecourt, 1975; Tiles, 1984). The problem of a social epistemology is also in the work of Bourdieu (1977, 1984). The problem of change is what is constituted as the knowledge of the world, and how that knowledge shifts and is modified as a result of changes in the social practices in which cognition occurs. For Thomas Kuhn (1970), change was present in the ruptures in traditional methodology that transformed normal to revolutionary science. Kuhn recognized that change occurred not only as a cognitive process born through the advancement of information and fact, but as a political process by which one paradigm (disciplinary matrix) replaces another. Kuhn's notion of scientific change, however, is idealistic in that it focuses on the ideas themselves without acknowledging the social conditions in which those ideas were spawned and challenged.

Foucault's contribution in this discussion is twofold. First, his work introduced the history and philosophy of the scientific tradition of epistemological studies into the realm of social theory. Second, the relationship of power to knowledge is a central focus of social study. Foucault reverses the traditional belief that knowledge is power and defines power as embodied in the manner in which people gain knowledge and use the knowledge to intervene in social affairs. Power circulates through the macrogovernance structure of the state and in the microgovernance of the individual. While most U.S. post-structural work places Foucault in a literary and discourse tradition, it is his philosophical and historical grounding that should be considered his central contribution to the study of social power. (I use *social epistemology* instead of Foucault's notion of *episteme* to locate my work in this larger field of scholarship because my emphasis is on knowledge and institutional relations in historical settings. I have done neither an archaeology nor genealogy of knowledge in the sense that Foucault does. See Dreyfus & Rabinow, 1983).

Foucault argues that power is embedded in the governing systems of order, appropriation, and exclusion by which subjectivities are constructed and social life is formed. This occurs at multiple layers of daily life, from the organization of institutions to the self-discipline and regularization of the perceptions and experiences according to which individuals act. This entails consideration of the ways that knowledge promotes certain truths as they are inscribed in the problems, questions, and responses that secure and enhance social life and its well-being. My interest in the knowledge of curriculum, teaching, and teacher education, for example, is in its creating not only the distinction, categories, and organization of the world, but also the wants, desires, bodily acts, and cognitive interests that form identity. This concept of power does not focus on physical coercion, nor is it directly concerned with one group's sovereignty over others, although domination is always a background issue. The power, in this sense, is productive of social identity rather than instances of repression, violence, or coercion (see also Noujain, 1987; Rajchman, 1985).[7]

This concept of a power/knowledge relation provides a methodological focus for the study of reform as an aspect of institutional development. To focus on institutional relations and the knowledge of schooling as social practice is not to deny the individual but to consider the ways in which our subjectivities have formed and are forming. Concern with the interplay among various social patterns, as well, does not undermine a recognition of structure as a historically formed object as well as a method of analysis. In an important sense, we need to be sensitive to the patterns that seem permanent and unchanging, if only as a benchmark by which to determine the points at which the interplays and discontinuities occur in the relations being produced. (See Callinicos, 1989; McLennan, 1989). Power cannot be viewed as totally ubiquitous but as part of the architecture that occurs in social fields. For example, I discuss in this book the coalescing of fractions within and across institutions through the production of contemporary reform. The fractions include state government agencies and groupings among university faculty, philanthropic foundations, and research "schools." These fractions establish power relations among institutions, but are understood through the dispersal of interpretation and the regularity in which the production of school reform occurs.

I have been using the phrase *social epistemology* in reference to a layer of analysis that directs this study: the relation of knowledge, institutions, and power. I use *epistemology* as a historical, social, and pragmatic concept. In contrast to much American philosophy, I seek to explore the interrelation of mind and material condition rather than to characterize them as "dualistic." Further, I have sought to posit a theory of knowledge as a historical theory of society and individuality. Philosophically, American epistemological studies have separated these, giving priority to knowledge as the foundation of all science and ethics. Finally, I define epistemology as an exploration of the relations between the form and style of reasoning and various historical configurations and trajectories. With pragmatic philosophy, I argue that there is not a common ground on which to locate a true consensus or a permanent neutral framework by which to evaluate a rational argument. There are no universal schemes of reason and rationality but only socially constructed epistemologies that represent and embody social relations.

KNOWLEDGE AND POWER
AS EPISTEMOLOGICAL PROBLEMS

Social epistemological questions enable us to move closer to a methodology that explores reform as an intersection of knowledge, power, and historically situated practices. In this context, it becomes apparent that the acquisition and alteration of knowledge (social epistemology) occurs when the continuities and discontinuities of structural relations are joined with institutional practices and events. Let me explore this further through a discussion of changes in epistemology that I believe are central to modern schooling and the ways in which reform is constituted. I present the following historical discussion to highlight important themes of the relation of power and knowledge that are embedded in pedagogical problems. The discussion moves beyond U.S. schooling to more general shifts and transformations that I believe are significant to the social reforms in which mass schooling in the U.S. is embedded. The discussion, however, is meant not to provide universal descriptions but to orient the narratives in subsequent chapters.

A central assumption in the practices of reform is the epistemology of the European Enlightenment (Foucault, 1973). Beginning in the 17th century, there was a shift from a classical view in which the word was representative of the object to a world in which people could reflect and be self-conscious about their historical conditions. A view of change occurred that tied progress to reason, and self-criticism and systematic human intervention to social institutions. The new sets of relations between knowledge and social practice inhered in a variety of social relations. Accompanying the emergent Enlightenment was the creation of the nation-state, where, for the first time, people were assigned a collective identity that was both anonymous and concrete. Abstract concepts of civil liberties and constitutional, democratic rules produced new sets of boundaries, expectations, and possibilities of the general notion of citizen. At the same time, people could be considered in specific and detailed ways as populations that could be categorized into subgroups distinct from any sense of the whole. The concept of population made possible new technologies of control, since there was greater possibility for the supervision, observation, and administration of the individual.

The previous discussion highlights certain tensions that are legacies of the Enlightenment and the particular ways of "seeing" that we can call *modernity*. (The discussion draws on the work of Michel Foucault and the conception of the modernization of the mind by Berger, Berger, & Kellner, 1973.) Within a context of changing institutional organization of knowledge, it becomes possible to speak of rational change, social progress, and mass schooling. The hope of modernity is to create more democratic, just, and equitable social arrangements. It also becomes possible to construct pedagogical forms, teacher education, and social science as they become historically interrelated in the production of mass schooling and its modern forms of discipline.

From Representation to an Analytic World
of Self-Reflection and Individuality

The idea of reform and intentional change is an outgrowth of a fundamental shift in epistemology that occurred in Western Europe and, later in the United States, between the 17th and 19th centuries. To understand the significance of the epistemology, we need to focus on the prior ordering that was assigned to the relation of self and world. Before the 17th century, the Classical Age maintained a direct relationship between the word and the thing that it represented; indeed knowledge was predictable and stable. Existence could not be called into question by individual rationales, since language was not about interpretation but part of a nexus of representation and being. In secular law, theology, and literature, the word was taken as literal. The locus of creation was God, and people provided clarification of His work; the epic murals decorating church walls and ceilings, for example, were viewed as the depictions of the teaching of the Bible and the image of God. It was the role of the intellect to construct a universal method of analysis by which secular symbols and representations could mirror a natural order, thereby yielding a perfect certainty about man's relationship to God.

Education was to inculcate in students an understanding of the relation of language to the world and a commitment to the religious, moral, and social tenets of Christianity. Pedagogy was designed to regulate moral unity and human disposition. There was a tendency to envelop the child entirely within a system that would take control not only of the child's intellectual existence but also of the physical and moral life, in order to be able to penetrate more completely and more profoundly into the child's deepest nature, to prevent any part of it from escaping.

The conversion of the soul depended on a particular epistemology of representation. The teaching of grammar was to instruct the mind to obey specific laws and rules that dictated forms of expression. Rhetoric and dialectics were to defend truth, which was thought to reside in the rules of language found in texts. Grammar, then, represented a microcosm of the larger processes and situations by which human vision and intellect could be ordered and organized to achieve a moral, stable world.

Thinking as representation was replaced as individuals turned their scrutiny inward, to their own nature. From the time of Kant, an analytic orientation emerged to show how representation is possible through an analysis of language, social practice, and history. The attempt to treat facts as existing within contextual boundaries and then to establish the condition of the possibility of all facts was an entirely new notion of the 18th century.

> The modern themes of an individual who lives, speaks, and works in accordance with the laws of an economics, a philology, and a biology, but who also, by a sort of internal torsion and overlapping, has acquired the right, through the interplay of those very laws, to know them, and to subject them to total clarification—all these themes so familiar to us today and linked to the existence of the human sciences were excluded by Classical thought. (Foucault, 1973, p. 310)

The ability to critically reflect and promote individual self-betterment contained an epistemological break with previous ways of ordering.

The shift to a mentality that makes problematic the world of nature, social institutions, and self was part of a transformation that included the construction of diverse structural relations.[8] A secularization of the conception of salvation contained a focus on people's work on earth and the governing of society. Conceptions of progress, science, rational planning, and the state became presupposed elements of social practice. Ideologies of democratic states emerged as individuality was postured as a political doctrine of governability. Reform became a public effort, first to bring God's word into the organization of individual life, and later, as a rational strategy for social amelioration.

But to speak of change in social consciousness as involving secularization and the development of science is to accept a progressive view of humanity. In this sense, modernity would seem a logical outcome of the Enlightenment, with human cognition and volition steering change. The historical developments, however, did not occur in a rational or predictable manner.

Science as Progress and Ideology

The concepts of progress are central to the shift from a representative to an analytic perspective. While there are moments of discontent (Almond, Chodorow, & Pearce, 1982), the notion of rational progress is taken for granted. People believe that through hard work our social situation can improve. This belief that the social and material world has evolutionary qualities that can be positively influenced through people's intervention is a recent historical development. The modern state, developmental views of individuality, conceptions of science as bringing a better world, and invention of planned reform are part of the cosmology of Western Europe and the United States. In more recent years, the focus on progress in the United States has emphasized quantity of practice as a means of school improvement. School reform is reduced to such remedies as increased homework or more stringent certification requirements as evidence of teaching competence. Reports of change or activity regardless of their nature or depth are considered testimonials of progress.

In our hope that rational action can produce progress, we lose sight of the fact that the very notion of progress embodies a particular set of assumptions about intellect and power. Theories of progress from the 17th century onward reflected the newly established institutional relations of religion, state, culture, and society. Earlier millennial views involved a critique of the present and the creation of a new world that departed drastically from the present. By the 17th century, however, these utopian views were being challenged and the millennial dream no longer included a sharp break with the past. From the new priests of Bacon's science to the utopian visions of the Saint Simonians, the possibilities of the future were inextricably tied to the organization and interests of the present. From one utopian perspective, human purpose could be realized as a powerful positive force that derives from suffering and pain. Hegel's dialectics were tied to a universal spirit that was allegorically related to the crucifixion and resurrection, the latter producing a brotherhood of love. Marx saw progress in the elimination of capitalism and the birth of a new society based first on socialism and later on communism.

Change was to be evolutionary, incorporating notions of commercial and rational time and space (DeGrazia, 1964; Landes, 1983; Nisbet, 1969)—but a particular kind of evolution in time that was to be contained and incorporated into a manageable space. Progress, it was assumed, resulted from a logical, sequential movement among and within existing institutions. Change became additive; modification and adaptation were tied to previous structures. Evolution, first a social and then a scientific concept, was a radical conception of the human condition as moving toward its own improvement through rational means of control. The control of nature, industrial development, and social amelioration, it was thought, would bring the new millennium. Individuals became responsible not only for their own faith but for the development of material and spiritual goods that improve one's life.

This notion of progress is fundamental to pedagogical thought.

Evolution meant that pedagogy should recognize and nurture differences through greater attention to the individual. Calvinist influences in Britain that were brought to the United States drew on a belief that there should be well-ordered forms of social organization, a belief that was manifested in 18th- and 19th-century instructional systems (Hamilton, 1989). Pedagogical knowledge was to provide more efficient systems of moral supervision and labor organization. The class system, grades, curriculum, and instructional methods were made part of the school order. They provided the mechanisms that ordered a sequential, hierarchical, and progressive system.

As we lose sight of the epistemology of progress, ideological constructions become incorporated into practices of research. The notion of evolution, at one level, made reasoning about change possible. European conceptions of world development and useful knowledge, for example, contained notions of progress. Change was seen as a "natural" social evolution from primitive to modern, heathen to enlightened. The "natural" history helped to make sense of the 19th-century Industrial Revolution, to justify the European colonization of the peoples of Africa and Asia, and to posit utilitarian values that would lead to both heavenly salvation and earthly reward.

In the 20th century, the millennial concerns were transformed into a secular focus on progress, a belief that is especially intense in social science (Ross, 1984). Prior to the Progressive Era (ca. 1880–1920), science as progress was combined with older, traditional values of community. The progressive view produced an optimism that reason and the rationality of science can be combined to produce social change. The scientists and philosophers of education, such as G. Stanley Hall, Edward Thorndike, and John Dewey, viewed the social world as rationally organized and amenable to progress through human agency (Curti, 1959). Dewey was most forceful in expressing the optimism of science. Change was defined in relation to existing patterns—functional and pragmatic in intent and drawn from Herbert Spencer's notion of an evolutionary process.

Progress was identified as a problem of science and society. Secularization replaced virtue and piety as the purpose of pedagogy with virtue and rationality. The rational control of nature and people would in turn organize the development and innovation of society. The social reform of institutions replaced an earlier moral concern with converting the sinner. It is at this conjunction that the creation of mass schooling and state building emerged. The discourses of state and schooling were similar: To govern is to provide strategies by which development and discipline can be meshed in the name of social welfare.

The 17th- and 19th-century views of "natural" evolution underlie contemporary school reform and research. More often than not, theories of progress are concerned with explaining stability and harmony rather than flux and the dynamics of social life (Popkewitz, 1984). As a result, theories emphasize such issues as overcoming resistance to planned change, circumventing impediments that prevent system equilibrium, and understanding of how innovations are adapted or modified by existing school relations. Models of change chart a world that seems sequential, hierarchical, and taxonomic. The classical view of representation is maintained. Progress can be viewed as a teacher's internalization and implementation of the model through behavioral practices.

Knowledge as a Technology of Power

The promise of modernity was to make people more responsible for and involved in their social conditions; the invention of mass schooling emphasized the project of Enlightenment in which knowledge of self and society would produce a better and more just society. Its proponents justified the individualization of knowledge by arguing that it made education accessible to all rather than limiting access to the elite.

But modernity also exerted power relations in a new way (Foucault, 1965, 1973, 1975, 1977, 1979a, 1979b, 1980, 1988). The battle of domination was no longer simply the relationship of rulers and ruled, dominators and dominated. Fixed in the rituals of the new social practices and the detailed procedures of social and political institutions were fundamental issues of power. While claiming to temper and prevent the violence that would supposedly exist without their civilizing constraints, the new rules and obligations created finer differentiations of everyday behavior that objectively separated and ranked individuals (Dreyfus & Rabinow, 1983). Individualization was coupled with new forms of the pastoral that made confession a secular event. Knowledge of self was to be organized and supervised by a professionalization of social affairs; psychology, an invention of modernity, is a central discipline for defining new patterns to supervise individuality. The knowledge of progress was itself a social practice that tied issues of power to the construction of identity. It is these relations of epistemology, institutions, and power that I believe guide the study of the structural relations that define school reform.

Reversal of the Political Axis of Individualization

The new power relations reversed the political axis of individualization (Foucault, 1979b). In feudal and monarchical systems, individualization was greatest at the summit of society. Power was visibly embodied in the individual—the king or his court. Crime was indistinguishable from the sacredness of the regime. Punishment was a ritual to express and restore the sanctity of the law and to provide retribution that emphasized the unlimited power of the king; punishment was not intended to reform the offender. Similarly, education was to exhibit the overt characteristics of knowledge as a form of display rather than to pay attention to the intrinsic "qualities" of the individual.[9] These displays were symbolic of the established order and the illumination of its proper administration.

With modernity, individualization and culpability assumed new meanings. There was a shift from the idolatry of those at the top of the social hierarchy (such as in the case of burial rituals and tomb art) to an individualistic focus on those at the bottom, who could be surveyed, observed, and controlled. *People* came to be defined as populations that could be ordered through the political arithmetic of the state, which the French called *statistique*. State administrators spoke of social welfare in terms of biological issues such as reproduction, disease, and education (individual development, growth, and evolution). Human needs were seen as instrumental and empirical in relation to the functioning of the state.

A particular set of relations emerged in education. New systems of monitoring children developed in the 17th and 18th centuries that are still incorporated into the public school systems of Britain and the United States (Hamilton, 1989). Education's social purpose was defined as the preparation of the child for a useful role in society through individual discipline and self-government.

The new pedagogic forms of the 18th century onward were tied to pastoral processes previously associated with Christianity. The use of clinical methods in medicine and psychiatry reformulated the religious concepts of progress and self-discipline into a secularized pedagogy about the individual. The intention was to make institutions less physically repressive and more humane. The discourse posited that individuals can know and change themselves by evaluating their behaviors within an appropriate discourse of science. It became possible, therefore, for the individual to think about himself or herself in ways that valued personal feelings, thoughts, and attitudes; to use personal reflection to investigate one's self-worth and competence. However, the distinctions and management of personality were also to be made part of a public discourse that was to be scientific and helpful to the individual in the management of daily life and social relations. Psychology replaced theology and philosophy as the central social discipline. The "soul" was reformulated as the product of personality, motivation, and learning "traits."

New confessional devices, however, provided a means by which power could circulate within institutions through the body and mind of the disciplined individual. The individual's innermost thoughts were made the focus of the experts' gaze, transposing the person into the "other" that specialists have defined. Truth of "self" was separated from power and considered as a means by which the person could gain self-discipline.

> The conviction that truth can be discovered through the self-examination of consciousness and the confession of one's thoughts and acts now appears so natural, so compelling, indeed so self-evident, that it seems unreasonable to posit that such self-examination is a central component in a strategy of power. This unseemingness rests on an attachment to the repressive hypothesis; if the truth is inherently opposed to power, then its uncovering would surely lead us on the path to liberation (Foucault, "Afterword" in Dreyfus & Rabinow, 1983, p. 175).

The confessional devices and individualization of social affairs made power invisible by bringing the spotlight to bear on people's thoughts, attitudes, and behaviors. The pastoral gaze was related to the production of new forms of social regulation that was given organization through professional knowledge. Human needs were no longer conceived of as ends in themselves or the subject of a philosophic discourse that sought to discover their theological origins or essential nature. The lack of relation between means and ends was facilitated by the methods of discretion and lack of a history, confusing control with the broader concept of action. These residues are found in the discussion of pedagogical models of reforms in which there is a blurring of the relation of theory to practical reasoning (see Chapter 6).

The Professionalization of Knowledge

As with 18th-century humanism, the public rhetoric of late 19th-century schooling affirmed the noble myths of the Enlightenment but interpreted the world and individuality through particular scientific discourses formed within professional communities. Expert knowledge, organized around the rationalities of science, was to free people from the constraints of nature and offer paths towards a more progressive social world. If people could reflect about their conditions, they could also consider means by which to rationally improve them. In the United States, the idea of progress legitimated the social sciences as the spokesperson for providing a rational course to history (Ross, 1984). Rational means were to be employed to assist in planning, coordinating, and evaluating institutions. Yet the specific technologies of professional humanism reflected the tensions between emancipatory and social regulating patterns. Methods of social administration were invented to organize people and their thoughts, attitudes, emotions, and practices. The most detailed elements of social planning and human psychology emerged. Private domains that were only subtly reached through theological supervision were open to scrutiny by methodologies that could observe feelings, attitudes, and dispositions, as well as organize facts and information.

The hopes, ambiguities, and contradictions of the Enlightenment are reflected in 19th-century social, political, and educational reforms, with mass schooling as the major reform of the period. A commitment to social progress based on reason and rationality was conceptualized as an empirical rather than a moral or speculative problem. The new professional communities of the social and educational sciences embodied this epistemological break (Abrams, 1968; Haskell, 1977; Silva & Slaughter, 1984). The social practices of the professional experts placed them in an authoritative position in the process of reform. Sciences of social and psychological planning were to monitor institutional patterns and produce humanist interventions that would bring social and individual progress.

In the 17th century, Bacon had talked about the scientist as the "new priest." Newton saw science as a way to make apparent God's designs in nature and to ensure their fulfillment on earth. By the 19th century, notions of planning, guiding, and supervising individual life were being applied to social institutions. While adhering to rules of argument and styles of reasoning associated with the physical sciences, the discourses of the human sciences maintained distinctions and visions of social relations that tied them to the tensions and strains of material conditions. The first professionals to identify themselves as social scientists were concerned with translating their Protestant beliefs about salvation into institutional arrangements to perform good works and save the poor. Merit and democracy underscored the conviction about an individual and collective millennial. Efforts to collect information and to agitate for reform were to assist in bringing "manifest destiny" to the New World. By the 20th century, the discourse of the human sciences had been incorporated into the state as its power became more centralized and expansive.[10]

Changing relations among social, cultural, economic, and religious patterns produced a political arena that related the social sciences to the modern planning state. In an important sense, the modern state performs an evaluation that defines and organizes public space (Bourdieu,

1989b). To operate effectively, the administrative apparatus of the state needed knowledge that was concrete, specific, and measurable. Demands for information about the state's environment, population, resources, and problems required the development of a whole array of empirical methods to plan, organize, and monitor social activities. Statistics referred to the collection of a variety of descriptive and mathematical data about populations that could help state officials classify people and problems. The sciences of the state made private problems into public issues of administrative scrutiny and control.

Problems of state management at the macrolevel also introduced new management issues at the microlevel. This problem is most seriously articulated in the production of modern schooling. Exposure of the individual to public scrutiny was integral to the new pedagogies. There were conceptions of correct information (learning), attitudes (socialization), deviance (backward and disadvantaged), sexuality, domesticity, as well as measures of competence and incompetence. Through a combination of hierarchical observations and normalizing judgments, all human characteristics become potential categories of observation and social administration, as, for example, in the current language of federal intervention, the "at-risk student." The political focus on the individual made intention rather than transgression the central criterion of culpability.[11]

At a different level, professional communities were tied to the state as a response to the growth of capitalism (Haskell, 1984). Professional communities in the United States were to challenge the self-interest of an unbridled capitalism in which an individualism of the market dominated. These were seen by certain privileged segments of United States society as morally bankrupt. Professionalism was to take the rationalism and competitiveness of the market and modify its self-interest through rewards that were nonpecuniary (glory and recognition tied to epistemological achievement) as well as financial, thus tempering and altering self-interest to promote a common, moral community.

INSTITUTIONAL DEVELOPMENT, THE STATE, AND SCHOOLING

I introduce the state not as a Weberian concept of legal-administrative power of government but as a concept that directs attention to the changing relations in governing, of which schooling is one important element. Mass schooling emerged with the development of the modern nation-state in Europe and the United States, although with differences between the two places (Ramirez & Boli, 1987). Schooling is a concept that presupposes structures of governing in society in which the macro- and microproblems of the state are brought together.[12] My concern with the state involves not only the structured relations that exist between civil society and public authority. It also includes a focus on how management of the state assumes a crucial place in the formation of civil society, and how social regulation of the self is crucial to the production of will, desire, and value in society.

The two levels of management are directly and indirectly established in the formation of schooling. There is the direct supervision and certification of schooling by the state. At the same time, there is a social and epistemological organization of schools in producing a moral, cultural, and social discipline of the population.

A state commitment to schooling becomes an important moral and political concern in a just and democratic society. But the dual implications of the technologies of schooling must be recognized. The capabilities and sensitivities introduced by schooling were intended to enable individuals to manage and innovate in the new social and political arrangements; the pedagogies in the United States were to reconcile the new demands and possibilities of contemporary society with an individualism that focused on the obligations and responsibilities of the citizen and worker. At the same time, the pedagogies imposed new technologies to regulate the individual in a manner that interrelated with the multiple demands of the new economy, culture, and the expanding state. The therapeutic attitude toward the individual, a new recognition of the role of personality, and a definition of society as systems of abstract and discrete units establish linkages between the state and individual governance.[13]

In this sense, we can understand a relation of policing to policy. Policing, in its 18th-century French and German sense, referred to the specific techniques by which a government was able to govern its citizens as individuals significantly useful in the world (Foucault, 1988). Techniques included gathering demographic and other population data to steer its policies. In the modern state, individualization of social affairs and pastoral techniques provide a more sophisticated and subtle form of policing. Pedagogy is one form of this social regulation that ties the citizen to the state.

The power that underlies the processes of governance is twofold: It is the ability to assign or reassign meaning and practice to the organization of social affairs. Typically, this notion of power has assumed a sovereignty in which certain interests and social actors emerge to give direction to current practices. As power relates to the state, there is a concern with who rules and how that rule is exercised (Torres, 1989). Power's second meaning reverses this notion of sovereignty and focuses instead on how individuals are constituted and the mechanisms that censor the self; that is, the choice of one set of practices over its alternatives as a component in the production of identity. In this context, the dualism of community and individual that preoccupies much political theory erodes; power is found in the depths of activities that are *not* political in the sense that they belong to the forms of government or ruling elites.

The social formations in schooling, however, are not static but entail changing coalitions and alignments in governing that are interrelated with the discourse patterns of schooling. While I have focused here on central problems concerning the relations of power and knowledge in schooling, it is the task of the following chapters to pursue the relations and the ruptures that occurred in the past and that have been carried into the contemporary reform practices. These governing patterns establish an arena of the state as it relates to schooling. School reform is a history of the changing relations of the nexus of knowledge/power that ties individuals to problems of governance.

CONCLUSIONS

I began this chapter with a discussion of the problems of structured relations that exist among institutions. These relations contain particular problems of knowledge and power when focusing on schooling. Pedagogy has the dual quality of social regulation and recognition of the socially constructed potential of human capabilities. The discussion then focused on changes in the social epistemology that have implications for the study of school reform, giving attention to the centrality of the relation of power to knowledge. In this sense, the epistemology of schooling is a social practice that sustains and produces worlds for individuals. Concepts of progress and the state were also introduced in the study of the changing patterns of social regulation.

Positioning knowledge in structural relations provides a historical method to explore how epistemologies make life intelligible, how they discipline desire and will, and, at the same time, how they respond to social affairs to qualify and disqualify particular forms of reason and provisions of principle. The issue behind change is how and why forms of truth come to prevail and, at different points, are historically challenged. For the purposes here, the study of change asks how it is possible to speak about school, its sciences, teaching, and reform as we do. It seeks a notion of history in contemporary events that focuses on the heritage of social forms underlying social practices. In this context, the categories and classifications of school reform are relational problems.

By making problematic the standards of truth that underlie daily life, there are no individual heroes, freedom, or unique events in any absolute sense; the person and singular event are not significant in and of themselves. The approach does suggest an irony: To devalue what history presents as necessary or progressive is to reject the validity of precedence and to create the possibility of contesting and changing those broad practices that seem to constitute our nature. The critical engagement that places the individual within a history of social affairs can provide points of weakness in the "regimes of truth" and thus identify potential sites of transformation. In this manner, the collective and individual actor is brought back into the constructions of social life, a central element of the last chapter.

I will now consider how the problem of change is tied to various concepts of reform, professionalism, science, and the state. These terms provide a framework in which to explore the sets of relations between knowledge and the conditions by which social regulation is established in schooling. It is argued that the interplay of pedagogy, teaching, and teacher education in the late 19th to early 20th centuries established particular sets of relations that were challenged after World War II, with the current reforms bringing to the fore certain issues in those formations. The implication of these practices is to narrow the democratic contexts in which schooling is practiced. In the final chapter, the conceptual issues are revisited in terms of political projects and their effect on the work of the intellectual. While I am aware of the political agendas of social and educational sciences to "right" the world, I cannot accept the role of science as tied to a concept of progress in a democracy. Progress is overt in the political left, buried under the rhetoric of noninterest in the positivism of social amelioration; in both instances questions are raised about the implication of an epistemology about progress.

2

Social Identity and Professionalization

The Construction of 19th-Century Teaching as an Element of State Building

In Chapter 1, I characterized the problem of educational change as one focusing on the social epistemology of school relations. It is my intent to increase recognition of the variety of historical contexts that are presupposed in the current language of reform and to identify the issue of change among the disjunctions that are elements of the social formations of schooling. To articulate the problem in this manner is to posit a history of terms, categories, and techniques by which certain norms and concepts came to be accepted as reason and truth in the construction of the possibilities of schooling.

The remainder of this book pursues the social epistemology of change through consideration of three interrelated terms that describe central categories of contemporary reform in teaching and teacher education as historically constructed through the relation between knowledge and power. Chapters 2 and 3 consider the 19th-century institutional relations that give shape and boundaries to pedagogy, profession, and educational science as a means of focusing more sharply on the constitutive experiences that occur in the depths of contemporary schooling and reform.

I will argue that the social and economic transformations that occurred during the 19th and early 20th centuries intertwined the formation of the modern state with the problems of governance. The organization of schooling, work, pedagogy, teacher education, and educational sciences provided a social field in which the governance of the individual was to emerge and take form. The issues of school reform and professionalization are incorporated into these organizational relations. At the same time, there was a stratification within the occupation, with those at the top concerned about the knowledge production and administration of the occupation, and those at the bottom, usually women, concerned with the instrumental knowledge of the "profession."

Various institutional layers and contexts intertwine as threads in the fabric of reform. The organization of teachers' work and education, as well as pedagogy and the social sciences, are the social fields that give rise to social regulations. These transformations were neither evolutionary nor reflective of a functional necessity, but rather the product of interaction, debate, and contradictions. I focus on the 19th and early 20th centuries in order to consider the social epistemology of contemporary reform practices. The post–World War II school reforms, still much in evidence up to 1990, constitute a break, I believe, in the social practices of state steering of schooling and the social regulatory role of social science and professionalization from those of the 19th century. The history presented in Chapters 2 and 3 is intended to draw from the past to interpret the breaks and continuities that embody present practice.

This historical interpretation explores the complex relations among institutions and the different layers of school practice. Readers looking for new data will not find it in the following two chapters; rather, I reanalyze standard institutional histories from a perspective concerned with the social epistemology of schooling. This strategy led me to secondary historical sources, and in particular to the discourse of elites about the purpose and function of school. In part, this focus results from the documentation available prior to the 1880s. But this analysis depends less upon the speakers than upon the modes of expression— the ways innovation is placed in relation to existing ideas and the institutional authority that sanctions the ideas. The historian may be uncomfortable with the conceptual reposing of the typical narratives that detail particular events and their sequences. But the intent of the current discussion is not to trace the chronology of school development nor to argue the agendas of individuals, but to provide an interpretation of certain continuities and discontinuities in the social relations of contemporary school reform. For those who wish to consider the historical references that underlie this discussion, citations are included in the text.

THE FORMATION OF THE MODERN STATE
AND THE PROGRESSIVE REFORMS

By the late 1800s, the United States was experiencing tremendous social, cultural, and material change (see Bledstein, 1976; Davis, 1967; Hofstadter, 1955, 1962; Schiesl, 1977; Walters, 1978). In a short span of time, society witnessed vast changes. A massive influx of immigrants streamed into the United States, first from northern Europe and then from eastern and southern Europe. The problem of "Americanization" became paramount as the nation's urban areas were flooded with newcomers who spoke a variety of languages, practiced a variety of religions, and maintained social dispositions and cultural ethos that clashed with dominant Anglo-Saxon Protestant views. Material transformations also were occurring. Canals were constructed, population levels were dramatically increased, small-scale manufacturing grew, national industrial infrastructures developed, and commercial growth continued. The changes affected rural as well as urban communities. Technology and commercialization in farming prevented the development of a distinctively European rural, agrarian culture as land prices and speculation promoted Protestant bourgeois values (Hofstadter, 1955).

Different social institutions helped to redefine the relation of the individual to society during this period, and in the process reformulated longstanding patterns of social regulation and structural relations. The Progressive Era (1880–1920) in the United States provides an important forum in which to consider the social dynamics that were shaping social relations. I use the label "Progressive Era" as a convenient marker to describe what was, in reality, a series of uneven developments, conflicting paths, and breaks in social patterns that have longer durations; it also helps to locate "progressive schooling" in the structural relations and rupture that it presupposes.

Called the Age of Reform, the Progressive Era's major innovations included the formation of a state administration to coordinate, monitor, and regulate major segments of society (Hofstadter, 1955). Management structures were created for social welfare, government, transportation, and mass schooling. While not without contradictions, the period promoted a belief in institutional reforms as purposeful interventions to alter and improve social life. Reform became more and more a part of the normal regulation of social life.

The modern state in the United States was an invention of the 19th and early 20th centuries. Evident by the time of the Progressive Era but continuing up to World War II, a centralized state administration developed in the transportation, agricultural, industrial relations, and military sectors.[1] The logistical muddle caused by variations in the size of railroad tracks from state to state, as well as the inconsistencies in internal tariff systems, made the need for standardization readily apparent. Alternative models of administrative reform were designed to circumvent the predominant systems of local governance and party control that had been in place since the 18th century. New forms of governmental administrative agencies, such as the Interstate Commerce Commission, replaced the older networks of political parties and courts in managing the economic and social-welfare needs of the nation (Skowronek, 1982). The university and the social sciences appeared as aspects of the new patterns of social regulation emerging during this period.

Industrial society produced conditions that made its citizens more interdependent, thus demanding more institutional regulation and control. Government came to be viewed as an indispensable agent to support individual dignity, security, and the regulation of competition that was to underlie responsible personal initiatives. These changes in production, culture, and religion raised questions about a laissez faire policy toward industrialization, social welfare, and the role of the state (Fine, 1956). From the ideology of independence and distrust of state that drove the American Revolution, the new liberalism prompted a rethinking of the "progressive" relationship between a society and its policy (Orloff & Skocpol, 1984).

New political doctrines of democracy emerged in relation to economic ideology (see Dolbeare & Dolbeare, 1973). Early notions of governance, as defined by the face-to-face community interactions of individuals, were replaced by theories of democracy centered around interest-group representation. The New England town meeting of the 1800s became less and less representative of how the people and their government interacted. The new notions of democratic participation, however, also separated that which was public from that which was private and domestic. The male citizen acted rationally and with reason; the female cared for the home, drawing upon her natural attributes of sympathy and empathy. The new patterns of citizenship mirrored gender relations that brought politics and economic issues into the problem of governing at the family level.

The reconstitution of the state system entailed not only a modernization of the political system, but also new forms of participation, interpretation, social management, and amelioration that often incorporated contradictions and tensions. The political system had undergone fundamental revisions by the end of the Progressive Era: Universal suffrage for white adult males became law. At the same time, greater government regulation in everyday life was secured through new policies of social welfare. Social-welfare agencies became responsible for child labor, health, education, and social planning; these agencies established a link between the "macro" programs of state governance and the "micro" organizations of the family and the school (Foucault, 1979b).

The social gospel movement among northern Protestant churches helped to redefine the obligations of the society and state during this period of transformation (see May, 1949). After the Civil War, ministers preached a social gospel that absolved the poor of responsibility for their condition and characterized the social system as in need of reform. The individual was no longer considered personally responsible for his or her economic and social existence, nor for the salvation of his or her soul. A social environmentalism was stressed in which efficient institutions could instill in individuals the necessary notions of civility and ethics for success in the new world. The journalistic muckrakers gave secular voice to the issues raised in the social gospel movement, providing a popular avenue by which to uncover the evils and tyrannies of social institutions, and to improve the environment of the individual.

A crucial link in the changing patterns of social organization was the professionalization of knowledge. In the face of this burgeoning social-welfare network there emerged a new rationale and approach to public problems. Social amelioration was defined as a problem of secular, scientific evidence that could order and guide social planning. Science was to provide objective, nonevaluative descriptions of how social institutions worked. The authority of the expert was founded on evidence and dependent on the rules of logic and reference to the empirical, rather than on the social status of the speaker or the authority of God.

These trends in social governance were embodied in the changing meaning of reform. Initially, reformers were middle- and upper-class citizens interested in improving social welfare through such causes as abolition and temperance, as well as through the promotion of self-help and economic independence (Walters, 1978). Antebellum reforms had been "very much that of evangelical Protestantism, with a leavening of rhetoric from the American Revolution and a dash of scientific thought" (Walters, 1978, p. 214). These reformers thought they were attacking sin rather than social crisis, and they urged individual repentance rather than legislation and coercion. But as early as the 1830s, the crises of the cities and rural areas were increasingly seen as problems of institutional reform rather than of individual sin and salvation. Moral in purpose, civic reform was to engender a return to agrarian values as well as personal entrepreneurship and individual opportunity through private philanthropy and, later, through federal programs. The Populist movements in the mid-century, challenging business concentration and agricultural policies, were the first to call for federal responsibility in social reform (Hofstadter, 1955). In the 20th century, further changes occurred in the style of perceiving problems, strategies, and solutions for altering social conditions. Reform entailed a rationalistic approach to science that would turn deviants into model citizens.

The reformers throughout most of the 19th century tended to be Eastern patricians, children of merchants, clergy, physicians, educators, and editors, whose worldview decried a moral and social degeneration and the eclipse of democracy. They passionately believed in their public duty, which combined a Protestant Unitarianism with a philosophical transcendentalism.[2] By the end of the century, this patrician was replaced by the reformer who was typically the child of a clergyman and whose sense of religious commitment and duty was given direction by a secularized training in the new social sciences. New professions of social science were to direct the progressive reforms and, in the process, to transform popularist and democratic ideal of service into one of expert knowledge for charting material and social progress, a shift discussed in Chapter 3.

A faith that science would bring about social amelioration did come to dominate public policy in the Progressive Era and was sustained as part of a larger discourse of professionalism. Social sciences were brought into the spheres of social affairs to interpret the more complex social relations and interdependence among communities and to reassert moral, social, and cultural authority through the process of reform. This brand of reform combined a commitment to Christian ethics associated with the social gospel movement with the reorganization of social, cultural, economic, and governmental affairs. The social sciences also entailed forms of empirical analysis upon which to base interpretations that could guide reform.

The purpose of such reform was to establish the norms of a Protestant, industrial democracy that would guide all social strata and groups (see, e.g., Bellah, 1968). As Jackson Lears (1981) argues:

> The cultural dominance of the bourgeoisie was partly an unintended consequence of scientific (though often self-deceiving) efforts to impose moral meaning on a rapidly changing world—efforts led not by bankers and industrialists but by ministers and other moralists. The best term for this process is not social control but cultural hegemony. (p. 10)

The cultural and religious definitions of progressivism made it plausible for the business community to lend strong support to the new sociologies, social psychologies, and education that emphasized environmentalism. Social scientists provided advice about how welfare policy could be improved through studies of the ways in which individuals and institutions interacted (see Haskell, 1977; Karier, 1986; O'Donnell, 1985).

The emergence of a policy of reform generated much debate and spun off in several directions simultaneously (see Silva & Slaughter, 1984). Businesses argued about the "nature" of labor relations. Religious groups debated the ways in which social institutions could serve God's will. Elites argued about the most appropriate mechanisms by which to incorporate immigrants into a Protestant society. The traditional mores of local government and theories of laissez faire politics and economics were being pressed by new demands for standardization and regulation in a stronger state. Debate raged within the social disciplines about the knowledge necessary for governance and about the social scientist's role in the planning, development, and evaluation of policies of social amelioration.

It is important to recognize at this point that the general histories of U.S. schooling are those of the Northeast and Midwest, and mostly of the white population. Before 1865, blacks were treated as property, not having souls to be saved and therefore having no need to read the Bible. In the South, state school systems were not modernized until after World War II, with the reform movements of the 1980s being part of that process. (For historical discussion of southern urban education, see Plank & Turner, 1987; Turner, 1989.) While the northern leaders saw the forces of industrialism and science as part and parcel of a religious crusade, the South had a very different material structure and collective consciousness (Johnson, 1986). Its ruling elites and poor whites maintained traditional notions of individual responsibility for one's social circumstances. Southern whites used the early 19th-century view of sin to focus on the black as a scapegoat for the plight of the farmers and the white poor. Following a brief period of inclusion after the Civil War, blacks were excluded after the 1890s from even second-class citizenship and educational opportunity (Noble, 1970).

It is important to note that through this and the following chapters, I tie particular sets of northern Protestant beliefs to social reform practices. The role of this element in the formation of mass schooling, universities, and social/education sciences is typically omitted in U.S. school histories about the period after the 1880s. My intent is not to impute motive to the restructuring; neither is it to ignore contradictory tendencies among religious groups toward social policy. The following discussion places particular strands of religious practice within the complex relations and epistemologies that evolved into the reforms that produced mass schooling.

SCHOOLING AS LOCALLY ORGANIZED STATE ACTIVITY

To consider mass schooling as a social reform, it is first necessary to review the process by which the state assumed the problem of schooling. Since at least the Protestant Reformation, schools had been an instrument of moral control and individual discipline, based on the relation of the state, civil authority, and moral discipline found in the reforms introduced by Martin Luther. Childhood and literacy became institutionalized as a strategy to confront social disorder with a standard set of religious, social, and moral values. Luke (1989), considering German reforms of the 16th century, argues:

> Humanist values alone perhaps would not have led to a call for public, mass education; but the need for state and church unity in the face of apparent moral and social decline in sixteenth century Germany required a total reassessment of existing affairs and call for reform of the social order for which Luther became the spokesperson. (p. 97)

This commitment to schools was expected to promote true faith, service to the state, and the proper functioning of the family. It was rearticulated in a new field of social relations in the 19th century. The school was seen as providing a social form by which the problem of social administration and upbringing in the modern state was resolved. If the state was to be responsible for the welfare of its citizens, the identity of individuals had to be linked to the administrative patterns found in the larger society. Free public schools, for example, were maintained in colonial times by the Puritans in New England to teach all believers to read the Bible. Reading was a conservative strategy of Calvinism but also a progressive strategy to enlarge participation in the Republic (Kaestle, 1985). Faith in the self-sufficiency of the individual coupled with Protestant beliefs about original sin, which viewed poverty as due to personal failure, however, made the support of state schools difficult during the years following the American Revolution. The various models of 19th-century pedagogy augmented the family role in child rearing. State schooling was emerging as a major institution for transmitting the cultural orientations, values, and styles of the cognitive approaches associated with modernity.

Moral tenets merged with other components of the national set of beliefs to create an American myth designed to guide—and explain— the country's destiny. This worldview was defined by beliefs in the unique destiny of America, the existence of a providential guiding hand in history, the westward progress of civilization, and the supportive relationship between material and moral progress. These combined as a millennial belief that social reform would create good citizens, moral character, and work habits to promote individual advancement. The major reform that encapsulated this belief was schooling.

Citizenship, Upbringing, and the Construction of Schooling

Protestant culture in the 19th century helped to make possible the construction of state-supported local schools. A longstanding Protestant commitment to literacy resulted in high rural enrollments in comparison to those in urban settings during the first half of the century. The northern Protestant social gospel movement made schooling an important institution to enable the uninitiated to participate successfully in American society. There was, however, religious debate, arising from concern among Catholic leadership, about which Bible should be placed in schools and the specific moral tone that should be emphasized.

Issues of citizenship were important to debates about schooling. As early as 1786, Philadelphia physician and statesman Benjamin Rush had declared that communities should support schools to convert men into republican machines "so they can perform their parts properly in the great machine of the state" (Kaestle, 1983, p. 7). Reading was still essential, no longer as a means by which to master the precepts of the Bible, but as a tool to prepare enlightened citizens for their place in the newly emerging democracy.

The state school also provided a response to the intense social anxiety about creating harmony and stability (Conway, 1974). As early as the 1840s, problems of poverty, cultural diversity, and urban life had become more intractable and burdensome. The urban charity school system was expanded into a public, state-run institution because it was expected to reduce crime and disruption and to introduce domestic tranquility into the cities. A thoroughly American curriculum would establish a national language, unify the culture of the new nation, wean immigrants away from a corrupt Europe, and instill appropriate habits and bonds among social classes.

State schools were developed by the middle 1800s by the privileged for the good of the less fortunate, but they also were designed to serve the middle classes. The connection between schooling and careers became more explicit in public discourse, and educators expanded their popular base and tax support by appealing to the interests of the middle class (Kaestle, 1983). Curriculum changes that promoted individualistic goals of intellectual growth and personal advancement increased middle-class participation and support, and the introduction of academic subjects tied college preparation to middle-class patterns of social mobility (see Katznelson & Weil, 1986; Popkewitz, 1987c).

The tensions of poverty, cultural diversity, and urbanization, among others, defined an ideology of schooling that was nonpartisan and distinct from the issues of the state. A system of education supported by local taxes and regulated by a loose affiliation between state government agencies and local community school boards set schools apart from any formal governmental apparatus (Spring, 1988). A school civil service administration developed separately from other state agencies. Professional associations of teachers and institutions of teacher training became strongest in their provincial locations. The strengths of the local school bureaucracy were reinforced by state government superintendents who operated on shoestring budgets and wielded minimal regulatory control until the middle of the 20th century. Created in 1867 to gather educational statistics and to watch over federal reindeer herds in Alaska, the U.S. Office of Education was relegated to a minor position in government until the 1960s.[3]

By the close of the century, schooling was an institution to mediate the relations among the family, culture, economy, and state. Schooling was to promote political conformity by providing social stability, intelligent but acquiescent citizens, obedient children for anxious parents, and productive workers for an emerging capitalist economy. Schools also promised to confer opportunity and status through literacy and the development of character.

We can view modern public education as a response to, and part of the social formation of, what we now consider the state. "Modern public education and its changes are products of further reform. From its inception mass public education has been a rationalistic and scientific effort to reform society—to restructure the population and incorporate it in a rationalized society (and often the state organization)" (Meyer, 1986, p. 45). The rational planning, organization, and evaluation of such a collective and purposeful enterprise entailed the formation of new occupational practices and relations. These practices and relations are implicated in the social fields that underlie what we now associate with the professions and with professional knowledge.

A Decentralized State Schooling

Linking schooling to the state involved establishing local administrations and community school districts, rather than the single centralized system common in Europe. Liberal theories of laissez faire were coupled with the political and social strains of a nation confronting industrialization, urbanization, and "assimilation" of vast numbers of immigrants in a manner that produced particular local responses. Localized administration of schooling was sensitive to cultural variations in patterns of childrearing and notions of civility while, at the same time, redefining them through the organization of pedagogy and school discipline (Callahan, 1962; Conway, 1974; Tyack & Hansot, 1982). In various places and times, school responses to cultural, economic, and religious tensions included native language studies for immigrants, "released time" from school for religious instruction to accommodate non-Protestant groups, vocational trade schools to accommodate the needs and concerns of businesses and unions, and art appreciation programs for the new middle classes who sought to use the school to promote social mobility. At the same time, commercial textbook publishers produced schoolbooks that were distributed nationally and served as an unofficial national curriculum without legislation or public debate (Westbury, 1990).

A particular national selectivity emerged in the epistemology that organized the decentralized school administration.[4] The same forms of rationalization that organized government and business practices—efficiency, procedural consistency, and hierarchical organization—became important elements of school reform (see Weber, 1904–5/1958). The school administration assumed organizational control, first in establishing hiring and salary policies within local districts and later in developing and inculcating the curriculum (Callahan, 1962; Tyack & Hansot, 1982).

The administrative perspectives introduced particular interaction patterns into the organization of students, teachers, and knowledge, even in elite urban high schools in the East (Labaree, 1988).[5] Sciences of pedagogy defined teaching as a hierarchical ordering of information and the organization of the school class as the discrete planning of individual lessons (see Chapter 3). The "cult of efficiency," to borrow a phrase from the arena of school administration (Callahan, 1962), often dominated, despite the fact that it conflicted with a common liberalism that focused on a child-centered pedagogy or education as social service to the community (Tyack, 1974; Tyack & Hansot, 1982).

As one reviews the discourses about schooling, especially during the late 19th century, it could be argued that a formally centralized state school system was unnecessary. American republicanism, bourgeois ideologies, Protestantism, and a meritocracy that combined ascription with achievement were deeply rooted in the discourse that formed public education (Labaree, 1988). Networks existed among the state, business, religious, and "professional" communities in which the assumptions of modernization were debated and strategies of reform were sought. The social values toward schooling reached into the small town high schools of the Midwest, just as discussions drawn from large urban newspapers and universities were brought into local women's clubs and into school policy formulation (Tlusty, 1986; also see Cuban, 1984).

The resulting patterns of schooling did not develop into a linear fashion to merely "mirror" the constructions and reconstructions of the larger society, but reworked solutions through an interrelation of regional patterns occurring in teaching, pedagogy, and teacher education. It is in the interrelation of epistemologies and institutional policy that the concepts of reform and profession appear as an expression of these social formations. The introduction of administrative notions of knowledge and social interactions in the 19th century does not imply that these conceptions were immediately brought into school processes. Rather, my argument is that the discourses of administration and science were brought into institutional relations as part of different arenas of school practice. It was not until the post–World War II period that this particular type of knowledge had immediate consequences for day-to-day practices in school. This occurred in relation to a number of factors, including changes in technological know-how that organized classroom practices and teaching.

THE CHANGING SOCIAL AND
MORAL AUTHORITY IN SCHOOLING

Mass schooling is an important element in the formation of the patterns of governing associated with the modern state. Schooling was seen as part of the democratic development of society and its millennial promise. Citizenship was taught as part of the general belief of the Enlightenment that reason and rationality were to produce progress. Ideologies of individualism expressed a belief that institutions could be created in which all citizens were treated objectively and equally (Freedman, 1989a). Conceptions of individualization were imbedded into the organization of pedagogical knowledge. (For a discussion of the different visions, see Curti, 1959; Karier, 1967; Kliebard, 1986). A language of reform and professionalism tied moral authority to schooling and occupational development. Teachers were to be "moral overseers, political stewards and . . . parent surrogates" to respond to economic, social, and cultural dislocations (Finkelstein, 1975, p. 368).

We can approach the transformations and tensions of 18th- and 19th-century society by investigating the organization of authority in teaching and pedagogy. In the early republic, authority was assigned to the teacher. By the end of the 19th century, the external authority of the teacher had been relocated through pedagogical strategies designed to encourage children to develop individual discipline. That shift, it will be argued, tied individual goals to useful social and economic practices. The conception of pedagogy presupposed an epistemology of useful knowledge that could be part of the production of identity.

The Internalization of Authority as Individual Discipline

Schools in the early republic were austere places. Benches had no backs and often were too big for their smallest occupants. In rural schools, students were instructed en masse, as there was no notion of grades or pedagogical organization by age or grade level.

Instruction was based on a simple representation of information and formal didactics. (Much of the following discussion is drawn from Kaestle, 1983.) There was little of the modern conception of psychology that presented individuals as having attributes, skills, or a "need" for motivation. The pedagogy was tied to an external system of coercion. Children were trained through repetition, drill, and the threat of the rod. Students were to learn the facts, moral precepts, and routines associated with school. Lectures were formalized, and learning was a passive affair. The notion of pedagogy in the charity schools was similar to that in rural schools, although the focus of the clientele differed. Reading moral tales and Bible passages was intended to make children content with their lot rather than ambitious to improve upon it.

While teachers commonly reported that they taught values, the moral education of children was left to the church rather than to the state or to legislators as a matter of public debate. Despite a certain amount of talk about the need for children to understand what they were learning, the routines reported in school memoirs seldom deviate: Children studied at their desks in preparation for rote recitation before the teacher. "Repetition, drilling, line upon line, and precept upon precept, with here and there a little of the birch—constituted the entire system," recalled a student of a rural school (quoted in Kaestle, 1983, p. 18). The teacher's role was likened to that of an oppressive governor: to teach children to accept the pieties of the text; to teach the values of conformity to the law; and to provide an environment that was designed to suppress spontaneity, discourage peer communication, and derive its standards of behavior from the conduct of the teacher (Finkelstein, 1975).

By the 1840s, local school communities and the early state educational agencies strenuously asserted the authority of teachers—rather than parents—over children. To create social harmony and control, the school leaders sought to compensate for what they saw as the decline of the family by reestablishing moral instruction in the role of teacher (Conway, 1971).[6] Professional teachers' associations and state school commissioners assigned to the state the "parental" duty of educating youth, and the argument that "children are the property of the state" became more commonplace (Kaestle, 1983, p. 159). The changing social patterns also entailed shifts in the pedagogical forms of schooling.

Pedagogy as the Discipline of the Self

This expansion in the authority of the teacher coincided with changing notions of pedagogy. Instruction evolved from demanding a simple repetition of knowledge to imparting a secularized pastoral attitude. The attitudes, emotions, and feelings that developed alongside the mastery of information came to be considered important, and the new pedagogies were seen as more humane and effective than the impersonal systems they replaced. Children were to internalize discipline and moral values, just as they were to be protected and molded, rather than have their wills broken by external authority.

Two pedagogies in the mid-19th century illustrate the changing epistemologies. The Lancasterian and Lanarkian systems were to instill virtue and morality; with different notions of childhood and progress, these pedagogies were to harmonize children's natural inclinations with their environment through internal discipline rather than by appeal to external authority. While earlier notions of character molding are found in the Reformation, the 19th-century pedagogy promoted an individualization that combined and secularized issues of upbringing and labor socialization.

The Lancasterian system had become popular in the United States by 1850. It originated with a Scottish-born minister, Andrew Bell, who sought to instill religious and moral principles in children. Bell's conception of monitorial instruction was drawn initially from his army work and experience in a Madras asylum, which he brought to English schooling (Hamilton, 1989). There it assimilated the language and ideologies of the Industrial Revolution and was supported by the Anglican church as a means of maintaining the status quo. Every class was under the constant supervision of its own teacher; every lesson was connected to that which preceded it. The system's highly regimented procedures maintained order as well as inculcated discipline; its moral instruction was intended to instill not only the traditional values of hard work and obedience, but also those of precision, standardization, and elaborate routines.

Teaching at this point had begun to provide constant supervision of students in every school activity (Hamilton, 1989). The Lancasterian system provided catechism and lesson plans that facilitated the work of untrained teachers. Recitation was emphasized in monitoral systems; children continually engaged in competitive groups that increased motivation. To increase the pedagogy's effectiveness, evaluation became a part of the teaching process itself. Constant testing would insure mastery, while prizes and a competitive spirit would replace cruel corporal punishment as the central means of motivation.

The school of New Lanark shifted the emphasis to piety and inner discipline. It was popularized by the Scottish industrialist Robert Owen (Hamilton, 1981).[7] An educational experiment, the approach was a response to the industrial unrest that was sweeping Scotland at a time when Owen was seeking more effective industrial management. The New Lanark school subscribed to the political belief espoused by Calvin and Knox that an investment in schooling was an essential element in the creation of piety and social virtue. The moral purpose of the infant schools was to save children's souls through religious education; the educators were to be saved through their own good works.

The active pedagogy of the New Lanark school was tied to the Scottish strain of utilitarianism, which itself was an ideological response to the Enlightenment that stressed the importance of group dynamics. In contrast to the Lancasterian system's focus on piety, Owen's educational experiments were designed to instill character. Infant school rules prohibited scolding and punishment; instead they encouraged continual kindness in teachers and unflagging curiosity in children. Answers were always to be rational; instruction was to emphasize the examination of actual objects. The schedule included exercise in music and dance when children became restless. Teachers were constantly to supervise all class members.

The individual pedagogies of Lancaster and New Lanark symbolize the tensions of modernization that were emerging in the United States; they juxtaposed conflicting images of rural Protestant democracy and the coming of the machine. Both systems involved intrusive modes of childrearing. The Lancasterian system focused on standardization, hierarchy, and order in the social world, using the monitoring system to promote piety and republican discipline. The New Lanark pedagogy maintained a utilitarian outlook that enforced an inner discipline. The underlying structure combined an individual psychology with collective ethics; the identity of the individual could be harmonized with the operation of "natural" (market) forces through the intervention of legislators (Hamilton, 1980).

New Lanark was to teach the lower classes how to connect their own interest with that of others through learning virtue and rationality. It was believed that pupils would accept the inequalities of society if schooling demonstrated that such social facts had a natural or providential origin (Hamilton, 1989).

Focus on the characteristics of pedagogy sheds light on the interrelation of institutional forms of schooling, knowledge, and occupational formations. The Lancasterian and New Lanark pedagogies embodied the sensitivities and awareness related to the process of the reorganization of labor, although they had different strategies of self-regulation.

An Epistemological Architecture: Art Education

It is possible to pursue the evolution of the epistemological architecture by focusing on art education. Beginning in the 1870s, when it was first introduced into schools, two themes continually reappear (Freedman, 1989a). An ideology of individualism emphasized the value of preparing the student for a productive and well-adjusted life through the making of art. At the same time, there was an effort to promote a common culture, one that raised moral and aesthetic standards and promoted social mobility through elite cultural knowledge.

From the 1870s to the present, these two foci have been maintained, but their content, moral purpose, and cultural dispositions have changed in relation to social, cultural, and economic pressures (see Freedman, 1987, 1989a; Freedman & Popkewitz, 1988). The introduction of a state requirement for art education in 1870 was motivated by a concern with civic education, with the cultural dispositions as well as labor skills that an individual should have (Freedman, 1987; Popkewitz & Freedman, 1985). Art first became mandatory in the Boston public schools in the form of industrial drawing, training that would supply industry with qualified designers while providing students with marketable work skills. Dependent upon ideologies of commerce and industry, increasingly viewed as appropriate to social amelioration, the curriculum was constructed by experts around scientifically organized procedures that would teach subject matter efficiently.

The drawing program was based on the belief that children developed industrial skills by perfecting isolated parts of design in a sequential and cumulative manner. Skill was achieved through the precise and repetitive copying of linear designs originally drawn by adults. The designs were believed to possess an inherent and objective order and beauty. Originality was to be accommodated only insofar as alternative patterns could be produced by combining previously accepted designs. Art instruction consisted of the dissection and reconstruction of wholes, without the vagaries of human impulse or individuality.

By the end of the 19th century, art was to be democratized and made available to all students. Children were exposed to the formal notions of aesthetics, including the principles of design, color, and shape found in all art. Art had inherent truths that could be learned by practicing the step-by-step processes of presentation in drawing composition and arrangement. For the middle classes, there was also manual training in which boys learned do-it-yourself skills that broke down the craft skills of production into a specific and hierarchical organization of work. For young adolescent immigrant children, art class was to teach them productive skills associated with their eventual work situation.

While the art curriculum involved skill training and had class differentiations, its more subtle implication was related to the form of its discourse. From the late 19th century to the earlier years of the present century, the moral qualities perceived in art education shifted from an ethic of behavior to a discourse of mental fitness and vocationalism. The character or will of the individual became conceptualized as traits of personality that were to be identified, supervised, nurtured—or changed, where deemed appropriate.

These dispositions toward pedagogy were maintained as art education evolved through its changing approaches to the individual: Art was to provide marketable skills through the development of technical skills; it was to incorporate theories of intelligence, eugenics, and the interests of the middle class through notions of talent and the "inborn potential" of the individual; and it was to provide a therapeutic context in which to overcome the imposed pathologies of culture, personality, and society found in individuals.

The art program as a curricular model contained a shift not only in the content or subjects of schooling but also in the rules of construction by which individuals define purposes, goals, and interests. By the end of the 19th century, pedagogy had shifted away from physical coercion to induce obedience and turned instead to social and psychological pressure (Finkelstein, 1975, 1989). At one layer, the curriculum was to be professionally organized by introducing rules and priorities of a particular style of knowing related to technical production and scientific management (see, e.g., Berger et al., 1973). At another level of analysis, the pedagogies contained new forms of social regulation and new ideas about the potential for the individualization of social relations. The pedagogies were to provide a way in which a child's "identity" would be disciplined to conform to contemporary social relations and to enhance individual potential (see Durkheim 1938/1977).[8]

Pedagogy, Epistemology, and Social Relations

The construction of individualized pedagogies was not new to the Progressive Era, but it was rearticulated in the 19th century in a new field of social relations. During the Lutheran pedagogical reforms of the 16th century, Luke (1989) comments that

> The precise and rigid organization of time, space and bodies in the school, coupled with the confessional procedures of the examination and punitive procedures of classroom control combined to constitute the site of early modern pedagogy where the calculated—prescientific—deployment of disciplinary power and knowledge intersected. (p. 120)

The epistemological meaning of the individual in school during this period is highlighted by Boli (1989) in a European context. The individual in the 17th- and early 18th-century context was both "irresponsible and indistinguishable" (p. 111). Related to a traditional subsistence economy in which the household was the unit of production, the individual was required only to follow the rules established by cultural patterns. One farmer is indistinguishable from another. "Their lives consist equally of the activities of primordial cultural rules in the seasonal cycle of sowing, cultivating, harvesting and so on" (p. 111). Labor was differentiated according to collective categories rather than by individual skill or interest. The head of the household received his authority from divine sovereignty without reflection of his own individuality. "His is representational (enacting) authority; his commands invoke the presence of God in the household but do not express his personal desires, goals, or needs" (p. 111).

The pedagogy of the late 19th century inscribed the teachers and the child in newly institutionalized discourse practices. The discourse practices about learning and teaching established a transformation of concepts about the discipline of the individual. The circumscribed constraints were positioned as classifications of performance, segments of learning stages, and sets of regulations. Boli (1989) argues that the conception of the individual in these new relations was related to a shift away from the household as the center of cultural and economic affairs. There was a need for a highly expanded sphere of knowledge to engender in workers the capacity to make rational calculations in daily labor situations. In addition, the idea of a social contract that is presumed in liberal economic and political theories "depends for its validity on the trustworthiness, discipline, competence, and honor of the individuals involved" (p. 112). Traditional authority and rules located in a sovereignty external to the individual was replaced by an autonomy and responsibility located in an individual who acts competently. Hamilton (1989) extends the discussion of pedagogical forms by suggesting that there is a close relationship between changing pedagogical practices, changing conceptions of labor processes, and changing assumptions about the individual and the state in cultural arenas. The relation is of school and society, not school in society.

Child-development literature can be understood in a social context. Children were portrayed as innocent and vulnerable, but also as malleable and capable of great moral and intellectual accomplishments. Childhood was connected somehow to the lost Garden of Eden and to all that was idyllic in humanity (Kliebard, 1986, p. 53). The literature ranged from the persisting Calvinist view of children as inheriting the original sin of Adam, and thus as innately depraved, to a view argued by Locke that the mind begins as a clean slate and that children were morally neutral at birth. The pedagogy of Froebel, influenced by Pestalozzi and Rousseau, held that children are naturally innocent and good, and that educational strategies should shield children from the dangers of a corrupt world.[9] As the new pedagogies redefined teaching, they also sanctioned the changing social conditions of bourgeois families and the distinction between the private (domestic and womanly) and the public (manly) that was given legitimacy in political theories (Pateman, 1988).

Pragmatism and Issues of Social Regulation

A seemingly different epistemological relation was offered by the pragmatist tradition associated with John Dewey. This approach rejected the separation of moral philosophy and science, and of individual and society, that was common to the other strands of pedagogy. Dewey's pragmatism was to interrelate community norms and rationally controlled progress in dynamic social conditions.

Dewey combined a number of different themes for the construction of schooling as it confronted the emerging processes of modernization. His ideas drew upon Emersonian democracy, which was permeated with voluntaristic, ameliorist, and activist themes. These themes were pervasive in the intellectual, urbanized, professional, and reformist components of the middle class to which Dewey belonged. Rejecting the evangelical elitist roots of Emerson's ideas, Dewey grounded his ideas instead in radical contingency, the variability of human societies and cultures, and the idea of communities as the center of contemporary thought. His epistemology combined "a mode of historical consciousness that highlights the conditioned and circumstantial character of human existence in terms of changing societies, cultures and communities" (West, 1989, pp. 69–70).

Dewey's pedagogy was to serve as an impetus for change related to the social commitments embodied in his pragmatism; it was to provide for a practical intervention against the concentration of wealth and power that resulted from industrialization. His pedagogy was also to give direct vitality to the themes of voluntarism, optimism, individualism, and amelioration that were part of the professionalized, reformist element of his time. While Dewey saw the main authority of pedagogy as based in its being an experimental science, he recognized that science was only one of the many forms of knowledge useful in determining social affairs and its possibilities. His concern was to expand and define a creative intelligence that would work toward a democracy.

The pedagogy was to replace fixed customs and feudal ideas with a more dynamic vision of social progress and harmony. The pedagogy of Dewey promised "to purge the child of the excess social baggage from the past, the erroneous and harmful traditions which kept him from being a cooperative and productive member of society" (Noble, 1970, p. 74). Each individual could discover and verify truth through science and thereby not only direct his or her own conduct, but also become an influential and decisive factor in constructing the environment.

The pedagogy, Dewey argued, contributed to industrialization by developing moral enlightenment and social harmony. Dewey feared class conflict and believed that science and technology would provide the guiding spirit by which schools, as one spectrum of a broader society, would produce social reconstruction (Karier & Hogan, 1979). Progressive pedagogy was to assist in the quest for rational change and the development of a classless, meritocratic order. Dewey argued that

> The conception of a social harmony of interests in which the achievement of each individual of his own freedom should contribute to a like perfection of the powers of all through a fraternally organized society is the permanent contribution of the industrial movement to morals. (quoted in Noble, 1970, p. 56)

The regulation of pedagogy was viewed not only as a means of purging the child of medieval traditions, but also as a way to prevent the radical ideas of Europe from finding their way into the ghettos of the city and the beliefs of the immigrants' children. The pragmatism of progressive education, political and economic leaders believed, would eliminate radical ideas and replace them with a faith in rural democracy, scientific rationality, and Protestant conceptions of civility. Pedagogy was to eliminate Marxist and socialist ideas brought from Europe by the new immigrants.

Dewey's intellectual position does not escape his particular professional, universalist view of a creative democracy (West, 1989). It posits a homogeneous community in which conflicts of structure and power are ameliorated only through discussion. Small rural communities, a consensus of artisans, and experimental methods of the natural sciences to guide social change are favored. Social change is viewed as a gradual process centered around a pedagogical content. Dewey saw the cultural tensions of his times as the product of distraught individuals, and he wanted to construct a public sphere that would create a revitalization of liberalism.

Dewey's ideas did not work. Within academia, his professional constituency found more appealing the managerial ideologies of corporate liberalism and Marxist ideologies of class struggles, both of which had the advantage of identifying a single embracing cause to explain social tensions (West, 1989).

While Dewey's pragmatism spawned an expansive pedagogical program, its impact was limited to a few school programs. Its epistemology contained an intellectual tentativeness that could not be easily evaluated, which made it difficult to implement in mass schooling, unlike the testing-and-measurement or child-development movements. But just as important, the social organization of schooling and teacher education separated moral philosophy and theology from teaching. These relations mitigated against a social psychology that would revise the control patterns established for both student and teacher. What occurred was the transformation of pragmatism into technical exercises of unit planning and a child-centered curriculum that focused on the individual making of meaning rather than the social construction of knowledge.

Pragmatism as it was incorporated into schooling became an exegesis; science replaced theology as practical knowledge was to empower individuals to know and to change themselves and their communities. It was a nonhistorical pragmatism that focused on the internalization of external norms as part of the discipline of self. Its evolutionary view of change and its notion of problem solving denied history in the formation of reflection, and possibility was reduced to problem solving about that which already existed.

This is not to minimize the importance of pragmatism as a uniquely American philosophy nor its position within a social field that made it a plausible alternative for the social regulation of schooling. Dewey's strategies, while sensitive to the various roles science and psychology play in schooling, were complementary rather than oppositional to other pedagogies as they related to issues of social regulation. G. Stanley Hall (1905/1969a; 1905/1969b), a late-19th-century psychologist, promoted a pedagogy that held that the natural order of child development was the most scientifically defensible basis for the construction of school instruction. The sociologist Lester Frank Ward (1915) saw the school as a principal force in social change and social justice. It was the role of the curriculum to make the school a leading institution in progressive social change. Pedagogies were to preserve tradition while being responsive to the transformations in rural and urban societies; in a broad sense, the pedagogies articulated strategies for responding to concerns about harmony, community, social change, and social regulation of the individual.

The pedagogies that had emerged by the early 20th century valued cultural definitions that stressed individualism and the importance of personal inner control and motivation. They responded to the pressures that were redesigning social life and the demands for a sanctuary that would provide a secure, caring relation; one that, according to the prevailing ideology, was to be offered by the bourgeois home. At the same time, the epistemology of school was based on a discourse about the individual. Since children were educated and protected through schooling, the new normalizing patterns of pedagogy organized the subjective definitions of happiness, pleasure, and advancement. Moral education, once characterized as public presentation and didactic moral insight, involved guidance and spiritual direction of an individual's most specific actions, behaviors, and thoughts.

While there were debates about how to preserve the traditions of Protestant rural democracy in the face of the new metaphors of machine and science, the new pedagogical strands created moral frameworks according to which people could be treated in seemingly objective and equitable ways. At the same time, the rational conditions were to be made less intimidating or homogenizing by the pedagogies' concern with the individual's unique qualities and traits. The pedagogies responded to the plurality of realities that had come to dominate, thereby enabling the individual to consider the "self" in concrete ways and as a functional and anonymous member of larger systems.

PROFESSIONAL IMAGES AND OCCUPATIONAL IDENTITY

Shifting views of pedagogy were coupled with changes in the social organization of teaching. Throughout the 19th century, there was reference to teaching as a profession, even while the social meaning and practices of schooling were being drastically transformed. To make schooling more appealing to immigrants, as well as to the industrial working and middle classes, the ideology developed of teaching as a "classless profession," one that muted social distinctions in considering issues about achievement and success (Mattingly, 1975). A professional was deemed to be above or outside consideration of social class and political maneuvering. A school professional was characterized as treating all students equally, with success determined by personal competence and hardwork. Teacher education required only efficient skill training. At the same time, the older networks built on face-to-face interactions and interpersonal relations were to be replaced by more abstract patterns of communication, which, in turn, created the generalized categories of the individual abilities, skills, and attitudes. These were the hallmarks of the larger movement of professionalization that was to be incorporated into teaching (Haskell, 1977).

Character and Career

The epistemological changes in schools were related to demands for teachers' preparation. Where the traditional definition of *professional* had limited it to a given ministerial style, the late 19th century saw a new emphasis on the concepts of organization and occupational career—a change that initiated what would become a continual struggle between the older theological conceptions of teaching and the instrumental concerns of the new professions. Training procedures originally called for an institutional overlap of a moral focus with science; but they later maintained a hierarchy between expert knowledge and classroom teachers, who, as I will consider later, were largely women.

The early educational reformers (1830–1860), such as Frederick Barnard, the nation's first Commissioner of Education, and Horace Mann, a superintendent of the Massachusetts school system, focused on the problem of inadequately prepared professionals. They sought to develop a loose system of voluntary associations, such as institutes, lyceums, and literary societies; similarly, lectures, observations of experienced teachers, and practical experience were offered to aspiring teachers.

Mann, in the twelfth annual report of the Massachusetts Board of Education (1849), focused on both secular and religious purposes in the improvement of teachers. The school, Mann argued, cannot be successful,

> without the living teacher, equipped to be consecrated for his great work. His mind replenished with knowledge, his heart effusive of virtuous influences, and all his faculties trained and devoted to the

one purpose of fashioning character after a high and enduring standard of excellence, without such a supply of such teachers for our schools [other school expenditures and activities] . . . will be in vain. (p. 27)

Professionalization focused on the character of the teacher. Teaching, it was believed, embodied a quasi-spiritual property that drew upon the moral potential within each student that was susceptible to improvement and refinement under the proper influences. The "character" of a teacher referred to her specific attitudes of intellectual discipline and self-possession.

The first teaching institute was, in fact, called a seminary, to underscore the relationship between the ministerial and pedagogical. The seminary was to enlist the Christian sincerity of the young in benevolent enterprises. The moral and personal qualities of the instructor were viewed as responsible for the intellectual growth, moral conviction, and social consciousness of her pupils.

Acceptance at a teaching seminary implied that an applicant's desire to cultivate moral discipline had been certified by the institution, and that the applicant had been identified as successful and of unquestioned character. Training in one's profession provided an opportunity for manifesting Christian sincerity by "professing" that sincerity. It was an apprenticeship to consecrate one's devotion to work and to an expression of Christian sincerity, virtues that it was thought, could only be achieved through some form of specialized training.

The process of teacher preparation was viewed as an awakening, which meant that everyone was capable of professional improvement and would profit from attending an institute or seminary. The institutes were to inspire the inner person and to train for minimal competence in actual classroom performance. More important, training was to shape an individual's potential for good. For Barnard, teaching was the "chosen priesthood" of society, and the Reverend Thomas H. Gallaudet spoke of a teaching seminar as a religious quest (Mattingly, 1975). Discussion of technique was placed in a nonmechanistic context, such as the development of moral character (Mattingly, 1975). Associating teacher education with moral character shifted its focus to a range of special motives inherent in Christian morality and away from a series of special consequences or achievements.

Training of professional teachers involved their recognition of larger principles of the republic and their inner submission to them. In addition, it was the role of the institutes to train teachers to extract total obedience from their students (Finkelstein, 1975). This focus on character also assigned importance to the individual's exercise of rational choice in selecting a career, a choice that was fraught with operational ambiguity: On one hand, the early institutes preached self-control and submission; on the other, they prodded young professionals toward self-motivation and self-improvement.

The notion of character was related to a transformation of the conception of the individual within the U.S. middle class (Bledstein, 1976). In the 18th century, the middle classes viewed character as moral qualities of the individual. Discussions about teachers were related to the conception of the curriculum as external adornments of the individual. By the end of the 19th and the early 20th centuries, however, character was no longer considered part of an individual's attributes, but an incarnation of the secular "self." Industry and frugality were equated with mental initiative, self-reliance, and utility. The individual had a personality that could discover reason, perceive a rational order, and become self-reliant in a world that was thought to be lacking in social authority. The self was conceived of as "capable of personal change; impressing others and gaining their approval became an important aim in life, far outstripping the value of doing the morally correct act" (Cushman, 1990, p. 602). Revelation was internal to the individual and tied to the discipline of self, a corollary to the epistemological changes in the conception of pedagogical knowledge. By the first two decades of the 20th century, for example, advertising was invented to capitalize on the belief in personal change through consumption.

The changing meanings of self and profession can be considered more explicitly by focusing on the meaning of career. Whereas the word *career* in the 18th century was concerned with a physical track characterized by rapid and continuous action and movement, its usage had evolved by the close of the 19th century to refer to occupational movement and the relation of the individual "self" to one's occupational labors (Bledstein, 1976). Careers involved preestablished patterns of upward mobility through organized professional activities. Professional communities developed as semiautonomous associations in which individual competence, knowledge, and preparation were judged important. Together, career and character ascribed a sense of identity that separated individuals from the particular physical community in which they lived.

We can juxtapose these notions of character and career with those of the early educators and social scientists. Horace Mann, a leading educator in the 19th century, was a lawyer and politician. The early social scientists were philanthropists, biologists, journalists, and men of wealth who were concerned with a horizontal mobility that had no structured or graduated career pattern. The American Social Science Association, established in 1865, included the Boston gentry, who valued trust, permanence, honor, reputation, and righteous behavior that related their personal obligations to the welfare of the public (as they saw it). Later generations of social scientists and educational leaders, in contrast, were educated within an occupation and looked to vertical mobility through a career structure that narrowed their intellectual focus and redefined their social commitments.

Character and Science

The shifting meanings of character and career within a profession relate to epistemological breaks in what defines a pedagogy of teacher preparation. The definition of occupational identity was tied more and more to social science and experimental psychology in order to produce the skills and dispositions of good teachers. The goal of improving native ability that motivated early teacher seminaries was transformed into a drive to introduce a rational order that compensated for natural talent and insight. The focus on abstract relations, individual attributes, or skills tended to locate the pedagogical concerns of instruction in terms of the sensitivities and dispositions found in the newly forming professional culture. The epistemologies of an individualized pedagogy were to become part of the social organization of teacher education.

Teaching institutes assumed responsibility for a new standardization of training that was to move from a concern about individual qualities to external standards that could be universally applied to evaluate individual competence. Experienced teachers began to assume that the profession was to be advanced not by individuals improving themselves but by the identification of minimum standards for professional efficiency by new state offices and new professional organizations, such as the superintendency and the teachers associations (Bloch, 1987; Mattingly, 1975). Anecdotal manuals of hints and suggestions were replaced by highly simplified and systematic guides; booksellers, once considered a disruptive influence because salesmanship competed with teaching for class attention, were now accepted as providing a professional service. Teachers who had never ventured beyond the boundaries of their own districts began to travel to larger cities, as if giving expression to the new expertise, association patterns, and impersonal knowledge that were to define professional careers.

The secularization and individualization did not preclude, but rather sustained, new forms of evangelism and religious fervor in the schools, but now as a generalized Unitarianism. Teacher institutes were a type of revival agency, modeled after the traditions of the ministry rather than the existing college structures. The institute leadership stressed professional training as a union of consecration and science. Education was viewed as a subject with scientific properties, "to be advanced like every other science, by experiment, whose principles are to be fixed, and its capacities determined, by experiment, which is to be entered upon by men of philosophical mind, and pursued with a philosophical spirit" (Mattingly, 1975, p. 93). Morality and pedagogical technology were seen as mutually supportive.

By the middle of the 19th century, conflict emerged between the view of a teaching career as a moral awakening and as a scientific organization of work. The new reformers came from a less-advantaged class than had their teachers. They focused instead on the practical grasp of work and production that could be useful in the new social organizations of schools.

The 19th-century notion of a pedagogical science, however, was different from later and more utilitarian definitions. In the earlier context, science involved a cooperative deliberation among practicing members of the teaching profession that would make teaching as scientifically exact and as socially prestigious as medicine, law, and theology. William Russell, a leader in the earliest national association for professional schoolmen, the American Institute of Instruction (1830–1918), and the influential editor of *The American Journal of Education*, argued that proper pedagogy would produce a person more independent and free to choose for himself. The science of teaching was to create methods of "constituting the mind, as far as possible, as its own instructor" (quoted in Mattingly, 1975, p. 123). That mind, however, was to be disciplined by certain rules of discourse. Russell conceived of a larger universal law of learning and drew on the notion of mental discipline current at the time to argue for exercises to identify generalizations and principles that would guide pedagogy.

> Any given mind became an individualized variation of the general law of knowing rather than a phenomenon which senses experiences uniquely shaped. Professional training precluded a mental fix upon either these principles or upon the particular experience; instead, it implied a mental culture, a continuing associate exercise of the mind, one which dwelt on the relations between both. The product was scientific, meaning for Russell a refusal to acknowledge the authority of principles over particulars or vice versa. (Mattingly, 1975, p. 124)

Russell's theory of training was drawn from the work of John Jardine, a teacher at the University of Glasgow and a successor of John

Stuart Mill (Hamilton, 1980). The utilitarian theories of laissez faire economics were applied to Scotland's industrial school classrooms as a
faculty psychology and then, as we see here, appropriated for the formation of teaching in the United States.

The notion of character serves as a springboard to discuss a changing epistemology of professionalization. Character, which Barnard described as self-sacrifice and a freely chosen commitment to a holy cause,
had become self-discipline and a dutiful acceptance of rationally developed talents by the beginning of the 20th century (Mattingly, 1975).
There was greater insistence on qualities and dispositions that slowly
matured, an orientation that by the turn of the century had become
commonly accepted by such educational leaders as the psychologist G.
Stanley Hall and St. Louis school superintendent William Torrey Harris,
who was to become a U.S. Commissioner of Education.

The construction of teaching as a career can be viewed in the context of new standards of reason and truth that emerged. Normal schools
were promoted in lieu of traditional teaching institutes to emphasize
more explicit standards for selecting professionals and long-term study.
Professional training now looked to the "aptness to teach" as evidenced
by behavior that could be measured by standards of time and actual
service. Teacher instruction was to depend in large part on the development of uniformly effective measures of instruction rather than on morally informed personal styles, and on the exercise of skills rather than
on the strength of commitment to a cause. Teaching was to transfer
technological knowledge, which previously had been subsumed as a
component in the inculcation of character. The science of education bore
little relation to that of the early 19th century, which mixed religious
beliefs with a search for laws about human behavior; it was a science
that valued a sense of orderliness, measurability, reproducibility, and
hierarchy, all considered essential to the reform of social and personal
affairs.

The standards and rules of truth are exemplified in the interpretation given to Herbartian theory in teacher education (Herbst, 1989). The
earlier 19th-century theories of normal school teaching drew on a view
of learning that was borrowed from Prussia. Based on the work of Pesto-
lozzi, instruction was to communicate Christian faith in a context of a
commitment to republicanism and a common school. Teaching was to
develop the human soul by providing opportunities for the individual
to actively discover and invent all truths. Herbartian theory, which replaced Pestolozzian approaches, was to be more systematic. Instruction
was divided into five steps that could practically guide teachers. Concepts, such as apperception, which said that children learn best that

which is related to what they know and are familiar with, were related to a cultural-epoch theory in which school subjects were organized into and integrated around historical periods.

Instruction stressed methods rather than mastery of a set of subjects. This concept of teaching methods was related to an 18th-century Calvinist need for well-ordered forms of social organization (Hamilton, 1989). It assumed a particular, scientific meaning within contemporary institutional relations. Teaching methodology was to order and control the processes of schooling through rational and standardized procedures, rather than through a more general approach in which strategies are reactive to the problem at hand and to the ambiguities of the situations in which people live.

The normal schools integrated their evangelical origins with an academic tradition; teaching was assigned a special place in their curriculum. At its base was a formal course of study, including the most professionally useful study, psychology, in which the process of mental discipline could be examined and its methods defined. Rationalization produced departmentalization, the preeminence of the college instructor and superintendents, and the method of teaching. The principal and trained faculty no longer shaped and defined the heart of the training institutes and normal schools; a literature and a special set of inquiry procedures developed quickly to enhance teacher study.

It is ironic that university education, which was to transform secondary teachers into professionals who enjoyed high status and intellectual rigor, soon became job-oriented, practical, fragmented in terms of curriculum, and committed to a scientism that included testing and measurement. For example, Horace M. Witlord of the Howard Seminary in West Bridgewater, Massachusetts, argued in 1890 for university education that would reorient secondary school teachers who had worked in isolation with mechanical routines and been subject to intense control and monitoring (Powell, 1980). University schools of education were to recruit the ablest students from the upper classes and then educate them in an environment of the highest intellectual order. However, the expansion of secondary schools, the feminization of teaching, the specialization of training to shape school careers, and the importance of research—all of which occurred at the turn of the century—combined to relegate teaching to a subordinate role within an occupational hierarchy.

The development of teacher education institutions contained a number of ironies and paradoxes. The normal schools were democratic institutions in an important sense. They were academic centers that provided higher education for the children (men and women) of rural

America and its working classes (Herbst, 1989). At the same time, the democratization included multitier and differentiated education systems that separated research universities, state colleges and, in the 20th century, community colleges.

The democratization also included a paradox as teaching was organized into a "profession." By the turn of the 20th century, most teachers were women of lower-class origins at a time when the definition of status and privilege was tied to middle-class male conceptions of character and career (Sedlack & Schlossman, 1987). The notion of profession, however, came to apply to those at the top—administrators and academics concerned with educational planning. It was those in the classroom—most of whom were women—to whom the organizing principles, directives, and assessments of professional knowledge were to be applied. The practices of teacher education were but one component of the changing social field that redefined professionalization. The concepts of character, career, and professionalization were intertwined with the changing patterns of work and knowledge associated with teaching. While moral and social in significance, professionalization reformulated the social order and regulation in the occupational patterns of teaching.

Feminization and Professionalization

The complex relations in the changing epistemologies of teaching entailed social constructions that interrelated gender with institutional patterns. In 1800, most teachers were men; by 1900, most were women. The feminization and professionalization of teaching, however, contain certain tensions which, at times, were useful to women teachers. Teaching was a calling that offered new status to women; later, bureaucracy was viewed as a way of protecting women from the multiple demands of their work (Mattingly, 1987). The organization of schooling also involved women in providing a family-like environment for younger children that bridged the widening gap between family, culture, and school. This new role for (primarily) unmarried women produced tension. It also meant a subordinate role for the classroom teacher, with less status and lower salaries than those available to men.

The tensions surrounding the role of women in schools were articulated in the Troy Female Seminary, which operated from 1822 to 1872 (Scott, 1988). It was the first permanent institution offering women a curriculum similar to men's colleges. The course of study emphasized both traditional and innovative values. The seminary's purpose was to train women for motherhood and some as teachers. Studies encouraged intellectual development and self-education that did not tie a woman's worth to her domestic role. The founder and head, Emma Willard, was a pioneer in teaching training and the systematic study of pedagogy.

The movement of women into teaching was related to societal attitudes about the family. Anxiety about maintaining virtue and discipline in a republican society placed the family unit in an unprecedented political role (Conway, 1974; also see Strober & Tyack, 1980). It was the only social institution that could be relied on for both moral training and discipline. A new division of labor emerged: Males assumed political and economic responsibilities; women were responsible for the administration of the domestic establishment (a task European and 18th-century American men expected to share with their wives). Their primary role as moral guardians made it plausible to have women in control of children's education.

The feminine teacher corps helped mediate the relation of society, school, and home. It eased the separation of child from home and made possible the supervision of the "self" as the modern welfare state developed. Schooling incorporated the intense childrearing patterns of the home into what had until this point been a secondary pattern of socialization.

New occupational hierarchies were sensitive to gender relations. The status hierarchy placed the superintendent at the top and the teachers at the lowest levels of professional status. Graduate schools of education, such as the Harvard Graduate School of Education, were established to provide occupational routes for men who wished to become administrators (Powell, 1980; also see Mattingly, 1981). Educational research focused on processes and technologies by which male administrators could organize and monitor the tasks of a mostly female teaching corps. Herbst (1989) argues that as normal school educators sought to replace citizen educators with professional classroom teachers, a hierarchy of institutions developed. Women were separated from men, who were the educational specialists, administrators, and normal school faculty.

There is some evidence that women teachers contested their roles in schools as there was a shift in the notion of teaching from calling to a profession. Women teachers formed coalitions with other groups concerned with social amelioration and progressive reforms (Clifford, 1987; Reese, 1986; Scott, 1988; Urban, 1982). The unionization of teachers after the 1890s spawned organizations created specifically to articulate women's interests in teaching, and some women union leaders did define the problems of teaching as related to larger social movements and gender relations.

The feminization of teaching lent a particular form to professionalization. School administrators, university teacher educators, and researchers guided occupational development and the technical knowledge by which both teachers and children were governed. Teacher education, in contrast, was to focus on problems of implementing and executing pedagogical practices that were conceived elsewhere in the school hierarchy.

CONCLUSIONS

The reforms of professions and pedagogy were tied to the changing problems of knowledge and regulation in society. During the 19th and early 20th centuries, mass schooling addressed the rupture between production and reproduction in economy, society, and culture. Definitions of teacher competence and skill were altered from those prompted by previous church pastoral education. The occupational work was reconstituted to include an organization associated with patterns of bureaucracy, technical production, and gender. At the top were groups that formed associations and maintained social and cultural authority over institutional domains, such as those in the educational sciences and school administration. At the bottom was a workforce, mostly women, whose labor was very different from the professional responsibilities of those at the top.

A network of relations linked teachers' work, pedagogy, teacher education, and educational sciences. The epistemology gave reference to a rationally planned organization of schooling based on an individualization of social affairs and a secular notion of pastoral care. Teaching and professional education maintained dispositions and cognitive organizations that redefined the notions of pedagogy, social relations, and identity. Diverse foci emerged, producing curricula based on a range of concerns from child development to scientific management to pragmatism.

The epistemological formations of schooling are of greatest significance as we consider the problem of professionalization. The institutional patterns of schooling related the occupational identity of teaching to the modern welfare state. The epistemological relations in schooling represented a major intrusion of the state into the daily lives of citizens. The traditional family role in childrearing was to be replaced by the teacher, as school became the major institution of socialization. Children's attitudes, abilities, and emotions were scrutinized through intervention schemes related to some notion of societal "needs" and cultural priorities.

School patterns, while related to state formation, embodied unique lines of development, peculiar strategies of organization, and sources of tension and contradiction. Multiple threads of meaning were located within different layers of schooling in which the degrees of choice and their outcomes were nonlinear and nonevolutionary. Debates and conflict among various segments in society appeared continually. At different times and with varying intensity, conflict emerged between urban/rural, corporate/small business, North/South, white/black, male/female, scientific/religious, and classes. These different interests interrelated and clashed in the process of occupational formation.

Teacher professionalization maintained inner contradictions. Beliefs in humanism and democracy were maintained. The goals of professionalization were tied to the search for enlightened, creative individuals who would contribute to social and material progress. Professions could focus on greater complexity and promote more humane institutions.

At the same time, the distinctions contained more subtle possibilities for the self-governing of individuals. The sciences of education, discussed in the following chapter, provided practical technologies of social amelioration while simultaneously inventing techniques of human engineering and social management that would make the intrusions seem less objectionable. The creation of a therapeutic attitude toward the individual, as well as notions of systems of abstract and discrete units of social and personal life, normalized the intrusions. The dispositions were such that administration of the individual at the microlevels of society was possible.

The discipline of "self" was intended not only to influence children but to guide teachers through processes that we associate with professionalization. Self-discipline was embedded into teacher education through the notions of career and character. Pedagogies and professional preparation normalized the control patterns necessary for the new regulation of self in culture, economy, and politics.

The institutional patterns considered here raise the question of how we should entertain a notion of reform. We tend to associate it with progress that links professional knowledge with social improvement. What counts as reform, however, are responses that tie the organization of knowledge to larger issues of social transformation and power.

I raise these themes as part of a framework for considering the epistemological relations by which certain occupations gain social and cultural authority over knowledge in a society. While teaching never achieved a position of authority equal to some other occupations defined as professional, its centrality in the production of order and identity brings to the fore an accounting of its social and epistemological relations.

3

Social Science
During the Formative Years
of Mass Schooling
State Policy and the University

The social sciences (in which I include psychology and education) have long served as an important dynamic in the production of reform and the structural relations that tie schooling to issues of governance. The social sciences and social reform became interrelated as part of state practices to resolve complex social tensions and conflicts. The rules and standards of problem solving, methodology, and the concepts of inquiry in the late 19th century, as now, were inextricably linked to social agendas and social movements. To the extent that we view social science historically, the emergence of discrete occupations was significant in that they merged the diverse interests of power, achievement, and salvation into a discourse that appeared universal, progressive, and beyond human reproach.[1]

Silver (1983) argues that social science and educational reform were related concepts as early as the mid-19th century in the United States. Increasingly, complex social tensions and conflict were brought into the schools and reconceptualized as problems of science and reform. Knowledge was to be standardized and professionalized in order to facilitate the planning, coordination, and evaluation of teachers' work. Professionalization, however, was a strategy not to give teachers autonomy but to lend organization to the regulatory processes of pedagogy, largely for the benefit of school administrators and social scientists.[2] The production of a disciplined workforce to effect the new pedagogy demanded new strategies to mobilize teachers as professionals.

To understand the social epistemology of the social sciences, I focus here upon both the logic of knowledge and the institutional conditions in which the sciences of reform emerge; in Chapters 7 and 8, I concentrate on their manifestations in contemporary practice. Social scientists became part of an expanding university in which resources were being directed toward state issues of social amelioration, especially in an emerging school system.[3] In particular, the discipline of educational psychology emerged in response to the development of mass schooling. The disciplinary organizations and the interests that came to dominate, however, were not a foregone conclusion but the product of extended debate, unanticipated consequences, and institutional conjunctions. In subsequent chapters, as we move into late-20th-century reform movements and shift our attention to new sets of relations, the specific epistemological concerns change but the overriding issues of the relation of science to governance do not. The rules and standards of problem solving and the organization of methods in educational sciences remain dynamics in the production of social regulation.

As in the previous chapter, the discussion here is meant not as a chronological history but as a social epistemology that relates professional knowledge to the interplay of culture, universities, social sciences, and the state. The argument is drawn from traditional sources in multiple disciplines but recast in a manner that directs attention to the issues of power and knowledge. Because of the concern with issues of how power is mediated, I have not sought to survey the fields of each of the institutions, but have reinterpreted existing work in light of the questions posed here. Discussion of certain nuances in the struggles that underlay the periods under scrutiny is limited because of space constraints, although attention is given to the nonlinear ways in which conduct emerged.

PROFESSIONALIZATION AND THE AUTHORITY OF SCIENCE

The formation of schooling entailed changes in the social and cultural organization of professional authority. Earlier conceptions of professions were tied to the gentry and were devoid of any sense of occupational regulation or explicit definition of technical tasks. As discussed in the previous chapter, there was no notion that character was tied to career. Professional life was cast in broad social and moral terms that linked one's station in life with community obligation and service. By the middle of the 19th century, a discourse of professional practice had developed, predicated on a more focused and rationalized, less religious sense of the world, although concerns with obligation, social order, and preservation of harmony remained. Debate juxtaposed traditional notions of community and rural Protestant democracy against a new professionalism that came to mean science, expert knowledge, and an ideology of objective, nonpartisan public service.

Faith in this new professionalism was sustained as part of a discourse that tied social progress to science. Scientific discourse was brought into the spheres of social affairs to interpret the more complex social relations and interdependence among communities and to reassert moral, social, and cultural authority through the technologies of reform. The idea of progress legitimated social science as spokesperson for determining the course of history (Haskell, 1984).

The new expertise was gradually introduced, and it flourished within the nation's universities as social scientists came to play an important role in state and social planning.[4] One of the most important correlates to the rise of the modern state was a shift from a normative and philosophical view of society to a reformist approach grounded in factual knowledge. University-based social science emerged to meet the state's demand for knowledge about the social processes and organizations that state intervention could seek to affect (Wittrock, 1988). The search for order, control, and social harmony became an explicit focus of scientific inquiry (Franklin, 1986).

A crucial phase in the development of social regulation was the professionalization of knowledge, which, in this context, refers to an instrumental way of reasoning about problems that is secular, abstract, seemingly objective and disinterested; it is, in particular, an approach to knowledge that yields order in response to certain types of scientific analysis and planning. The expertise of research became a strategy for rationalization and social innovation, especially during the Progressive Era. The currency of the new "professional" expert was a knowledge based exclusively upon rules of logic and reference to the empirical, rather than on the social status of the speaker or the authority of God.

The conceptual challenge facing the nascent social sciences was the production of overarching symbols of order and the organization of appropriate motivating and cognitive structures that meshed with the reform tendencies of the state. Direction came not only through explicit state intervention but also through the incorporation of a discourse about useful knowledge into a science of public policy and, later and indirectly, through research funding provided by foundations and businesses.[5] The technologies of the social sciences were methodologies designed to grapple with the complexities of social administration and individual self-governance.

The establishment of professional knowledge as a discourse of state reform involved the interweaving of a number of institutional developments that brought together the new occupations of social science within a reconstituted university. It is to these developments that I would like to give attention.

The University and the Management of Society

It was not until the early years of the 20th century that the disciplines of social science established itself as an integral element of a growing research capacity of the university. Previously a place where elite men learned the character and the habits of mind that would prepare them for their station in life, the university was transformed by state development and the use of philanthropic foundations into a training ground for science and professional education as well as for character development.

With the philanthropic support of such new industrial leaders as John D. Rockefeller, the U.S. university began to shift focus by around the turn of the century (Curti & Nash, 1965). Excess capital, changes in inheritance laws, and religious commitments related to the social gospel movement combined to produce a new institution of philanthropy, the "foundation." Wealthy industrialists sought to provide for the social good through private organizations that could dispense capital to affect social welfare (see, e.g., Lagemann, 1989; Wheatley, 1988). The Social Science Research Council, for example, was financed by John D. Rockefeller in 1925 to develop an expertise about policy research. In addition, philanthropic efforts were directed toward reforming professions through the development of professional education and social science within the university. In general, the philanthropists were concerned with practical knowledge that would advance social, cultural, and economic institutions.

State action also promoted a university that would provide students with the more practical knowledge needed in a society in which both rural and urban settings were experiencing rapid change. The Morrill Act of 1862 created land-grant colleges, requiring that land be set aside in each state for higher education to promote "agriculture and mechanical arts . . . in order to promote the liberal and practical education of the industrial classes in the several pursuits and professions in life." The resulting land-grant colleges were endowed financially as a result of their ownership and subsequent sale of agricultural land, and, with the passage of the Smith-Hughes Act of 1917, they expanded their agricultural and engineering programs, later to include such practical and applied courses as ones in education.

In both private and state-funded universities, research became an integral element of the organization of disciplines. In the context of the university, science was organized to promote social and material welfare and to provide for the management of social harmony. Graduate programs emerged to provide ongoing research and to produce the technical expertise that could, in turn, develop social and economic agendas. Linked to the nascent social sciences were such "helping" professions as public school teaching and social work. The elite of these occupations shared a common view that scientific knowledge was essential to the solution of social-welfare problems.

This early professional expertise was gradually introduced, and it flourished within the nation's universities in departments of political science, economics, sociology, psychology, and education. The university provided an institutional base from which resources could be drawn and training supplied for the new state functions in social welfare, a symbiotic relationship nonexistent in many European nations, which had entrenched humanist traditions in their universities that devalued practical knowledge.[6]

The changing character of the university was related to a number of historical peculiarities in the United States. The worldwide economic depressions between 1873 and 1896 provided unique opportunities for industrial advancement in the United States as compared to most of continental Europe and Britain, but they also posed new problems associated with immigration, urbanization, race, poverty, and class (Manicas, 1987). The academic traditions and strong labor movement so firmly entrenched in European society did not exist in the United States. It was still possible for the social sciences to develop within the organizational structure of an independent department, much as their counterparts in the physical sciences had developed, and to become a central part of academic life. The professorate could feel secure in dealing with middle-class issues, first as moral concerns of the day, and later, as unspoken values through a technical emphasis on programs of social amelioration.

An explicit and direct relationship between the university and the management of society emerged during the Progressive Era (see Bledstein, 1976).[7] Various elements in society turned to the state university systems to provide the expertise necessary to make government and policies of social amelioration efficient. Referred to initially as the "Wisconsin idea," this conception of the role of the university emphasized its contribution of practical knowledge that could be applied to problems of commerce, industry, agriculture, public affairs, and government through expert advice (Curti & Carstensen, 1949; McCarthy, 1912). The university provided the setting and resources necessary for the development of occupations that valued instrumental knowledge and an expertise that avoided a radical political involvement, especially as it related to socialism.

To a great degree, goals characterized by politics and administrative agendas guided the development of the social sciences. By 1902, University of Wisconsin President Charles R. Van Hise had moved to restore a measure of autonomy to the university by rephrasing the democratic notion of public service into a progressive vocabulary of reform through the development of expertise. Van Hise, a friend and classmate of Wisconsin's Governor Robert M. LaFollette, and economics professor Richard Ely were influenced by the social gospel, which sought to use the teachings of Christ as a guide for social reform (Hoeveler, 1976). Replacing faith in the isolated individual to perfect his or her community, the social reformer turned to the state as the truest expression of beneficent power. The "Wisconsin idea" of Van Hise, shaped by the ethical commitments of the social gospel movement, rejected its gospel elements but accepted its social content. The university was to be "the epitome of the intellectual and moral power of the state" (Maraniss, 1990, p. 15a). The reforms were to be directed toward the growing concentration of power and corruption that bred unethical, un-Christian goals.

In keeping with the progressive commitment to public expertise, Van Hise encouraged the social and psychological sciences to assume an activist role in social amelioration, a role that would prove to be as lucrative as it was enlightening. Joseph Jastrow, a leading Wisconsin psychologist at the time, "discovered that applied psychology was 'the pay-vein that supports the mine.'" Jastrow changed the direction of psychology at Wisconsin into "an advertising agency of applied endeavor," focusing upon the fields of education and mental hygiene (O'Donnell, 1985, p. 217).

The reformist role of the university tied expert knowledge to the organizational demands for efficiency emerging in state, social, and economic institutions. The belief that rational, administrative ordering of priorities and the collection of data would define and resolve social issues came to dominate the prevailing view. Political conflict between social values and special interests was moved to a peripheral place; moral philosophy, theology, and political economy were to be supplanted by the more narrowly gauged sciences of psychology, group organization, economics, government, and teaching. The instrumental concerns underscored a shift in social epistemology from a normative and philosophical approach to a reformist tendency that was grounded in factual knowledge.

University involvement in social formations can be more specifically articulated through a focus on the emerging state school system. By the turn of the century, the university had shaped the categories and content of the school curriculum. Replacing subjects tied to church concerns of literacy, the 1893 Committee of Ten's recommendations for modern academic subjects in the high school were designed to impose greater standardization on the pattern of college admissions (Krug, 1972). The university's control over admissions standards gave it direct authority over what was considered to be knowledge in the public high schools. In addition, the university began to train public school elites. University schools of education replaced the normal schools in defining the careers of school administrators and teachers, especially by providing graduate research training as a career path for men in a heavily female teaching occupation (Mattingly, 1981; Powell, 1980). Finally, and the chief concern of this discussion, scientific research traditions developed in the university as part of the planning of schooling.

The multiple functions of the university are illustrated in the development of school mathematics education between 1900 and 1920 (Stanic, 1987). Central to the debate about the purpose and organization of school mathematics was the issue of what type of instruction should be given. One group focused on instruction that would teach children how to think and reason properly. It was assumed that mathematics in public schooling would provide the mental discipline and character of mind appropriate for eventual leadership in social and economic institutions. A second orientation to curriculum focused on functional requirements for those who would never go to college. From this perspective, the curriculum was to provide students with practice in managing everyday life, such as using mathematics for household budgets. Research programs were developed to justify and organize the curriculum around each type of instruction, including task analyses to identify the mathematics needed in the home and in industry. Both orientations translated values about social purpose and differentiation into more scientific and seemingly neutral questions of psychological development and learning (see, e.g., Kilpatrick, in press).

The professionalization of school knowledge makes apparent a long-term process in which both epistemology and notions about the legitimate "holders" of authority were redefined. The work in curriculum tied moral values to secular interests of vocationalism. School placement came to validate both the importance of curricular structure as a means of organizing solutions and the role of the new experts in producing social knowledge.

The development of the university as a dynamic in the management of society did not occur in a straightforward manner or without debate and conflict. Initially, social scientists did not view their responsibilities as tied to academic settings. The decentralized quality of higher education produced flexibility, diverse foci, and different trajectories among state and private universities. Further, notions of tenure and academic freedom, developed to protect the expert role of the new academic during the Progressive Era, gave legitimacy to diversity in academics, including dissent within carefully circumscribed social boundaries. (See Silva & Slaughter, 1984. For a less political analysis, see Hofstader & Metzger, 1955.)

Reformism: Science, Religion, and Commerce

Two sets of beliefs give focus to the reformist tendencies that existed in the university social sciences in the late 19th century. One set of beliefs viewed reform as a link between national identity and progress. The country was seen not only as a new world but also as the biblical promised land. Professionalization and notions of progress permeated a search for a reorganization of material life and a cultural disposition that would lead to a new millennial world (see Popkewitz & Pitman, 1986). A second set of beliefs redefined the relation of the individual to society; the view of sin as a fall from grace shifted to a focus on the "environment," a central tenet of the social gospel movement, combined with an evolutionary belief that directed efforts could alter and improve the immediate world.

These beliefs gave rise to the first program of 19th-century U.S. social science. Because of the social gospel movement, poverty was no longer seen as an embarrassing contradiction of the assumption that the United States was a Garden of Eden. The influx of immigrants, most of whom were quickly enmeshed in urban industrialism, made reform the problem of the day. Notions of civility, manners, and the work ethic associated with the dominant society would be inculcated into the newcomers through schools, settlement houses, and other social-welfare institutions. Social institutions would help to improve the conditions of the poor as well as create a stable environment that stressed particular social and cultural values.

Civil service reforms were designed to create an efficient government. At one level, these reforms provided avenues for the participation of men, and later women, who previously had been disenfranchised. They were to also make it possible for government to provide greater service to the poor and immigrants of the cities. In so doing, however, reform directly attacked and undermined the organizational apparatus that industrial workers could use to gain power. Immigration from eastern and southern Europe at the turn of the century had introduced socialist ideas more directly into the U.S. urban context. Local government was seen as increasingly influenced by immigrant and lower-class groups whose values conflicted with those of the older patrician leadership. The reformers were fearful of

> an enfranchised emerging "political proletariat." A nub [was a fear] that recent immigrants whose labor powered the rapidly industrializing economy would organize and displace their kind of socioeconomic power. To counter this threat, they developed schemes to control these immigrant workers and rhetoric to justify the schemes. Their rhetoric styled the emerging working class as potentially a "close combination of vice, ignorance and brute force, wholly inaccessible to reason or the dictates of public virtue." (Silva & Slaughter, 1984, p. 55)

The predominant moral outlook intertwined science, religion, and commerce. The cultural and religious definitions of progressivism made it plausible for the business community to lend strong support to the new sociologies, social psychologies, and education, all of which emphasized environmentalism. Jackson Lears (1981) argues, however, that the sciences, to direct social ameliorative efforts, imposed a particular cultural dominance of the bourgeoisie. This occurred through the values contained in the categories, distinctions, and differences used for social planning. The moral meanings embodied in the social sciences, Lears continues, were provided through the efforts of "ministers and other moralists" rather than bankers and industrialists (p. 10).

As will be argued later, many of the early social scientists and school reformers were driven by missionary purposes. (See, e.g., Karier, 1986; Joncich's bibliography of Thorndike, 1968; and Noble's discussion of Dewey, 1970). The problems of an urban society were related as much to the problem of salvation as they were to institutional reform, and the task of the secular expert was to help those at the lowest levels of society to expunge the evil within. Efforts at civic reform were approached with a religious zeal. G. Stanley Hall (1905/1969a), for example, spoke of the soul in describing the focus of psychology. Social scientists provided advice about how welfare policy could be improved through studies of the interaction of individuals and institutions, with their advice maintaining certain Protestant Unitarian beliefs about individual works producing salvation (Haskell, 1977; Karier, 1986; O'Donnell, 1985).

To this point, business and political ideologies and social science have been juxtaposed to the social gospel movement in progressivism. This has been done, in part, to point out the religious motif as an important element of the early social reform movements and professionalization. As Weber (1904–5/1958) noted, Protestant religious cosmologies were integral to processes of modernization. (For the ties of science to utopian thought, see Manuel & Manuel, 1979.) My focus in this chapter is on a particular set of social practices and beliefs that emerged within a segment of American Protestantism and that were part of a particular conjunction in social and cultural formations. In describing such a relation, it should be noted that there were diverse Protestant denominations, including the evangelical churches of the South and West (see Hofstadter, 1962). This divergence, however, should not detract from the importance of the interplay of religious conceptions with our secular world.

Social Science: From Redemption to Disinterest

The first professionals who called themselves social scientists emerged after the Civil War. They were from many different professional backgrounds and had no special higher education or "methods" to certify them beyond a shared belief that the purpose of the social sciences was to guide social amelioration through more direct state action. By 1900, the character of the social sciences had shifted such that they were associated with professionals in particular disciplines and with methods of historical and empirical analysis. The social scientists recognized an increased power of the state, sought to provide more effective ways to bring Christianity into the civilizing institutions of U.S. life, and worked to develop occupational associations that could guide and interpret politics. They helped to popularize the troubles of the lower classes and people of color by drawing the attention of the middle class to the problems of urbanization, illiteracy, and poverty. Science, it was thought, would produce systematic public provisions, coherent public policy, and rational government intervention.

Charles Sanborn, a founder of the American Social Science Association (ASSA) that was the forerunner to many of the specific social science organizations, acknowledged that the association anticipated the state's post–Civil War expansion, which included public education, legislation in child and adult labor, banking and tax/tariff regulation, transportation, and the development of national parks and museums. The state's expansion, Sanborn said, "contemplated our own more special work, the combination of private and associated activity with whatever governments might undertake" (quoted in Silva & Slaughter, 1984, p. 52).

The papers and records of the ASSA are characterized by the dominant theme of "the science of reform or reform as science" (Silver, 1983, p. 115). Science was viewed as a form of philanthropy. The early social scientists came from privileged backgrounds but shared a sense of social obligation to help those who were culturally and religiously different and less fortunate. Sanborn, for example, viewed the role of the social scientist as one of mediation between private power and an activist state that interrelated older notions of a gentry with a professional knowledge (Haskell, 1977).

The concern of science was related to its political commitment to improving conditions of life and to eliminating misery (Manicas, 1987). The collection of data, usually statistics, was viewed as a device to identify the sources of such social ills as crime, poverty, and illness. The emphasis on investigation and method was considered an approach that could determine the right course of action for social betterment. Research methods were combined with Puritan notions of redemption, cooperative self-help, and social ethics in a science that would also agitate for reform.

The particular view of a profession of social scientists was related to the experiences that these men had when they traveled abroad to the German universities where basic research was in the forefront. The U.S. social scientists had been infused with a German view of political economy that was historically and socially broad. This view was incorporated but modified by the organization of U.S. politics and culture to provide a more functional science (Herbst, 1965; O'Donnell, 1985).

As the social sciences became organized into disciplinary professional organizations, intense debate arose about the role of the social scientist in the processes of social amelioration. Some tied their expertise to social ethics in that they believed that the social obligations of Christianity were to be related to the conditions of the working class. The initial charter of the American Economics Association reflected the economist Richard Ely's interest in a more effective forum to promote advocacy of Christian values in the economists' concern for reform. Other social scientists, such as the economist John Commons, argued for an approach that integrated social, economic, and cultural issues into the study of institutions. Over time, however, the activist orientation generally lost favor and became marginalized. Most professional organizations adopted the stance that scientists were disinterested observers and that knowledge of science was neutral toward the world of politics and social values. The knowledge of social science was to be useful to policy making by guiding the administration and evaluation of social agendas, but that knowledge was to be nonpartisan.

This stance is well illustrated by the development and activities of the American Economic Association. In the face of a great deal of political maneuvering and social pressures, the reformist bent of the organi zation's founding charter was transformed within approximately three years of its initial acceptance. The new wording emphasized a more technical approach, one that focused on disciplinary concerns. The 1885 Statement of Principles, Article IV stated:

1. We regard the state as an agency whose positive assistance is one of the indispensable conditions of human progress.
2. We believe that political economy is still in the early stages of its development. While we appreciate the work of former economists, we look not so much to speculation as to the historical and statistical study of actual conditions of economic life for the satisfactory accomplishment of that development. (quoted in Silva & Slaughter, 1984, p. 83)

The function of expert knowledge was articulated as part of a general belief that science was a disinterested endeavor for the advancement of society. The association's third principle gave reference to the need of church, state, and science to combine their efforts in solving the social problems caused by the conflict of labor and capital. In the study of these issues, however, economists were to be viewed as nonpartisan, as stated in the fourth principle.

4. In the study of industrial and commercial policy of governments we take no partisan attitude. We believe in a progressive development of economic conditions, which must be met by a corresponding development of legislative policy. (quoted in Silva & Slaughter, 1984, p. 83)

Part of the association's increasing recognition of nonpartisan professionalism occurred in response to the influences of university presidents. In the late 19th century, university presidents were developing strong administrations to steer the growth of higher education. As they sought to establish ties with business and community leaders as a means of gaining political and economic support, it was feared that these relationships would be undermined by radicalism and pro-labor professors if social scientists continued to stress social values and agitation for reform. The search for status and resources also produced more caution about activism and advocacy (Furner, 1975). Debate about the role of capitalism, unionism, and the state in bringing material and spiritual progress emphasized the role of specialized experts in guiding intervention. In a number of instances, professors who urged social and institutional restructuring were fired, with those more aggressive advocates often losing any future chance for academic positions.

Within this social and psychological milieu, a certain epistemology soon came to dominate professional fields. A uniquely U.S. positivism developed as part of the practices of science, even prior to the philosophical work of the Vienna School and British analytical thought of the 1920s. The world was viewed as governed by deterministic laws that could be identified only through scientific inquiry (Lears, 1981). Beliefs that the physical sciences subdued and controlled the material world provided organizational context to the work of social scientists as they sought to advise policy makers. Science was to function as an instrument of control: "Central was the vision of a science which would make society as amenable to analysis and certain kinds of mastery and reform as was the world investigated by the natural sciences" (Silver, 1983, p. 104).

At this point, we can understand U.S. social sciences as integral to the particular organization of social affairs associated with the Progressive Era. At one level, social science contributed to the Progressive Era's reworking of political institutions; it helped formulate a changing structure of participation and a new bureaucracy that provided access to many Americans previously denied involvement in social and political affairs. The working class was enfranchised by the broadening of standards of what constituted legitimate decision making. Expanded primary, secondary, and higher education included minorities and ethnic groups that had been excluded. State institutions implemented more extensive regulatory practices regarding problems of social welfare (see, e.g., Peterson, 1985).

At another level, one which is often overlooked, new epistemologies of interpretation were formed as part of the new systems of social regulation and innovation. The new patterns related the organization of society to the individual and the family; in this context, the problem of governing involved two distinct processes: the administration of the state institutions, which would produce social progress, and the production of a domestic economy in which the family and individual would display inner restraint and discipline of purpose in the emerging social order (Foucault, 1979b). Alongside the social sciences would come the social technologies needed to grapple with the complexities of social administration and individual self-governing.

Social Science and Social Agendas

It was the goal of social science to ameliorate social conditions, but professional expertise became a part of the social agenda itself, as illustrated by the creation of the domestic sciences. As part of longer patterns of change in the United States, as well as in France, Britain, and Australia, influences of technology were brought into the home and school, material production was moved outside the home, and suburban growth combined to alter the patterned relations of the private and public worlds (see Donzelot, 1979; Lasch, 1977; Poster, 1978; Reiger, 1985; Shorter, 1975).

The separation of production and reproduction, combined with the other elements of social transformations that were occurring prior to the late 19th century, produced new demands upon the processes of childrearing in the family and school. The dominant bourgeois familial ideology characterized the family and home as a place of intimate and personal relationships.[8] The home was to be a place of rest for man, a haven that nurtured an expressive relationship that was not permissible in the rational world of business. For women, the home was the forum in which they were to provide the formative influence on children's character.

The new sciences of domestic life challenged these values in the name of preserving the ideals of the home and family. The principles of the emerging domestic economy movement stressed scientific housewifery in which the domestic skills of planning, preparation, and execution of meals, proper hygiene, nutrition, and housekeeping were taught. The science of the new professional invaded at every point the separation of sexual spheres and the privacy of the home by ''demanding that women learn and apply the principles of the capitalist industrial world'' (Reiger, 1985, p. 55). As the literature about the period suggests, conflicting ideas about the home placed stress on women from the middle and lower classes, since the bourgeois ideology contradicted the demands of the scientific ideologies of industry and commerce, resulting in points of confrontation and resistance.

The changing professional definitions of the family, however, were incorporated into the school curriculum. Nutritional science, hygiene, and sex education became classroom topics. The curriculum was to regulate the private lives of middle- and working-class families as moral standards were reconceptualized into problems of health.

Just as significant was the incorporation of the ideologies of the family into pedagogy. From Dewey's notion of community to the task analysis of domestic work that was undertaken as part of the social efficiency movement, the private and public sectors addressed the issue of how individuals could be self-governing, productive members of society. The pedagogies not only provided ''facts'' about daily life; inherent in them were dispositions about the appropriate standards for reasoning and effecting outcomes. In this context, the concern for individual self-regulation as an element of the formation of human capability was a presupposition of the psychological sciences.

A rhetorical style emerged in the social sciences as they became central to the formation of reform practices; the language of social amelioration became one of science and administration. Many progressive reformers, civil leaders, and social scientists viewed their basic values about society as fundamentally accurate but nonetheless under siege as they sought to find novel solutions for making institutions more responsive to social problems. Scientific expertise was to devise technical and administrative strategies to make government, social welfare, and education more efficient. Knowledge itself was reclassified: Moral philosophy, which included the study of political economy, was redefined as a normless science that included philosophy, politics, and economics as distinct disciplines.

These normless sciences were met with considerable opposition, both in and outside the professions. Those within the social sciences who challenged existing structures of inequality were placed in marginal positions or excluded from their fields. The arguments that modern science should combine reform activism with social Christianity were deemed unrigorous and unscientific by the professional organizations. Unions, Catholic organizations, and socialist political leaders who were suspicious of the policies of the civic and educational reforms did not use the arguments of science until much later in the 20th century; instead, their language focused on the moral, ethical, economic, and political dilemmas of their particular institutions (see Reese, 1986).

SOCIAL SCIENCES AND
THE EMERGENCE OF MASS SCHOOLING

The state's agenda for social amelioration made mass schooling particularly important.[9] The school was seen by reformers as an institution that could mute class distinctions, one in which success was to be defined through objective criteria of merit. A common school was to be an institution in which all social classes could mingle freely and harmoniously. The Carnegie Commission on Higher Education, founded by the industrialist Andrew Carnegie's philanthropic foundation, for example, asserted in a 1927 report that the schools "consolidate and advance" U.S. civilization. That "both U.S. theory and U.S. practice have furnished a powerful antidote to the class discrimination long characteristic of European procedure is beyond dispute." The coupling of the U.S. economic and social conditions with public schooling brought the possibility of a "full return for every child concerned" (Learned, 1927, p. 3; see also Herbst, 1989).

The university-based sciences of schooling would provide a means to develop and implement policies that responded to ideas of progress produced in the Progressive Era, as well as to the emerging social discontinuities that characterized urban living. The psychologies of individualization and testing would provide practical technologies that testified to the objective and meritocratic quality of schooling. The school sciences promised to increase the functional efficiency of schooling and to introduce a mechanism for progress that would permeate the whole of society.

The Psychology of Schooling: The Sciences of Pedagogy

While psychology had been an aspect of education since at least the Middle Ages, it assumed particular disciplinary focus and professional organization at the turn of the century (see, e.g., Karier, 1986; Lears, 1981; O'Donnell, 1985; Sennett, 1978). Psychology was the first discipline to develop solely within the university (Napoli, 1981). The new discipline of psychology provided a direction for concentrating on the individual as part of the modernization of society by focusing on the attributes of self-reliance and moral outer-directedness and by assisting in organizing the processes of pedagogy in schooling. It provided a symbolic system through which to interpret the material and cultural transformations that underlay the Progressive Era and, at the same time, it reconciled the social challenges to dominant Protestant theology posed by the development of the theory of evolution.

A science of psychology emerged as a subdiscipline of philosophy to give focus to the natural development of the mind and spirit, as described in 18th- and early 19th-century writing. By the end of the 19th century, psychology had become distinct from moral and mental philosophy and was positioned to reconcile the theological issues of Protestantism with the material issues of evolution. University presidents who had previously taught the philosophy course as "the crowning pinnacle of college education," especially in Eastern private institutions, embraced psychology as a way of reconciling faith and reason, Christian belief and Enlightenment empiricism (see Leary, 1987, p. 317). Psychology also provided an opportunity for people like William James, G. Stanley Hall, and James Cattell, father of the mental testing movement, to resolve personal conflict concerning science and religion, materialism, spiritualism, determinism, and free will (Leary, 1987). Psychology maintained the dualism of matter and spirit and could perform the service of inculcating belief:

> After Darwin, the essential philosophical task of philosophy was psychological: to offer convincing proof for the evolution of consciousness in order to extricate mind from the implications of mechanical determinism and to allow ethics to be rewritten in evolutionary style. (O'Donnell, 1985, p. 58)

The role of psychology, however, was more than the inculcation of belief. The emergence of the modern state at the turn of the century exploited the new conception of self as secular, rational, divided, and conflictual through the new discipline of psychology. U.S. psychology incorporated and expressed a key cultural belief in the power and significance of the individual. Literature and art of the era tended to affirm a continual harmony and progress through the efforts of individuals and to deny the conflicts in a modern capitalist society.[10] The key to progress was thought to be the disciplined, autonomous self that emerged from the proper bourgeois family upbringing. Psychology integrated these themes into its scientific programs and research methodologies.

Psychology also had the tasks of dissemination and advancement of a practical knowledge in an emerging industrial nation. By the Progressive Era, the corporate drive for efficiency and the state mobilization for intervention had intensified. Demands for social amelioration were premised on the Victorian ethic of self-control and the extension of the processes of rationalization into personal conduct. Industrialization involved a press for "systematic methods of self-control . . . beyond the work place into the most intimate areas of daily experience—perhaps even into unconscious wishes, dreams, and fantasies" (Lears, 1981, p. 13; also see Berger et al., 1973).

It was the control of "self" that U.S. psychologists returning from Germany adopted as a major disciplinary interest. Many of the early U.S. psychologists had visited the laboratories of Wilhelm Wundt in Leipzig. While committed to the development of experimental techniques, Wundt theoretically defined the mind as active, and consciousness as having an objective social-historical source (Manicas, 1987, p. 183). Here we can consider how particular intellectual traditions are, in fact, series of structured relations in which practices are neither evolutionary nor solely functional. The broad perspective of thought and consciousness formulated by Wundt was reformulated in America into a synthesis that linked institutional developments in schools, advertising, and social welfare (see, e.g., Cushman, 1990). Psychology focused on the assessment of personal capacities that would produce the successful adjustment of the individual to the environment.

The development of behavioral psychology central to school research needs to be understood in the context of the institutional conditions in which it occurred. While Wundt's experimentation was concerned with human purpose and the objective conditions in which thought processes are formed, American psychologists narrowed their focus to attitudes, attributes, and skills. What Americans observed in Wundt's laboratory was the study of psychological processes through individual case descriptions about subjects' thoughts. American psychology redefined the problem of individualism to consider statistical distributions and group experimentation that would identify population characteristics. (I am reminded here of the first American translation of the Soviet psychologist Lev Vygotsky. While Vygotsky sought to develop a Marxist psychology after the Soviet revolution, the English translator left out all references to Marx because they were considered irrelevant. This was corrected in later editions.)

This shift in procedures had little to do with the issues of scientific progress or knowledge accumulation. The American approaches to psychology were related to demands for collective data about aggregates of students attending schools. The "audiences" that provided the resources to support the research influenced the scientific paths that were followed rather than any "inherent" quality of the knowledge or scientific approaches themselves (Danziger, 1987).

The two major strands of U.S. psychology that developed within the university—behaviorism and pragmatism—asserted the criterion of usefulness as the value of the discipline. William James, a pragmatist, said, "What every educator, every jail-warden, every doctor, every clergyman, every asylum-superintendent asks of psychology is practical rules. Such men care little or nothing about the ultimate philosophic groups of mental phenomena, but they do care immensely about improving ideas, dispositions, and conduct of particular individuals in their charge" (quoted in O'Donnell, 1985, p. 67). Cattell declared that behaviorism was a science of social control: "Control of the physical world is secondary to the control of ourselves and of our fellow men" (quoted in O'Donnell, 1985, p. 77).

The general and applied concern for psychology imbued the discipline with a uniquely U.S. character. "Psychology would flourish neither as a mental discipline nor as a research science but as the intellectual underpinning and scientific legitimater of utilitarian pursuits, especially in the field of education" (O'Donnell, 1985, p. 37; see also Napoli, 1981).

Pedagogy as a Psychological Problem and
Financial Basis for Occupational Development

The field of pedagogy became the primary focus of psychologists. Schooling, which was expanding at a phenomenal rate in terms of both numbers and resources, was thus becoming a major U.S. institution. Between 1902 and 1913, public expenditures for education doubled; between 1913 and 1922, they tripled. During these decades, more public funds were invested in education than in national defense and public welfare combined (O'Donnell, 1985). Clinics, child study research, and curriculum development projects provided jobs and financial support for psychologists.

Psychology responded directly to concerns about moral upbringing and labor socialization posed by the social gospel movement and business leaders but positioned them as problems of attitude and thought, as well as interaction, between the individual and the environment. A functional view of knowledge, the focus on individual differences, and the apparently objective methods of psychology offered an approach to social regulation that could enable school professionals to deal with large population increases and issues of socialization. While sociologists also were concerned with issues of schooling, they did not have access to the practical technologies of organization that were eventually provided by the application of learning theories, measurement, and testing.[11] By the 1920s, psychology had replaced the efforts of the early sociologists to monitor and organize the upbringing tasks of modern schooling (see Franklin, 1986).

The career of G. Stanley Hall, a leading psychologist, illustrates the increasing importance of psychology in school matters. Hall worked at the first U.S. graduate university, Johns Hopkins, and later became president of Clark University. He sought to make his work in psychology accessible and useful to educators. He sponsored workshops for school superintendents, teachers, and normal school principals on the scientific pedagogy; convinced the reformist elements of the National Educational Association (NEA), an organization dominated by school administrators at the turn of the century, that the new psychology provided the scientific basis for the study of schooling; created the *Pedagogical Seminary*, a journal devoted to child study; and, in seeking to regularize relations between the NEA and his psychology department at Clark

University, founded the American Psychological Association in 1892. The professional organization was to lend legitimacy to the applied strategies (O'Donnell, 1985).

In his massive, two-volume work *Adolescence* (1905/1969a, 1969b), Hall argued that psychology and pedagogy were inseparable and that the latter is a field of applied psychology.

> The largest possible aspect of all the facts of life and mind is educational, and the only complete history is the story of the influences that have advanced or retarded the development of man toward his completion, always ideal and forever in the future. Thus psychology and the higher pedagogy are one and inseparable. Not only the beautiful and the good, but the true, can have no other test of validity that they appeal to and satisfy certain deep needs; and these are many. From this general viewpoint I have tried to show how truth about things of the soul, in a unique sense, is never complete or certain till it has been applied to education, and that the latter field is itself preeminent and unlike all other fields of application for either scientific or philosophic conclusions. (vol. 1, p. ix)

The experimental psychology of Thorndike, the child study of Hall, and the behaviorism of Watson, among others, were consistent with the new role of the social scientists within the university: that of providing expert advice about the formation and implementation of policy. Much of the early research sought to establish an inductive approach to curriculum, based on the regularities of existing patterns of behavior found in schooling.[12] However, it was the concept of measurement that was to be most instrumental in the formation of schooling.

That particular focus of educational psychology related to the rise of administrative and specialized training within graduate university programs (Powell, 1980). Research provided large-scale assessment of student groups and indicators of the quality of an entire school system. It was also to provide school administrators with a way to monitor and control the work of teachers and students. Quantitative measures were used as means ''for establishing unchallengeable administrative authority in a time of growing school enrollments and expenditure'' (Powell, 1980, p. 10). Paul Hanus and A. Lawrence Lowell, professors at Harvard, viewed educational science as a contributor to professional authority rather than as a scholarly activity. Educational research was to be ''a professional tool for all responsible school officers'' (Powell, 1980, p. 103).

New research strategies served to certify mobile careers of specialists and administrators (both typically male) in school districts as well as to provide credentials for the educational researcher in the university. At the same time, teachers (typically female) were relegated to ancillary status as a subject of inquiry.

Educators' acceptance of psychology occurred amidst debate and questioning. William Chandler Bagley, for example, was trained as a psychologist and initially believed in a functionalism by which observation of teaching would provide a body of laws and principles to identify the successful practices and valid principles in effective schools (Johanningmeir, 1969). Later in his career, however, Bagley acknowledged the complexities of school practices and viewed psychology as contributing to, but not the sole discipline for, the organization of schooling. Science was to have a restricted role in the formulation of curriculum.

Educational Psychology and Social Amelioration

The development of educational psychology provided a new form of expertise for selecting, organizing, and evaluating school knowledge. Psychologists believed that they had sufficient knowledge and political neutrality to promote institutional change.[13] Acting as "an evolutionary cadre," the psychologists "asked the public to have confidence not merely in their knowledge and skills but in their ability to construct a better world as well" (Napoli, 1981, p. 41). There was a belief that science was the "mainstream of inevitable progress" and that an individual "could make and remake his own world" (O'Donnell, 1985, p. 212). Promising what utopian thinkers had long sought, Hall (1905/1969a) saw psychology as the means to overcome the problems of urban life, family stress, and inadequate social development:

> Along with the sense of the immense importance of further coordinating childhood and youth with the development of the race, has grown the conviction that only here can we hope to find true norms against the tendencies to precocity in home, school, church, and civilization generally and also to establish criteria by which to both diagnose and measure arrest and retardation in the individual and the race. While individuals differ widely in not only the age but the sequence of the stages of repetition of racial history, a knowledge of nascent stages and the aggregate interests of different ages of life is the best safeguard against very many of the prevalent errors of education and of life. (vol. 1, p. viii)

In later life, Hall (1923) was less sanguine about whether science had lived up to its promise; but he still believed the goal was attainable, although progress was slow.

At the center of the new scientific pedagogy was the expert, who was well trained in the efficiency of science. Thorndike (1910) argued that education should be based on sound scientific fact rather than opinion. The human mind was considered subject to precise measurement, similar to that of the natural sciences, but such measurement was viewed as beyond the capacity of kindergarten teachers; as a result, the formation of curriculum was considered best left in the hands of experimental psychologists (Bloch, 1987). Hall argued that it was the scientifically trained psychologist "who could devise and administer tests to determine such motor and 'mental' skills, as sensual acuity, muscular strength and coordination, speed of reaction, perception of movement and time, and simple memory" necessary for the proper functioning of schools (O'Donnell, 1985, p. 156).

The new ways of constructing curriculum established specific patterns of reasoning and acting about children's socialization. At the center of scientific pedagogy was Hall's Child Study Project. Drawing on revised assumptions of phrenology, Hall used an exhaustive empirical compilation of children's behavioral traits and patterns of explicable individual differences. The study involved a massive empirical compilation of mental tests, questionnaires, and teacher and parent reports. The statistical composite of cognitive and emotional development of the normal child was to form the basis of a pedagogy that would conform to the developmental sequence of the child.

To understand the scientific language of curriculum as a discourse of power, we should realize that psychology is not "natural" to the selection and organization of school knowledge; nor are the psychological disciplines of education in the United States the only way to classify and frame problems of subjectivity and consciousness. The choice of curriculum involves philosophical, political, and ethical questions that can be interrelated with those of science (see Popkewitz, 1982a; Soltis, 1968). Yet by the 1920s the dominant paradigm in curriculum had become one that was articulated from functional psychological and social-psychological perspectives (see Franklin, 1986). Psychology was a unique blend of pragmatism and individualism that responded to—and was a part of—the larger structural relations that existed within the United States.

Educational Psychology and Decontextualizing Power

One implication of the particular psychological form adopted in pedagogy was the decontextualization of the social and political issues involved in the forming of school practices; they were largely reformulated as policies of administration and efficiency. The sciences mobilized a bias in favor of a particular methodology that obscured the interplay of social class, religion, ethnicity, gender, and geography that underlay the formation of schooling. The invention of the psychological categories of "backwardness" and "need" during the late 19th and early 20th centuries illustrates this phenomenon.

School leaders invented the notion of "backwardness" in response to the special problems they confronted in educating immigrant children (Franklin, 1907a). The conception of backwardness acknowledged two different "causes" of student failure. One involved the physical deficiencies of children, such as brain damage. The sciences of measurement and testing, developed as an integral part of the eugenics movement, were offered as "proof" of the mental deficiencies of those who came from non-English-speaking countries (see Gould, 1981). Backwardness was also viewed as the result of environmental conditions that produced in children a debilitating "self-concept" or unsatisfactory school attendance. The immigrant children spoke a language other than English, had styles of dress and manners that were deemed "backward," and were thought to breed the corruption that they brought from the old world.

Policy debate drew on the scientific discourse about backwardness to describe and prescribe resolutions to moral and economic issues. The sciences of testing and environmentalism drew on dominant cultural and social sensitivities to offer distinctions among and solutions to the problems. It was believed that functional curricula would address the products of unrestrained immigration, urbanization, and industrialization. Science, it was thought, would help prepare people for jobs and identify those individuals who should be granted access to social mobility. At the same time, the scientific curriculum would provide seemingly objective criteria by which knowledge was selected and judgments made about children's success or failure.

The reformulation of social issues into those of functional science developed concurrently with the curriculum concept of "need." Walter Smith's 1879 plan for an art curriculum in Massachusetts schools referred to the different "needs" of children, with "need" embodying a class concept. It divided children into those who were "gifted," "privileged," and from "working classes" in constructing an art curriculum (Smith, 1879, reproduced in Wygant, 1983; Freedman, 1987). By the late 1800s and early 1900s, the concept of need had emerged as part of the charity movement, a group of reformers concerned with the abuse of government expenditures in and the influence of political corruption on social-welfare programs. The reformers would give the unfortunate city dwellers new forms of organization that were considered more precious than money, food, or clothing (Lybarger, 1987). Charity was to bring character, self-respect, and ambition to the poor. The settlement house movement, as well, sought to instill character, virtue, and social unity through teachings about American social institutions and customs.

While the reformers' intent was complex and sometimes confused, the educational activities of the reform groups were structured around what they thought the immigrants "needed" to know. This included recognition of the purpose and utility of one's work, ways by which social betterment of one's conditions could be achieved, and the larger visions and higher ideals of Anglo-Saxon culture that could be given by the leadership of the charity/settlement house workers (Lybarger, 1987).

Reformers, social scientists, and wealthy philanthropists and social-ites saw their mission as instilling in the poor a strong appreciation for class differences—in particular between the wealthy and the poor—and, where possible, providing social mobility to the middle class. The re-formers were joined by labor unions and ethnic welfare organizations that saw the school as a way to improve their own social conditions (see, e.g., Peterson, 1985). Similar to Adam Smith's notion of education as emulation and sympathy (Hamilton, 1980), the curriculum was to help the poor and immigrants assume a productive and rewarding life within a scheme organized by American Protestant Unitarian values and scientific reasoning. The organization provided by science would teach proper sanitation, nutrition, and habits of daily routine that would uplift the lower classes and thereby improve the society as a whole.

The motivation of the reformers and social scientists was uplifting and noble; the consequences were contradictory. Conditions of some of the poor and the immigrants were improved, and social mobility was both an ideal and a reality for many. But the value of social mobility also eliminated consideration of a social policy seeking equality of conditions rather than equality of opportunity.[14] The former presupposed a differ-entiation and hierarchy in society; the latter contains differentiation but equal value across occupations.

The notion of "need" implied dependency and defects in the moral, intellectual, and personal makeup of segments of the school clientele. The reposition of "need" from a social to a psychological category made the selection of social priorities seem to be dictated by considerations of efficiency in achieving predefined goals. It was the psychological notion of need that was incorporated into the work of the Committee of the Social Studies in 1915 and that underlies many strate-gies for the selection and organization of the curriculum today, in-cluding the reforms of teacher credentials and the label of "at-risk" children, especially as these educational policies are related to minority groups.

CONCLUSIONS

The social sciences are firmly positioned in the relation of schooling to the state. Psychology provided a discourse that could attribute the problems of state governance to the individual. The professionalization of knowledge contained technologies that made the intentions of the person subject to scrutiny and supervision. As part of those arrangements, the social sciences have developed a rhetoric of persuasion about structures of power. They have also created social technologies that have implications for the production of self.

While the early discussions about schooling focused on moral and political issues, the sciences of schooling redefined pertinent considerations into issues of instructional procedures and administration. The reformist role of the professions combined scholarly work with applied procedures for organizing structures of meanings and relationships within institutional contexts. A social consequence was technologies that stipulated rules for determining competence, social responsibility, and authority.

Psychology became a central dynamic in the production of power relations and, as it moved into the 20th century, provided the dominant discipline around which a school discourse about pedagogy evolved. The scientific distinctions created an appearance of a common school as universal for all. The official debates came to center around curriculum management, individual development, classroom community, and effective schools. Political and economic issues were transformed into manageable education problems that focused on the creation of teaching strategies, testing procedures, and a search for effectiveness, thus obscuring the social predicament of schooling in a diverse or differentiated society.

The transformation of curriculum into problems of modern psychology yielded important political implications as to the social organization of institutions and individuals. A decontextualization of moral and political issues formulated reform as "helping" individuals through greater efficiency and administration. The problems of success, failure, and self-worth were reattributed to the individual through the methods of classification of pedagogical sciences, thereby establishing a social focus on self-discipline and individual motivation. At the same time, patterns of classroom discourse normalized social relations through an organization of neutral-appearing tasks that focused on a pastoral care that was to supervise attitudes, skills, and behaviors. Clinical methods rationalized the personal and private, subjecting individuals not only to the control of others but to an inner accountability and discipline for which they were personally responsible.

Despite these influences, as we have argued, at no point is the relation of social science to institutional power total or complete. A series of alternative choices could have been made that would have altered the relations that evolved. The creation of educational sciences as an object of schooling and pedagogy resulted from multiple trajectories in sites such as the university, state, and schools—all of which joined at a particular historical moment. The positioning of science entailed the consideration of multiple threads that intertwined and characterized the social tensions and conflicts that were emerging. My intent here is not to assign educational scientists power in society or to define the problem as one of voluntarism; rather, it is to locate the movement of power and regulation through the distinctions and categories of institutional settings.

I have included a review of the 19th and early 20th centuries in a book about contemporary school reform in order to understand how the present is part of a continuum that shows both a continuity with and breaks in the patterns of social regulation. In this and the previous chapters the emergence of mass schooling is described as a rearticulation of practices inscribed in a complex social field that included the state, religion, social science (especially psychology), philanthropy, and the university. Central to this history were epistemologies incorporating a liberal individualism that were developed and given form through teaching, teacher education, pedagogy, and educational sciences. The formation and formalization of discourse around schooling occurred unevenly, following various trajectories at different layers of institutional transformation as schooling was internally constructed and interrelated with sectors of culture, politics, economy, and society.

Our focus on the social epistemology of these practices helps bring to the fore important issues of the current situation. We can interpret the construction of mass schooling and educational sciences as a series of breaks with previous patterns; reform is associated with a professional knowledge, school is tied to the role of the state in producing progress, and the individualization of the person is given a particular institutional form through the practices of pedagogy. These constructions persist. Today they are inscribed in a new field of social relations and processes of production. It is to the rearticulation of reform in a new social field—not as a chronological history but as one of changing relations of institutions, knowledge, and power—that I now turn my attention.

4

Contemporary Teaching and Teacher Education Reforms

Reconstituting a State Bureaucratic Apparatus and Forming a Political Discourse

The reform movements following World War II, which were given a particular shape during the 1980s, show certain continuities and discontinuities with the social fields of schooling formed throughout the 19th and early 20th centuries. Discourse practices about individualism are retained, but the renewed pressures of modernization produce new institutional relations that guide, direct, and evaluate the governance of schooling. Professional and scientific practice are defined in new sets of cultural patterns that frame curricula and provide strategies for defining teaching and teacher education. My argument about contemporary reform in this and the following chapters is that the processes that govern schooling have at least two dimensions. The first, the social regulation of schooling, constitutes a break in patterns in which dichotomies of centralization and decentralization are no longer adequate to explain the phenomena; the second, the patterns of relations, contain practices that narrow the range of democracy. My purpose in moving from the previous discussion about 19th- and early 20th-century schooling to the present is not to describe the progressive development of schooling. Rather, it is to consider current practices as the residues of their predecessors at an institutional level, while at the same time signaling breaks in those relations in the present context of school reform.

In this and the following chapters, I draw attention to the work and quality of teachers' practice that has become a part of the national political agenda. Government, foundation, and professional reports have called for a reappraisal of teaching and teacher education (Carnegie Forum on Education and the Economy, 1986; Gideonse, 1984; Holmes Group, 1986, 1990; National Commission on Excellence in Education,

1983). In nearly every state, this reexamination of teaching and teacher education has resulted in increased admission requirements, more liberal arts education, expanded field experience for new teachers, and a system of ongoing supervision that extends into the first year of teaching (Kalfayan, 1988; Wisconsin Department of Public Instruction, 1984). An explicit purpose of the reforms is to increase teacher professionalism; this is to be achieved by increasing the professionalization of knowledge through administrative changes and research that interrelates various layers of institutional life. These reforms of teaching and teacher education respond to certain transformations in social, economic, and cultural conditions in the United States. To view the reform proposals as objective, disinterested plans for action is to obscure the social significance and political implications of the discourse that spawned them. The current reforms are not simply a formal mechanism to respond to events but are part of the events that serve to structure loyalty and social solidarity.[1]

I examine these reforms as an important rupture in the traditional meaning of state as it applies to the arena of schooling. Institutions interact to orchestrate new agendas and relations in the field of schooling. The strategies are designed to promote system maneuverability and to redesign the bureaucratic priorities and presuppositions of the work of teaching and teacher education. At the same time the policy language about federal systems, about local control and decision making, mystifies rather than illuminates these new patterns of regulation, which are both institutional and epistemological. Standardization and regulation occur not through a geographic centralization but through the interrelation of diverse institutions and discourse patterns.

This chapter provides an outline of the patterns that give shape and fashion to contemporary reform practices; subsequent chapters subject these patterns to further analysis to consider the forms of knowledge and power relations produced. The discussion considers both the apparently disparate reform practices of federal, state, and local governments and philanthropic and university institutions as interrelated in the production of the social regulations in schooling. These patterns of institutional relations produce forms of social regulation through the types of problem-solving strategies applied. Later chapters focus directly on the practices that construct those relations, establishing priorities not only in the organization of social life but in the patterns in which individual actions are structured and administrated.

As in the past, my concern is with those practices that are part of the dynamics of social regulation and serve as important hallmarks of schooling. The practices of reform link prescribed social changes with the public knowledge of the world in a manner that enables people to feel satisfied that the processes will effectively attain their personal as well as social ends. Here, as before, I am concerned with systems of relations and not with individual intent, teleological conceptions of cause, or notions of conspiracy. The argument considers reform as a practice of schooling and challenges the commonly accepted notion of schools as loosely coupled organizations with reform policy as a ritual separate from practice (Meyer & Rowan, 1977).

PREVIOUS STATE MODERNIZATION IN EDUCATION: AN INCOMPLETE PROCESS

An understanding of the process by which particular forms of social regulation emerge requires consideration of the long-term processes of state modernization as they relate to schooling. Attention to the structural relations of the political system reveals an external facade of decentralized decision making driven by an increased movement toward standardization and regulation.

The movement from a highly decentralized system of control to one that embodies centralized steering patterns in educational practice developed slowly in the United States, especially as compared to European systems. During the Progressive Era (1880–1920) and up to World War II, the public sectors of transportation, labor, banking, industrial relations, and the military were reorganized under federal administrative agencies as a means of mobilizing and coordinating agencies of political influence or control. This approach to state development, as discussed in Chapter 2, was unique among Western nations and was a pragmatic response to the power relations that existed with local political parties and the courts after the forming of the new republic.

Educational policy and practice remained outside the realm of these processes of centralized administration as a result, in part, of strong beliefs about local control of schooling (Fine, 1956). In addition, local school administrations developed their own mechanisms for delivering services, and homogeneous textbooks helped to produce a national curriculum without federal intervention (Westbury, 1990). The widespread rationalization of school processes incorporated the characteristics of standardization and regulation associated with state formation, but cast them into the context of local school administration. The "cult of efficiency," to borrow a phrase from administration research (Callahan, 1962), involved developing a national infrastructure of school control through the incorporation into each school building of particular management systems for organizing people and pedagogy.

While this administrative organization produced a certain type of problem solving across school processes, a degree of flexibility was retained in responding to the tensions unique to each community. The political and social strains of a nation confronting industrialization, urbanization, and "assimilation" of vast numbers of immigrants produced particular demands that could be addressed effectively through local initiatives. These demands included native language studies for immigrants, religious "release time" from the school day, vocational trade schools to accommodate local businesses and unions, and art appreciation programs for the new middle classes, which viewed education as a prerequisite to social mobility. Locally controlled administrative organizations were constructed to respond to local conditions and to help ameliorate tensions emerging in the larger community (see Mattingly, 1975).

World War II is a watershed for a number of social upheavals that were occurring in an uneven fashion in the decades prior to and following the war years. The New Deal of the Roosevelt presidency linked professional knowledge more firmly to the planning of the welfare state, and executive government in the person of the president assumed a greater role in domestic and foreign policy. This strong executive role was further established by war planning and the new global role of the United States. Following the war, the expertise that organized and directed the military was brought into the civilian economy and social planning. Men who had applied system analysis to rationalize and give efficacy to the millions in the military were influential in the reform programs created in sectors such as education after the war (see Popkewitz, Tabachnick, & Wehlage, 1982, especially Chapter 2).

The decades following World War II brought substantive changes in economy, society, and culture (Cushman, 1990). The economy was based on continual production and consumption of nonessentials and quickly obsolete products, often reflecting transient fads. The urban population moved from 77 percent of the whole to 95 percent by 1970. An important segment of the urban population were blacks, who moved in increasing numbers from southern rural areas, and Hispanics from Puerto Rico, Mexico, and later Latin America. Widespread automobile ownership and new technological industrialization transformed business capacities and cultures. At a different level, suburban and urban dwellers were living in more crowded environments but experiencing much more secluded and secular lives. The numbers of people living in the average household decreased as the extended family unit, and later the nuclear family, declined.

Culturally, there was greater focus on the individual as the source of salvation, but this individuality had a particular configuration. Personal fulfillment came to be seen in relation to "the culture of narcissism" (Lasch, 1978). Community, tradition, and social meaning were decontextualized and recontextualized, with attention given to the discrete attributes of individuals and with fulfillment sought through immediate consumption. The new economy, social relations, advertising industries, and the field of psychology contained a configuration of the "empty self" (Cushman, 1990). Cosmetics, media, diet industries, and pop psychology, among others, suggested that self-improvement was among the most important of social values.

The "empty self" was related to the reformation of the welfare state. The purpose of governing was no longer to repress or restrict, but to create wishes and desires that could be satisfied immediately. The social sciences, particularly psychology, produced theories and practical technologies that would enable individuals to find satisfaction through consumption.

After the war, the federal government began to play a significant role in key decisions concerning school curricula, organization, and teacher education. Through diverse financial incentives and research and development projects, the curriculum became more responsive to larger economic, military, cultural, and social interests (Spring, 1976). The National Science Foundation (1950), National Defense Act (1958), and the Elementary and Secondary Education Act (1963) were some of the legislative vehicles by which these actions were initiated. Indirect federal influence in teacher education was established in undergraduate and graduate programs through student loans, grants to teachers who taught in federally defined priority areas, and funding for teacher institutes concerned with improving university programs and subject-matter teaching (Cushman, 1977). The Borden Act (1946) initiated these projects, with later programs such as the Teacher Corps and Teachers of Teacher Training (TTT) providing focus to preservice education and minority educational improvement.

The federal government began to sponsor research and development centers throughout the country that served to mobilize an educational science community in a manner that previously did not exist.[2] The creation of 27 research centers and developmental laboratories in the mid-1960s, for example, was intended to strengthen federal administrative capacity as the modern curriculum movement gained impetus; at that time, however, available expertise was inadequate to meet the requirements of the tasks under consideration.[3]

National research and administrative strategies established boundaries and set priorities to monitor those considered in need of special help. A program of remediation was established for poor and minority groups through nationally funded projects. A commonly accepted psychological language of school success and learning was produced that formally defined populations of low achievers. Nationally defined categories of "socially disadvantaged," and later "at-risk," students "in need of remediation" became commonplace in the vocabulary of schooling.

While legislation in the late 1960s seemed to originate from a ground-up concern about the poor and disadvantaged, its long-term effect has been the inculcation of a political doctrine of governability into the everyday world of schooling. Social concern about poverty and inequality was placed under the purview of existing governmental agencies and refashioned to align with administrative priorities (Rose, 1972). Racial and class relations were redefined as issues of poverty, disadvantage, or later, "at-risk" students. This discourse of school remediation was also one of social regulation. Professional knowledge embodied a series of differentiations that objectively separated and ranked individuals from different social and racial groups (Franklin, 1987b; Sleeter, 1987; for a more general argument abut the discourse of power, see Foucault, 1975, 1980). To establish remediation for the poor was also to incorporate languages of clinical medicine, behavior modification, and therapy into the general curriculum. Diagnosis and prescription became methods for treating all children, but especially those of the poor and minorities. Rather than challenging the powerlessness of the poor, the reforms simply expanded the bureaucracies that defined the rules of that powerlessness and incorporated the discourse of remediation into the priorities of the communities that were "targeted" for help (Popkewitz, 1976a).

To summarize, after the Second World War, traditional mechanisms were pushed to their limits as dramatic social transformations precipitated a recasting of educational policy and practice (Kaestle & Smith, 1982; Spring, 1976).[4] Strains were increasingly apparent in the face of new types of industrialization and militarization, the "cultural revolution" of the 1960s, the reactions to the Vietnam war, and the civil rights movement. Drastic social and economic changes challenged the steering mechanisms of the school system; a shift in the relation of federal policy and practices toward schooling followed. The local organization of school practice, which had withstood the centralized patterns of state development in other arenas, began to change. This change reflected new economic commitments in the face of the U.S. international position as well as social commitments toward minorities and the poor. These new patterns produced new institutional capabilities and social regulation, which I now explore.

SOCIAL TRANSFORMATIONS AND
THE STEERING OF SCHOOLING

We can think about the intense efforts toward educational reform in the 1980s and the beginning of the 1990s as part of transformations that have national and international dimensions. Certain analyses have labeled the current cultural-economic situation as part of the crisis of governability (Offe, 1975, 1984). In part, it is argued that the state is unable to meet the demands of the economic sector to create conditions for commodity production while at the same time responding to escalating demands in the noncommodity sectors, such as those for social welfare and education. A common prescription has been to diminish the overloading of system claims, expectations and responsibilities. At the same time, tensions and strains in these cultural systems are producing new demands on schooling and teacher education.

This notion of "crisis" is, I believe, overly dramatic and ignores the long-term transformations that influence the social organization and social regulation that occur in schooling. In the following discussion, I will focus on certain economic tensions, cultural patterns, and demographic changes in the United States that are intertwined in the patterns of social regulation occurring in the educational reforms of the 1980s. While educational reforms retain a focus on the development of individual capabilities, they are part of patterned practices different from those preeminent at the turn of the century. This discussion is intended to provide a horizon from which to view the administrative arenas of schooling that are discussed in the final sections of this chapter and in later chapters. To consider the changing notion of the state and of the particular historical tensions of society and schooling is to consider the reforms of the 1980s and early 1990s as part of broader, long-term transformations.

Economic Tensions and Demands on Schooling

As early as the Great Depression of the 1930s (Zolberg, 1989) and following the postwar European recovery of the 1960s, there has been concern about the decline of the U.S. economic power and authority in international commerce (Krasner, 1978). A globalization of the world economy in the postwar period that links Japanese, U.S., and European businesses, as well as relations of these economies to the southern hemisphere (Silk, 1990), has implications for the social process of schooling. The current debates about the decline of foreign markets, trade imbalances, and the burgeoning obligation of a welfare system are part of long-term transformations. They are given new immediacy by the rise of the Pacific ring, the European Community, and changes in Eastern Europe, all part of an international economy that reaches directly into the nation's domestic production and fiscal policies. The report on U.S. education, *A Nation at Risk* (National Commission on Excellence in Education, 1983), noted these long-term changes but defined them as a national problem of loss of power and in terms of instrumental relations of schooling to economic issues.

Public discussion suggests that the current reform proposals in teaching and teacher education are positioned as a response directly linked to economic issues. There has been increasing economic inequality in the United States from 1969 to the present, with a shrinking middle class. Blacks have fared particularly poorly in these changes (Levy, 1986). While unemployment among urban black youth (aged 20–24 years) averages 40 percent, government national unemployment figures place the general unemployment rate at about 6 percent, the lowest in more than a decade (U.S. Department of Labor, 1986).

An issue of the national magazine *Business Week* ("Help Wanted!," 1987) focused on employment changes from a shrinking core of traditional jobs in blue-collar industries to occupations that require increased education. The inability of schooling to provide adequate labor, it is suggested, was muted in the past decade by the bountiful supply of workers, the "baby boomers." These children, born in the years following World War II, entered the labor market between the early 1970s and the mid-1980s. Because this labor supply is no longer available, more direct national administrative controls of the school-work relationship are sought. But "even with the best efforts, it will take years to upgrade the educational level of the U.S. workforce" (Garland, 1987, p. 61).

What is significant in the current economic situation is the uncoupling and recoupling of elements of socialization and labor processes. Economic transformations, including multinational corporations, technological production, and the growth in service industries contain demands for workers who are more flexible in their ability to function productively within the context of constantly changing work situations and requirements (Kantor, 1989). This autonomy remains clearly bound and disciplined in a cognitive study of technological production and bureaucracy. Individuals need to be more skillful in working within the constraints imposed by rapidly changing conditions; that is, they need to have a "problem-solving ability" that enables them to identify flexible solutions within rationally bound systems (Berger et al., 1973).

While schooling assumes political significance in the formation of new economic patterns, an outcome of the economic pressures and dislocations has been repeated calls for a restructuring of social and economic arenas. Efforts to achieve school reform combine with other practices to place less restraint on business (privatization of the economy), to reduce the financial burden imposed by demands made by the noncommodity systems (such as welfare), and to increase attention to the effectiveness of socialization and vocational processes. Business discussions as well have considered redefining corporate culture from bureaucratic networks to smaller, more flexible and innovative organizations (Kantor, 1989).

It would be misleading, however, to view the current reforms as exclusively economic. The seemingly clear relation between education and the economy is less straightforward than it appears. The relation of schools to the national economy is exemplified by legislation that justifies school aid and by teacher unions that have linked teaching to a production model as part of a strategy to gain material and social benefits. The relation between economy and schooling, however, is not a one-to-one correspondence; it is instead the product of the subtle tensions that occur as culture, labor, and politics interrelate (see, e.g., Bourdieu, 1984). The complex relations among cultural, economic, political, and social patterns are a key part of the production of the school reforms that are occurring.

Cultural Tension and Demands on Schooling

Demographic changes, shifting social boundaries of cultural institutions, and political pressures from liberals and from the New Right have produced demands for reform in schools and professional education. But what have been viewed as changes in business expectations about an educated worker are also related to expectations and patterns of production found in the arts and the political system. These transformations involve complex social relations and multiple patterns that produce and define social solidarity—a process Durkheim refers to as part of modernity (DiMaggio, 1987; Kantor, 1989).

A rapidly changing U.S. demography is an integral aspect of the current reconstitution of social regulations.[5] By the year 2000, one of every three U.S. citizens will be nonwhite; 38 percent of the school population will be black, Hispanic, Native American, or Asian (Mirga, 1986). These minority populations will continue to experience greater disparities in major social welfare indicators as compared to the majority population (see Massey, Condran, & Denton, 1987; Massey & Eggers, 1989).

Recognizing the central social, cultural, and political role of the school, the program officer of the Exxon Education Foundation, a major corporate-funded nonprofit group, argues that changing school demography demands the reimposition of a "nation-building" effort in schools. The new effort is analogous to that which occurred in the early 1900s in response to European immigration (Miller, 1986). The current nation-building agenda for nonwhites is "a matter of even more pressing concern for the overall moral, political, and economic health of the nation" (Miller, 1986, p. 40). Miller argues that the role of the contemporary school is to produce social progress and a moral citizenry and to eliminate social strife through a seemingly classless institution based upon merit.

Current demographic changes are coupled with cultural tensions that together have implications for the construction of school practices. Traditional notions of social solidarity are threatened by transformations in family structures and sexual practices, fears about public safety, and challenges to conceptions of a national manifest destiny in which the U.S. provides moral, political, and economic direction for world affairs. These social and cultural changes can be identified in multiple layers of society. Feminism and altered gender practices have subjected cultural definitions, mores, and labor relations to ongoing critical scrutiny. Social response to homosexuals in the context of the AIDS epidemic; the conflict between whites and blacks in the Bernard Goetz, Howard Beach, and Bensonhurst cases in New York; the growth of fundamentalist religions; and the resurgence of patriotism expressed in the 1988 presidential election and in widespread public approval of Colonel Oliver North—all exemplify cultural tensions about cherished beliefs.

At the same time, these multiple points of conflict entail constructions of belief and social expectations about the conduct of schooling that are coded in reform practices. For example, the rhetoric of the New Right calls for preservation of the family, but its social practices are not a return to some previous model; the intent is to impose practices that respond to contemporary social conditions, technologies, and ideologies. As I consider in Chapters 5–7, the movement toward teacher professionalism, accountability, and national educational goals can be understood as institutional strategies of cultural regulation and occupational mobility that are part of forming structural relations.

The lines of cultural struggles are not clearly drawn as they intersect in education; there are multiple and conflicting interests. Efforts toward reform in teacher education, for example, have indirect links to the pro-family policy of the New Right. The New Right has sought to eliminate what it views as the pernicious values of feminism, liberal social welfare, and "secular humanism" (Hunter, 1988). Adopting a popular-ist rhetoric that combines notions of privacy, solidarity, and community with economic agendas, the New Right has focused on the school as a mechanism by which it can move to protect the family and maintain women's "traditional" roles (also see Omi & Winant, 1986).

The New Right's strategy is to rebuild society from its base to its peak. Federal and state government involvement in teaching and teacher education is one strategy by which nationalism, patriotism, and nonfeminist family values can be injected into the curriculum. The fed eral education bureaucracy supports state activism to set standards of "basics" whose effects are to steer schooling to conservative values by reducing social-welfare and "activistic" agendas, such as those of the 1960s reform movement. While specific data are unavailable, one legacy of the Reagan administration appears to have been the replacement of many of the middle-management people in federal educational agencies who maintained the liberal programs articulated by the Johnson War-on-Poverty agenda of the 1960s.

The agenda of the New Right is juxtaposed against the concerns of liberals. Accepting the role of the school in reviving the economy, liber-als project cultural priorities different from those of the New Right. They seek to improve the status of teachers, change bureaucratic work-ing relations within schools, and provide increased opportunities for minorities and the disadvantaged through the continuation of special programs. Attention is also given to "basics," standards, and school effectiveness. Liberal policies seek institutional reforms that include a broadened constituency by giving explicit reference to aiding minorities and the poor.

At points, there is a redrawing of liberal concerns into conservative political policies. The call for choice is an illustration—a political and economic metaphor that maintains a broad symbolic appeal. The fran-chise model of education is related to the privatization occurring in other sectors of economy, culture, and politics.[6] Its main proponents argue that if parents choose the school that their children attend, market forces will produce motivation and achievement among those who pre-viously had no choice; similar arguments are also introduced into teacher education. The franchise model has become a subject of schol-arly discussion, legislation, and specific school and teacher education practices that are sponsored by businesses, philanthropic foundations, and formal government agencies (see Clune & Witte, 1990a, 1990b). Although legislatively mandated in several states, the programs related to educational choice have drawn criticism concerning costs and the weakening of the common school where diverse groups have historically come together (Cohen, 1990). Some evidence points to its counter-effects: the production of new patterns of selectivity in schooling. A study of privatization in English schools, for example, found that only 10 percent of working-class and minority children used a grant program; the major beneficiaries were children of educated, "helping" professionals who had little economic but some academic capital (Edwards, Gewitz, & Whitty, 1990). The rhetoric of highly specialized schools and technological education, however, is framed to provide market options to those without advantage.

Liberal and New Right agendas appear to be in ideological conflict, but strategies for change produce similar assumptions and implications at many levels. As a result, a combination of conservative and liberal reform strategies are in place in many American public schools. Many school districts, for example, have incorporated discussions of religion into their curriculum. In 1989 the Arizona Board of Education included the teaching of "the religious roots and ethical convictions and cultural differences" as an essential skill (quoted in Steinfels, 1989, p. 1). The California Department of Education will test students in their knowledge of religion beginning in 1992. For conservatives, inclusion of religion in the curriculum helps to overcome what they perceive as a pervasive antireligious message; for liberals, it encourages students to learn about and accept religious diversity and pluralism (Steinfels, 1989).

The rhetoric of professionalism is an example of how liberals and conservatives produce similar strategies to pursue disparate agendas. The rhetoric about professionalism asserts a greater teacher responsibility and autonomy; values supporting individual creativity, flexibility, and critical reasoning are to be engendered. Yet attention is given to administrative, technical knowledge and to questions of teacher status, thus diminishing attention to the social and political issues that underlie teaching and standardization, and increasing centralization and control.

The merging of political agendas in educational practice is further exemplified in the practices of choice in teacher education. Teach For America (1990), an alternative certification program, was initiated by a senior at Princeton University who wrote an honor's thesis about the shortage of teachers in urban and rural areas. It is argued that shortages could be eliminated by recruiting liberal arts graduates from the top private and public universities. Supported by funds solicited from major corporations, over 500 students selected from private and public elite colleges entered this teacher education program in 1990. Following an eight-week summer institute participants will teach for two years in urban and rural areas while studying about teaching.

Teach For America provides an opportunity for the children of affluent America to express social commitment as did the Peace Corps and Teacher Corps of the 1960s. But that social commitment and expression is framed within a conservative political context concerning state social-welfare practices. The discourse of privatization of social policy that marked the Reagan presidential years is thus carried into the reform of teaching. Teach For America is privately funded through individual initiatives rather than through state commitments. The context for social action by youth concerned with the effects of social differentiation and inequities is defined through nongovernment funding and an organization that exists outside of institutional networks.

To this point, I have briefly described the relation of the current reform movement of schooling to larger economic, cultural, and political transformations. Educational reform brings to the forefront related issues of shifting structural relations in society. The predominant role of schooling is to control and minimize the fragmentation and disorganization resulting from structural conflict, while, at the same time, schooling remains part of the processes of production. My intent in this discussion is to provide a stance from which to view the changing patterns of institutional relations occurring during the 1980s and early 1990s. The brief discussion of culture, economy, society, and demography is intended to place the school as a dynamic *in* society.

RECONSTITUTING AN ADMINISTRATIVE CAPACITY

While it is clear that economic and cultural issues have produced a restructuring of certain school policies, change does not emerge in a straightforward manner from the larger external context. In fact, public discussions about a crisis may obscure the more subtle and institutional shifts that are occurring. From regional and dispersed sites emerges a specific and unique ensemble of mechanisms and clusters of procedures that, taken together, serve as a broad system of regulation and power. The federal role in education has been altered through an increase in its monitoring and steering functions. These changes are occurring within local and state governments. Less visible are the concrete arrangements and ordering patterns common to philanthropy, business, unions, and universities, especially as these are interrelated with governmental practices that steer school practices.

We can view the interrelation of patterns of governing as a reconstitution of the state in schooling. It entails a number of movements that do not constitute a single force or a direct correspondence among institutional patterns. Rather, it is a historical juncture that weaves together multiple patterns whose outcome is the reformation of the social regulations in schooling. Traditional notions of centralization/decentralization of government are no longer adequate to describe the current steering mechanisms; the current reconstitution of social regulation contains reference to professionalism but without referring to issues of power or involving notions of the state. The new professionalism contains elements of religious commitment and nationalism reminiscent of the late 19th century, but these assumptions and values exist in a different configuration of moral, ethical, and political relations.

In examining the patterns of steering and monitoring, my concern is the effects of power that occur through the strategies undertaken. The emerging standards are part of institutional relations and epistemologies that narrow the range of participation and responsibility—an argument running through this and later chapters. While the rhetoric calls for more informed public policy, community involvement, and teacher professionalism, the reform practices reverse these intents. The issue, then, is not standards but their assumptions, implications, and consequences.

The Reforming of a Federal Bureaucracy

The current reform movement is not merely a conservative restoration (Shor, 1986), but a continuing extension, yet reconstitution, of patterns of social regulation in schooling that developed in earnest following World War II. The extension of administrative involvement in school activities is considered first at the federal level and then as it relates to state and local government. Later, nongovernmental institutional relations will be explored.

The U.S. Department of Education became a central actor in the formation of school control in the reforms of the 1980s. Although initial executive policy during the Reagan administration sought to eliminate most of the programs of the Department of Education, congressional pressure intervened. Instead, many educational grants have been retained, such as centers to assist in bilingual education, but they have been recast as programs to address issues of school "effectiveness." The programs respond to national conservative priorities in economy and culture that merge certain liberal and conservative views about rational change and progress.

In this instance, the federal strategy does not expand federal legal power; instead, it establishes national standards and monitoring procedures and leaves it to the individual state agencies to meet the standards in their local jurisdictions. The strategies of setting standards and monitoring reconcile conservative ideological concerns about "big government" with demands for a moral and economic revitalization. The Department of Education has adopted a "bully pulpit" agenda in order to translate the issues of the New Right into concerns about school "content, accountability, character, and choice" (see Finn, 1988, p. 349). In certain respects, the U.S. Department of Education has begun to sound much like a European ministry, making general pronouncements about social values, conserving traditions, and economic recovery, while at the same time developing and extending its own administrative capacity and control.

At another level, new control mechanisms are developing through expansion of federal statistical and research capacities. For example, in the 1989 federal budget appropriations, funding for educational statistics totalled $31 million, a 61 percent increase, while educational research received $47 million, less than a 1 percent increase. The National Center for Statistics currently is redefining its sampling mission to assess "continuity" of school programs. Achievement, enrollment, and "opportunity to learn" data are to be collected in every school in the nation. Although resisted for 20 years by state governors, there is now a general political consensus favoring establishment of an assessment center for state educational systems in Washington, D.C. It will provide an interstate data system for comparative accounts of individual state achievement performances. The National Assessment of Educational Progress, originally funded by the Carnegie Endowment and administered by the Education Testing Service (ETS), received a fivefold increase in its funding (from $5 million to $25 million) in the 1989 congressional budget. The nation's governors have endorsed a program of achievement testing to be administered at grades 4, 8, and 12, a decision that lends further priority to increased statistical monitoring of individual schools (Fiske, 1990).

The categories that define educational research constitute a different arena of steering and monitoring. Current federal administrative efforts have redefined and extended government-funded research centers, typically located in universities around the country. The development of expertise occurred as part of the dramatic expansion of U.S. universities during the 1960s and early 1970s, extending faculty and graduate research programs in the social sciences and education. The availability of adequate expertise is no longer the issue it was in the 1960s. In addition to national centers on effective schools, teaching and teacher education, and policy research, there are research centers for such school subjects as mathematics, science, art, the humanities, and reading. In this context, it is important to recognize a theme that appears repeatedly in this discussion: the role of statistics and social science in modern state formations to monitor the processes of change, and as an element that produces a social organization as educational problems are defined and solutions sought.

The historically close relationship between social science and state development makes such extensive federal funding plausible (see, e.g., Silva & Slaughter, 1984). But the focus and emphasis of the research being funded has not been established in a top-down fashion. Instead, continual dialogue between leading educational researchers and the agencies charged with producing reform has established networks of groups and agencies in the social field of education. Many of the central academic players have a strong sense of the direction to be taken by government and foundations and are thus able to influence the specific formulas used to define the parameters of grant projects. There is also a mobilization of organizational bias that occurs as certain epistemological distinctions are given legitimacy by military, industrial, and cultural changes, such as the plausibility provided to cognitive psychology (see, e.g., Noble, 1989). In these contexts, new research foci are initiated to serve policy makers, such as the contemporary redefinitions to focus on "teacher thinking" and pedagogical reasoning in educational psychology discussed in Chapter 6. The resources made available through research grants are in turn used to fund and extend support staff and graduate programs, as well as to promote individual careers. Federal financing of teacher education research centers, first at the University of Texas at Austin and, more recently, at Michigan State University, is evidence of an organizational infrastructure that exists among the two dozen centers around the country. The production of subdisciplinary researchers in teacher education and teaching interrelates state reform agendas and production in educational sciences. The Wisconsin Center for Education Research, an umbrella organization for research in education where I have a part-time appointment, is also well funded and a part of the network and production patterns.

The new federal steering mechanisms exist in the context of intrainstitutional conflict that becomes submerged in the administrative construction. Debate continues between federal and state governments as to Washington's proper role in education. The New Right's focus on government's need to limit "secular humanism" and theories of evolution in the curriculum is juxtaposed against its distrust of central government. The struggle continues between the executive, legislative, and judicial branches, as illustrated in the previous discussion about the congressional pressure on the Reagan administration to maintain a Department of Education.

Despite these tensions, the juxtaposition of various governmental practices produces a pattern of relations. The advocacy role of the federal government establishes distinctions and categories by which national attention is focused on the input/output qualities of schools. Reform responses fuse liberal economic concerns about science and technology with cultural issues concerning values that have a relation to pro-family agendas of the New Right. The extension of the federal Department of Education, the creation of a new information-gathering apparatus, and an extended national research network, coupled with categorical grants, create an infrastructure that can more centrally respond to certain economic and social priorities. These steering and monitoring strategies, however, are not merely guidelines for technical compliance. The rules embody certain epistemological practices about schooling and produce interpretation and direction. Evidence suggests that the priorities established in testing and statistical comparisons do emerge in certain circumstances in local communities as criteria of school success and do give priority to classroom instruction (see Chapter 7 in this book; Popkewitz et al., 1982, especially Chapter 4; see also House, 1985).

Rationalization and Standardization: State Government

State government reforms are a related aspect of the reconstitution of the administration of teaching and teacher education occurring in the 1980s reforms. At one level, continual tension exists between federal and state governments as to the locus of control in educational decision making. At another level, interrelated practices do emerge to guide and supervise the everyday world of schooling. On the state level, policy research and analysis reiterate the need to make schooling and universities more directly responsive to governmental priorities. This includes restructuring teacher standards, altering school environments, and redirecting teacher training and other university programs (*Time for Results*, 1986; Newman, 1987). These public statements do not suggest that an explicit agenda is being implemented or followed; instead, the statements are elements within sets of institutional relations that have been established and are produced within a particular type of problem solving that I explore.

One of the important actors in the current reform movement is the executive branch of state government. In keeping with national trends toward the concentration of authority in the executive branches of government, governors have assumed a new and powerful role in formulating domestic policy and responding to changing global economics. The executive branch has accumulated more formal authority and influence than at any time since governors led the progressive movement in the early 1900s. The branch concentrates power that was once dispersed among independent agencies and the legislative branch (Stevens, 1988).

State governors, including the chair of the Carnegie Forum on Education and Economy, have focused on education as an immediate response to the pressures of the economy, nationalism, and international competition. As a response to the federal system of government and increased financial demands on local governments, comparative schooling performance is used as a political lever to increase individual state tax revenues and to attract new business. State and local governments bid actively against other localities for new industries in the current situation, as national and state boundaries no longer restrict or drive economic production. Governors proudly proclaim the achievement levels of their local school systems as they struggle to convince industries to relocate plants or high-tech research facilities. Schooling is viewed as a part of the "incentive" program that prepares students for future employment. A ready supply of properly trained workers is held out as an inducement to white-collar industry, and schools are touted as representative of a community environment that is appealing to professional workers.

Within this political climate, state departments of public instruction have developed administrative capacities based on principles of active reformation, long-range planning, and problem management. In contrast to previous reforms that focused on the broad content and categories of schooling, state educational agencies have sought to conceptualize and define practice. This occurs, for example, through increased rationalization of teacher certification and more stringent administrative rules for school graduation and university teacher education programs (Cronin, 1983; Kirst, 1984).

At both the state and federal levels, policies assume that the system can be guided in a *purposeful, rational* manner; that is, logical and discrete policy can define and direct practices with measurable outcomes. Legislative acts, administrative guidelines, local grants, and state agencies define a series of specific practices to address the various social pressures brought to bear upon schools, such as sensitivity training for teachers regarding poor and minority students (human relations) and teacher training for "mainstreaming" handicapped pupils; these elements also combine to emphasize greater labor efficiency and more stringent fiscal controls within the university and schools.

Purposeful, rational discourse should be viewed as a form of regulation that emerges as a consequence of the strategy applied. Through the application of various school and administrative sciences, consensus and stability become increasingly important (see Popkewitz, 1984). Procedures are viewed as universal and devoid of reference to specific purposes and goals. Standardized and routinized procedures are emphasized, while the relationships among the various elements and their relationship to the whole are exempt from scrutiny. The subdivision of practice into logical issues limits reflection and criticism to specific evaluation techniques. For example, in Chapter 7, I explore how administrative rules in teacher education create distinctions and hierarchies that seem to address all children through universal teaching practices, while they in fact legitimate new forms of supervision and regulation for minority groups. It is through strategies of purposeful rational discourse that political issues are reformulated into administrative concerns and conceptions of responsibility in teaching and teacher education are focused.

While I can identify a pattern of action emerging from state government agencies, these responses have not been developed without conflict or internal debate. Although governors and state legislatures have accepted the rhetoric of reform, they are concerned that increased fiscal control will mean decreased local autonomy; that the regulatory costs involved in the new administrative procedure will be prohibitive; and that rivalry among, for example, governors, state superintendents of public instruction, and legislators concerning policy and control may be detrimental to the political positions or future of all three groups.

The centrality of a purposeful, rational discourse can be gauged in personnel changes that have accompanied increased regulation by the state government bureaucracy. Bureaus concerned with school testing, evaluation, and certification have increased in both size and number. From an office of two workers in 1974, the State of Wisconsin Department of Public Instruction's Office of Teacher Certification now employs more than 20 people. Similar growth has occurred in the State Assessment Office. The agency, now called "school improvement," designs and administers tests, statistically analyzes test results, and disseminates this information to establish statewide standards. After the introduction of new Wisconsin standards for the public schools, auditors were hired in 1988 to visit school districts and assess compliance at a cost of approximately $200,000. In contrast, former curriculum consultants within the Wisconsin Department of Public Instruction have seen their resources and personnel reduced. Their tasks have been redefined from assisting in local curriculum design to developing state standards and monitoring the implementation of the new administrative rules.

At this point, it is arguable that the flattening of reality into technical dimensions is little more than commonplace in social science, psychology, and schooling.[7] Purposeful, rational thought and instrumental reasoning, discussed later, have been elements of school organization and curriculum planning since the Progressive Era. What appears in the contemporary situation is a particular appropriation of this style of reasoning in relation to various elements in the reconstitution of state steering and social regulation. My point in focusing on the instrumental quality of the reform practices, then, is to consider the specific and historical sets of relations in the multiple institutional layers in which reform occurs, with their multiple epistemological distinctions that give organization to reason and thought about progress. Thus, while I initially draw on the analysis provided by the Frankfurt School of social research (Habermas, 1971; Jay, 1973) to explore the instrumental reform strategies undertaken, I focus on the specific regional qualities and relations in which reason is formed, rather than identify a single, global concept of social relations, such as produced by capitalism. Here and in later chapters, I interpret the fluid grids of interrelation that include the production of reform discourses, the practices of educational research, state government administrative rules for teacher education, and local school district efforts to develop a more professional teacher corps. Each provides a particular specificity to the different layers and the epistemological distinctions.

The Patterning of Control in
Teaching and Teacher Education: Two Cases

We can explore the interrelation of state government and federal practice by studying the combination of circumstances under which the steering of teaching and teacher education occurs. At one level, countless federally and state government–sponsored conferences, commissioned papers, research articles, and media discussions have focused on the need for reform. These various forums, discussed in the following chapters, establish categories through which selectivity and agenda setting occur. At a political level, the production of rational standards, combined with an emphasis on local responsibility for determining fiscal policies and program regulations, is called *deregulation*, a political/economic metaphor brought into the school arena. But the new circumstances involve neither deregulation nor decentralization in that various forms of school steering occur in multiple institutions and at various layers, rather than as a homogeneous, single outcome. This can be explored by examining both state government–sponsored reforms and school financing.

One arena in which to consider the reconstitution of control is the relation among state government departments of public instruction, local school districts, and teacher education institutions. There is constant interaction between state educational agencies and local school superintendents through advisory boards, issue-oriented study groups, and financial incentives or grants for specified programs. The "participatory" arrangements establish a forum through which local districts can initiate reforms by assuming responsibility for developing strategies of implementation. Steering is accomplished through a system characterized by "functional" autonomy, in which policies set by state government establish general directions for reform while specific implementation is provided in local school districts. Reform becomes a constant agenda of the state government and local school district, a ritual that establishes the rationality, benevolence, and modernity of institutional practices (see Popkewitz, 1982b). I explore a set of these interrelations in Chapter 7 through analysis of an ethnographic study of three districts in the state of Wisconsin (Popkewitz & Lind, 1989). The Wisconsin Department of Public Instruction, after recommendations of advisory councils and study groups, established experimental projects to improve teaching. In 1986, eight school districts received matching legislative and local school district funds to monitor first-year teachers, to design programs that gave special monetary rewards for participation in staff development, to create awards for exemplary teaching, and to encourage continuing professional studies. These experimental programs were to serve as the basis for the development of statewide administrative rules concerning the conditions of teachers' work. Responses to the pilot programs indicated that participants viewed the reform as the result of local initiative. Yet examination of these local programs revealed values that were consistent with the more generalized national discourse about reform. The pilot program strategies were ostensibly intended to reduce bureaucratic tasks and to increase the professional autonomy of teachers. The practices actually intensified supervision and regulation. Increased routinization of teacher planning occurred, since lessons were to be evaluated on the basis of their conformity with predefined steps for organizing them. Monitoring procedures were increased during the school year to ensure that teachers followed outlined steps.

In this case, the implications of reform for the control of teaching were obscured by the reform practices themselves. The multiple levels at which the agenda was negotiated produced an aura of consensus and equality in decision making. The presence of state advisory committees and local structure projects combined to assign legitimacy to the new patterns.

The complex changes in school control patterns are exemplified by the relation between federal and state tax laws for school revenues. While the myth holds that schools are financed locally, centralized financing of schools has increased dramatically in recent years. In part, these changes date from the 1970s, when conservatives sought to limit local school district expenditures. The Jarvis amendment in California in the mid-1970s was intended to reduce local expenditures: Its effect in California, as of similar initiatives elsewhere, was the centralization of school finances in response to reduced local property taxes. In California the state contribution to school funding has increased from 35 percent to 75 percent as compared with the national average increase from 55 percent to 60 percent. The state portion of Wisconsin's local district budget now approaches 50 percent, with current legislation considering further increases.

Redistribution of funding responsibilities coincides with growing national demands for school steering as well as with strains on local systems of school financing. In many local districts around the country, school tax referendums are repeatedly defeated in local elections. Local politicians fear the property taxes to finance schools have been stretched to the limit. Local school boards, administrators, and teachers view state-collected taxes as the best way to increase and improve school programs.

To this point, the discussion has focused on the various patterns by which federal and state governmental agencies construct school practices. The interplay of federal and state government practices does not always surface within public view. Specified grants to local governments and particular research distinctions and categories establish directions that are not visible when explicit patterns of decision making are examined. But the multiple patterns of government action shape the institutional coalitions that organize current practices in important ways.

A POLITICS OF RECONSTITUTION:
PHILANTHROPY, PROFESSIONS, BUSINESSES, AND UNIONS

Reformulation of the state's administrative capacity in the 1980s was not straightforward, nor was it concerned solely with governmental agencies. Instead, a pattern of state control has been constructed through coalitions of civic, political, and economic interests that interact to establish practices as new structural arrangements are formed. Governmental agencies and nongovernmental organizations of professional groups, universities, philanthropic foundations, national businesses, and teacher unions interact as elements in the production of social regulation.

It is this interactive relation that, from an analytical viewpoint, is a reconstitution of the state in the context of schooling. There is no clear demarcation between governmental and civil institutions as they mesh in the establishment of social regulation in education. Current reform practices are products of the tensions that define the patterned relations among these institutions.

Nongovernmental Processes of Control: Professional Organizations, Philanthropic Foundations, and Unions

The current rationalization of educational practice involves consideration of at least four institutional contexts outside of formal governmental agencies. These four are philanthropic foundations, professional organizations, national union organizations, and universities. (The first three will be considered here, with universities the focus of a separate section.)

Foundations have been important institutions in setting agendas for graduate and professional programs since the turn of the century. They were instrumental in defining a focus for black colleges (Berman, 1990). Foundations are influential in defining school standards, through their sponsorship of organizations that construct tests, and as key actors in the mobilization of reform discourses through the production of reports (see Chapter 6; also Labaree, 1990a).

Essential in state steering since the progressive reforms of the late 1800s (see, e.g., Curti & Nash, 1965; Wheatley, 1988), foundations have made education and teacher education a priority since World War II (Cushman, 1977). More than 6,000 such foundations listed in the *Foundation Directory* describe the improvement of education as a major interest. The Ford Foundation and its Fund for the Advancement of Education provided $80 million in the late 1950s and early 1960s for school and teacher improvement. The Carnegie Foundation for the Advancement of Teaching and the Carnegie Foundation have sponsored a variety of publications to promote certain social agendas and supported the creation of the Educational Testing Service in Princeton, New Jersey. Professional organizations and foundations work with state governmental agencies to create a system of national standards. The National Council of Teachers in Mathematics (1989), for example, financed a project to define national standards in mathematics curricula and evaluation. The project is co-sponsored by the Mathematics Sciences Education Board, a group created by the Conference Board of Mathematical Sciences and comprised of presidents of major professional mathematical organizations. The board receives money from a variety of federal agencies and foundations, including the Carnegie and MacArthur foundations.[8] The professional standards advocated by organizations such as these, are acknowledged by state governors and the U.S. president as models by which school reform should be pursued.

Protocols for a national teacher test for occupational entrance have been developed at Stanford University with support from the Carnegie Forum on Education and the Economy, the group that funded a major national report in 1986 on reforming teaching and teacher education (See, e.g., Shulman & Sykes, 1986). The teacher examination may later be placed under the aegis of and be further developed by the Educational Testing Service, the private nonprofit corporation responsible for the National Educational Assessment Project and other examinations that serve as entrance requirements to colleges and graduate schools. The concept of a teacher entry examination has received support from state governors involved in the Carnegie Forum, who view education as a vehicle to make their states more economically competitive. Support also has been expressed by deans of schools of education and major teachers' unions, especially the American Federation of Teachers.

At first glance, union support for a national test might seem odd or tangential to the interests of governors and deans of schools of education. Although the idea of national standards provoked initial debate between the presidents of the American Federation of Teachers and the National Education Association (Carnegie Forum on Education and the Economy, 1986), the use of competency tests is expected to confer status on the professional organizations through control of entrance. Albert Shanker, president of the American Federation of Teachers, is calling for a national curriculum that would make teacher education more focused and serve as a foundation for better standardized tests (Flint, 1990).

A national teacher test and curriculum standards must be viewed within the broader context of the realignment of competing interests. National unions have become part of the structural relations that define the organization of teaching and pronouncements about national purpose and goals. There are serious discussions between the American Federation of Teachers and the National Educational Association about merging these national organizations. The teacher test will further centralize a system in which national teacher organizations can demand greater membership affiliation and control as the systems of teacher education, school output measures, and curriculum are tied more directly to national institutional practices. The national examination is only one element of reform that may affect statewide contracts and occupational entrance requirements, such as those being prepared by the National Board for Professional Teaching Standards. Thus national testing of teachers is part of a larger dynamic and entails a shift to the center, potentially replacing the local school district contracts that have historically determined teacher salary and work conditions.

The interrelation of foundations, professional groups, and unions has created a pattern of internal control of schools. The creation of standards is seen publicly as professional rather than political in origin; as based on scientific judgment rather than issues of global realignment and economic reformation; as administrative rather than positioned in a particular field of social/cultural power in which teaching and teacher education operate.

Nongovernmental Processes of Control: National Businesses and Local School Reform

Large corporations with international markets have been another key actor in the current reforms. This level of business involvement, however, occurs through locally derived projects rather than by way of a single, nationally organized program. The Ford, Carnegie, and Getty foundations, for example, have established staff development projects in secondary mathematics, science, and art education. The Ford projects, for example, are located in urban settings and are often administered through Public Education Funds, local agencies that represent national corporations in large cities. Public Education Funds are an example of organizations that lie outside the purview of regular school district policy-making procedures but interact with all levels of a school district's organization.

Critical thinking, problem solving, and *teacher empowerment* are key phrases in teacher education programs sponsored by the foundations through local business support. These themes have universal appeal and can support a wide array of assumptions formulated in response to contradictory interests. In the current climate, these key phrases have a mixture of references to functional or useful knowledge that relates to demands of the economy and labor formation, as well as more general claims about social inquiry and social innovation. The mathematics standards and notions of problems solving, for example, are drawn from criteria related to scientific and technological use that posit a particular vocationalism and practicality for knowledge.

Business involvement has different facets and does not exist in isolation from other institutional patterns. In the state of Washington, for example, corporate leaders created new forums to exert pressure for legislation to collect school attendance and performance data and to promote specific goals for schools (Trachtman, 1989). The state of Washington Business Roundtable, a task force organized by chief executive officers of major corporations, made recommendations for the improvement of teaching. These included all-day preschool for "at-risk" children, teacher evaluations and inservice training, increased graduation requirements and testing. These proposals, it is interesting to note, are consistent with other recommendations included in the plethora of reports published in the 1980s and early 1990s. The roundtable's language to distinguish educational problems incorporates an institutional discourse of effective schooling—"at-risk" children, teacher evaluation, testing, and so on. The roundtable's reforms were seen as directly and indirectly beneficial to the state's workforce. The roundtable agenda was not immediately taken up in the political arena but became influential only after some setbacks that necessitated their learning to work with other political groups to promote legislation.

To consider the impact of business on the process of school governance, it is important to recognize that its involvement in schooling is not new. Since the 1870s, the language of business administration has been applied to social affairs and cultural development to foster progress. It was the turn-of-the-century business groups that maintained the authority to support or reject the financing of mass schooling through local tax systems (Noble, 1970). National business groups represented by philanthropic corporations have responded in times of crisis to promote both conservative interests and progressive changes throughout the 20th century. Higher education, professional education, and curricula in public schools have been particular concerns. In the 1930s, business interests, national politics, and philanthropy shaped art education through the Owatonna project in Minnesota (Freedman, 1989b). Funded by the Carnegie Corporation, the project was to change the life of the community and to be a model for other school districts.

The current involvement of multinational corporations, however, focuses the agenda of schooling less on local economic assessments than on national production and internationally defined priorities. While traditional jurisdictions are maintained in school policy making, local assessment and the development of programs coincide with the priorities and assumptions determined outside the local area.

THE POLITICAL LOCATION OF
THE UNIVERSITY AS A DYNAMIC OF THE STATE

My concern in this chapter is to consider the reform practices in the relations among federal and state agencies, philanthropic foundations, businesses, unions, and, in this section, universities. We can think of the intersecting institutions as positioned in a social space in which certain types of practices are given sanction to guide and define the distinctions in contemporary educational reform. The university, in particular, assumes a position in relation to the multiple foci and strategies formed.

Social regulation is important in the arena of the modern state through its production and reproduction of knowledge. The U.S. university has multiple roles in the regulation of schooling. In addition to knowledge production, the university is responsible for the socialization of teachers through the processes of teacher education. Universities are also the site at which the disciplinary formation of educational science occurs. The universities are active agents in advocating social reform and providing corrective approaches to social problems. This occurs through systematic and empirical analysis, theoretical developments, and social/technological inventions.

To consider the multiple roles of the university, we must focus on the distinctions between elite and nonelite sites, the divisions of labor that occur, and the particular utilitarian values articulated by the current reform discourse. Distinctions among universities help to give focus to the manner in which diverse institutional relations are formed and facilitate an exploration of the institutional practices in which diverse actors compete for the authority to speak as the legitimate agent of change.

Colleges of education live in twin worlds of schools and universities, and, by definition, all universities are not equal (Powell, 1980). The prestigious teacher education programs are located within elite land-grant and private universities that combine the democratic service ideal with an emphasis on research and the production of knowledge. These roles are a legacy of the Progressive Era, when certain universities combined the character-building function of universities with professional and scientific roles that were important to the development of the modern welfare state.[9]

Schools of education within elite universities have attained status through their university affiliations, graduate programs, alumni from undergraduate programs, and service commitments. The relative stature of schools of education is also related to research grant money that produces jobs, generates extension services within the states, and leads to patterns of communication (theory and research) that are considered authoritative in the maintenance and reform of schools. These elements of cultural and social capital are assigned further importance because the land-grant universities are usually located in state capitals, providing easy access to state legislators and agencies.

The cultural status of elite universities provides a context in which to consider the central role assumed by schools of education in the current reform movement. The Holmes Group, comprised of deans of schools of education in research-oriented universities, issued a report in 1986, *Tomorrow's Teachers*, followed by *Tomorrow's Schools* in 1990. The reports can be read as an assertive and defensive reaction to actions taken by state governments and philanthropic institutions toward teacher education. The future of teacher education is to be developed in accordance with the leadership role provided by research universities. A priority is given, as in the Carnegie Forum on Education and the Economy (1986) report on teaching as a profession, to strengthening the liberal arts background of teachers, improving the rigor of professional courses, and differentiating staffing patterns to reward career teachers for excellence. More professional collegiality among teachers is also recommended.

While the Holmes Group does suggest tension and discontinuity between state government agencies and universities, the dissent nonetheless embodies epistemological assumptions similar to those that are rhetorically said to be dysfunctional for education. While many applaud the desire to improve teacher status, the assumptions of hierarchical differentiations reflect the style of thought associated with bureaucratic institutions.

The professional agenda is established through a populist rhetoric. A concern is expressed for teachers' developing strategies to improve their professional identity. The language of teacher improvement, however, is one of the expert in service of the democratic ideal: Professional knowledge is to elevate teachers and help them make appropriate decisions in their immediate environment. Research is to bring "active participation in community" (Holmes Group, 1990, p. 12), cultivating collaboration and teaching as "communities of learning" (p. 9); with the task of education to bring about democracy as "we in the Holmes Group are willing to wager on popular intelligence" (p. 21). That popular intelligence, however, is based on a formalized knowledge that describes effective practice and the university "distilling" from experience and linking teacher practices to the research produced by universities. The university research community, the Holmes Group argues, provides the expertise necessary for instituting new controls for schools.

The current reports, like those of the educational psychologists of the turn of the century, argue for the importance of an empirical, functional knowledge to direct education progress. The 1986 Holmes Group report, for example, asserts that the reform of teacher education "depends upon engaging in the complex work of identifying the knowledge base for competent teaching and developing the content and strategies whereby it is imparted'' (p. 49). The 1990 Holmes Group report gives greater paradigmatic specificity to that research by privileging a cognitive psychology concerned with teacher thinking, an approach I argue in Chapter 6 has certain implications for the patterns of social regulation in teaching and teacher education. The report calls for management guided by research and increased professionalization through greater stratification and differentiation in teaching. The dividing of teaching into discrete units that can be sequentially organized and monitored entails the further rationalization, regulation, and division of work (Popkewitz, 1987b). The Holmes Group reports maintain the epistemological assumptions of school administration, using the existing distinctions to guide the formation of the report.

Since the issuance of its initial report, the Holmes Group has increased data gathering and assessment that, on the whole, recycle traditional instrumental orientations but refashion them in the new language of the reforms. The report ignores the intense debate about knowledge that is occurring within the university by adopting a stance that ties schools of education to technological definitions of science and system approaches to analysis (see, e.g., Kimball, 1988). Its more recent report (1990) calls for the professional development school, but maintains a consensus view of knowledge and rational change. The report reverses the democratic intent of its rhetoric through a functional research that is to organize and monitor teaching and teacher education.

The Holmes Group reports can also be considered as social documents that exist within the social field and political economy of the university. At an institutional level, the changing demography of teachers (they are, as a group, getting older) and the retraining required for new social/labor expectations create opportunities for more teacher inservice and staff development programs, graduate degrees, and evaluation projects, each of which has great potential to generate university income and status. Prestige is also gained as university faculty establish social technologies to define and interpret the standards of school reform.[10] As Larabee (1990b) argues, the teacher and teacher education reforms promote the social mobility of teacher educators who have long been considered second-class citizens within universities (also see Schneider, 1987).

The irony of the Holmes Group's response is that the university's efforts to preserve its influence in the redesign of power relations in fact undermine and negate one of the strengths of its institutional position. Rather than arguing for a critical as well as mandarin role, the rhetoric of the report is devoid of intellectual content but rich in the folklore of schooling (Popkewitz, 1987a, 1987d). While alternative discourses do exist (e.g., Cherryholmes, 1988; Tabachnick & Zeichner, 1991; Tom, 1984), they tend to be marginal, since the dominant particular visions and distinctions are given legitimacy through the interrelation of the university with federal, local, and philanthropic practices. The reports accept myths of professionalism without considering the historical process by which professions gained and consolidated power, as well as the tendency since the 19th century for the reforms of teaching to introduce more hierarchical forms of control over a corps of mostly women teachers.

CONCLUSIONS

This analysis focused on the relations among institutions in order to consider current restructuring in education. Methodologically, this entailed decentering the events and individual actors by situating them in relational patterns over time. The concern here is with patterns and relations among institutions, not with the motives or intent of individual actors. The contemporary reforms are part of important transformations and ruptures occurring nationally and internationally. Economic realignment is a motif, but it is interrelated with cultural and political issues in such a way that analysis limited to simple cause-and-effect relations obscures the complexity of the conditions. As will be discussed in the following chapter, the reforms symbolically assert the role of global capitalism in a national destiny, a renewed spiritualism and nationalism, and liberal democracy as it is defined in the current social-political climate.

At an institutional level, the current reform practices change the meaning of the state. With different points of entry, coalitions within government, professional groups, universities, foundations, and unions have produced a specific pattern and direction for schooling practice. The relation between the discourse practices of different institutions and layers of action is part of the reformulation of the state as it relates to the arena of schooling. The new vocabulary of reform maintains traditional myths while forging new patterns of social regulation.

The reconstituting of administrative capacity assigns a particular U.S. pattern to the state. The state assumes corporatist characteristics in which sectoral interests form coalitions of distinctly different economic and social institutions. But the analogy of corporatism does not capture the dynamic relations and the regional, seemingly disparate, ways that power and regulation are reconstituted. The networks and patterns of interaction in the current reforms do not simply incorporate major interest groups into political structures. Nor are they only consultative relationships between public authorities and representatives of significant interest groups. Instead, the coalitions among institutions involve finer and more localized channels of social regulation. A series of discrete practices forms a constellation of civil and governmental institutions.

Through the combined practices of professional groups, foundations, businesses, unions, and state government agencies, multiple pressures have been introduced into the educational system. The research and professional functions of the university are part of the complex network of administrative arrangements that are being reconstituted to steer the practices of schooling. A possible consequence of these new coalitions is the limitation of the role of local school boards, administrators, business, and unions in schooling. A further consequence may be a realignment of coalitions among state governments, universities, and local schools.

This reconstitution of the state in the educational arena has implications for the conception of democracy as it exists within schooling. This has at least two dimensions. The first concerns the loci of actors. Centralization reduces the scope, responsibilities, and autonomy that operate at the level of school practice. The second is the instrumental reasoning that gives form to practice. The rules and standards of legitimate issues are conceptualized as being related to administrative concerns, thus reconceptualizing social, political, and moral issues outside the question-asking and problem-solving routines of institutional life.

In demonstrating concern here with the instrumental quality of reform, I am not viewing standards and regulations as evils to be rejected at all cost. As I argued in Chapter 1, social regulation is a condition of schooling and pedagogy. Social regulation is not to be fought against and eliminated; the continual concern of the science of schooling is to study changing ecologies and power relations. Part of the processes of regulation are the production of rules and standards through social practices. Public standards about schooling, at one level, can be helpful as guides that orient teachers and as points of reference in debate among the constituencies of schooling about what is appropriate and worthy of attention. The discussion of standards and regulation in the reform practices being mobilized, however, reveal social configurations and epistemological forms that narrow the foci of schooling to technical issues. The social/political/cultural contexts in which interests and values are framed become obscured.

In the next three chapters, the practices and relations of reform will be examined more closely to consider these consequences. The prescriptions of the different reform programs interact in a manner that redesigns the landscape of schooling to make it more standardized and rationalized. Public and academic discourses create patterns of communication that hide the social relations and power in the restructuring. Changes in conceptualizations and practices of reform, however, are not merely a continuation of process already in place but entail a reconstitution of the social field of regulations.

I realize that my argument contradicts the conventional folk wisdom of education policy researchers, which holds that reforms do not affect practice. In part, I think, the difference results from a shift in both foci and level of analysis. When particular behavioral qualities of schooling or substantive curriculum purposes are considered, such as developing intellectual curiosity, there is little evidence that such reforms are practiced in a universal way (Popkewitz et al., 1982). Over time and when considered relationally, however, there is evidence that schools and universities are being subjected to greater instrumental control (see Chapter 7). Evaluation schemes previously used by administrators have been taken up by teachers as a means to judge what is worthwhile in the classroom. The reconstitution of administrative capacity removes teachers and local communities further from substantive debates about the purpose and direction of schools. The functional orientations of teaching reforms and research become epistemologically and socially more important.

5

Educational Reform as a Discourse of Social Organization and Regulation
The Proposals of the 1980s

The institutional relations discussed in Chapter 4 are enmeshed in the discourse of federal, state, professional, and philanthropic reports on education that began to appear in the 1980s. Their sheer number is impressive;[1] commissioned reports related to mathematics education listed in the references of the National Research Council (1989) exceed 80. The reports are calls for institutional change that responds to and reflects certain transformations in American social, economic, and cultural conditions. The documents sanction social participation in educational reform (Edelman, 1964; Martin, 1978) and foster particular beliefs about the nature, causes, consequences, and remedies for institutional practice. They establish sets of parameters about which issues and knowledge are relevant to school change, excluding other relations and problems as existing beyond the scope of reform.

The current reforms assign a new importance to formal texts that was distinctly absent in previous efforts to reform U.S. schooling. In the past, control tended to be exercised through informal cultural and social patterns, with the "texts" of schooling relegated, for the most part, to the curriculum: readings of textbooks to understand social lore, morality, literacy, and citizenry. Those texts that were important to the 1960s reform were produced by academics, such as Arthur Bestor (1953) and Jerome Bruner (1960), or they were part of a popular literature about why Johnny could not succeed in school. The introduction of national texts about reform and the prominence of administrative texts in steering school practice suggest new patterns of regulation that are related to the reconstitution of the steering mechanism that was discussed earlier. The texts mediate the developing relations within and among the various institutions, describing the new coalitions that are forming and articulating their significance for cultural, political, and economic patterns.

To understand the assumptions and implications of the current discourse about change, this chapter examines the problems, causes, and remedies proposed in the public texts that call for educational reform; central to this review are the pedagogical recommendations these texts offer. The curriculum efforts of the 1960s, the previous period of intense educational discussion, will be juxtaposed against contemporary proposals, and the discourse patterns will be related to the cultural, social, and economic conditions of schooling.[2] The reports are viewed as an element of a new social regulation that entails the meshing of different themes, tensions, and contradictions. In fundamental ways, the reform proposals have significant implications for both the processes of legitimation and the construction of self.

EXPERTISM AND SOCIAL AMELIORATION: THE REFORM OF THE 1960s

If we juxtapose the current commission efforts with those of the late 1950s through the early 1970s, the previous era in which school reform became a national concern, both continuities and differences appear. The call for reform in the 1960s can be seen as a response to at least four elements in the transformation of society: increased professionalization, an increased emphasis on science, a dynamic economic expansion, and a spiritual hope brought about by the end of a World War II. These changes in social conditions provide a horizon from which to consider the current school reform discourse.

Increased Professionalization of Social Life

As argued earlier, one element of the 1960s reform movement was the enhanced status of professionalized knowledge. Since the Progressive Era, academics had had a long history of moving in and out of positions of social and cultural authority in the United States. Following World War II, academics as professionals again rose into national prominence after providing valuable technical direction to the war effort. It was the scientists' role to provide direction for social and material improvement. The public believed that the darkest evil had been destroyed and that a new world could be structured to meet both the material and spiritual needs of all citizens. C. P. Snow (1962) wrote about bridging the two worlds of science and politics. The sociologist Daniel Bell (1962) believed the world was approaching a new harmony that would bring an end to ideological debate. It was believed that the task of the social and physical sciences was to apply engineering know-how to produce a millennial world.

Professionalization gave prominence to particular occupational specialties located in the universities that served as the sources of the reorganization of school knowledge, the "discipline-centered curriculum" that included political science, physics, and specialized fields of mathematics popularly called the "new mathematics." The role of the social sciences and "helping" professions was most clearly evident in efforts toward social amelioration.

The managerial expert, an important actor in the American corporate structure, was transplanted into government and became a more forceful part of the political apparatus. Administrative theories gave direction to social reform. Systems analysis as well as cost/benefit and evaluation approaches became part of government policy to guide operating practices. A legacy of the Kennedy presidency was the incorporation of business accounting techniques directly into state planning, evaluative government agencies, and social reform. Systems analysis and budget planning were introduced into the Department of Defense and other agencies to provide for a more effective and efficient government.

Reforms focused on a general restructuring of social and political institutions. The War on Poverty was to help the poor and socially disenfranchised obtain the institutional support necessary to eliminate the psychological and economic conditions that contributed to poverty. The "war" effort was to bring the best expert knowledge of the social sciences to bear on the problems of society.

The school reform movement was one part of this concerted effort to make social institutions efficient, effective, and, at the same time, responsive to demands for social equity. The newly created National Science Foundation and, later, the National Institute of Education (now the Office of Educational Research and Development) were to direct scientists' efforts toward improving schooling. A major concern of the National Science Foundation was to make the schools more responsive to the changing knowledge of science and technology. The National Institute of Education developed a cadre of professional experts who were responsible for planning, implementing, and evaluating school reforms (see Popkewitz et al., 1982, Chapter 2). Monitoring systems and programs to achieve specific outcomes became an important byproduct of the development of the new expertise in schooling. In complementary ways, the two agencies supported the incorporation of professional knowledge into the schools.

Science in Cultural and Material Production

The professionalization of knowledge is related to a second dynamic of the 1960s reform movement, the importance of science to industrial and cultural life. Science and technology assumed great importance in the productive capacities of American industry. This trend began prior to World War II but was accelerated by the postwar demands of American industry and society. Day-to-day life became more dependent on science and technology, from more automation that changed work patterns to mass media, such as television. The discourse of the postwar years characterized science as a source of improvements in daily living and avenues by which human needs and wants were to be fulfilled.

Of similar importance was a new cultural consciousness that looked to a particular administrative, problem-solving science as a way of reasoning about the values of social affairs. A communications "industry," based in the new technology, emerged in ways that influenced the idioms of daily conversation, the nature of political debate, and the general sensitivities of mass culture. In part, an increased reliance on psychological manipulation of symbols, an increased attention to the presentation of issues, and a decreased concern with the content of issues became a part of American public life. Debate focused on the image of the candidates rather than on the actual practices of government. Public opinion polls and survey research became major instruments of politics; they were tools used to gauge the public's perceptions and views about its government as well as to formulate policy in ways that would be publicly palatable.

Professional science, in the narrowest sense, assumed a particular but culturally significant role; the precision and control that was thought to exist in the natural and physical sciences was to be directed toward social affairs. Professional journals, such as *The American Behavioral Scientist*, were established as a forum in which academics could seek unity in the social sciences through shared assumptions about the administration of social affairs. It was an idealized and mystified vision of social and physical sciences that enabled many to look for a new millennial world on the horizon; the idiom was to become one of technical solutions to political problems. While similar beliefs had existed during the years in which the social sciences first developed, the postwar period stressed the essence of science in cost-accounting procedures that would guide the organization of social welfare and planning.

The curriculum reform movement of the 1960s was born into this general euphoria about the role of science in world progress. This idealized and technical view of science was incorporated into the new curriculum, emphasizing scientific knowledge as produced by scientists who were disinterested in social values and based their research practice on consensually agreed-upon norms (see Popkewitz, 1977a, 1977b). The discipline-centered curriculum was intended not only to disseminate the knowledge of the academics but also to include the methods of arguing, thinking, and "seeing" the world that were considered the bases of these disciplined endeavors. Many of the leaders of the curriculum reform movement, such as Arthur Bestor, Simon Begel, and Jerome Bruner, were professors who believed that the existing school curriculum was irrelevant to the knowledge, skills, and ways of reasoning found in the organized disciplines. They offered their expertise to both redesign the subjects of the curriculum and to lend integrity to its content and teaching. Schools were to teach recent theories and problem-solving methods of physics, biology, mathematics, political science, anthropology, economics, and sociology.

The professionalization of school knowledge produced a curious anomaly. While the knowledge brought into the school was considered clear and unambiguous, science is concerned with the production of knowledge—a process that naturally involves ambiguity, tentativeness, and inventiveness as core dispositions. Also lost in the insertion of the social and natural sciences into the curriculum were the ways in which the internal and external factors of science interact to influence the production of knowledge. Further, the treatment of knowledge focused on the logical and procedural qualities of science. This removed from scrutiny the dual history of professionalization. While the professions have at times worked toward social reform and innovation, they also have tendencies toward increased rationalization and individualization through the ability of experts to define public and private space. This tendency helps to explain, at least in part, the credence so easily given to human-engineering techniques in the "helping" professions.

These tensions between the social motives of professionalization and science characterized the 1960s reforms. Much of the open classroom movement and certain kinds of curriculum materials, such as *Man: A Course of Study* (Education Development Center, 1968–76), stressed the productive quality of science and emphasized the tentativeness of knowledge, the social origin of our understanding, and the importance of community. A social focus on the ambiguity of knowledge and conflict of values created intense political issues, producing pressure on the National Science Foundation to withdraw funding from curriculum projects by the 1970s. In contrast, the school accountability movement emphasized science as producing the objects of knowledge that students should learn. A crystallized view of knowledge and procedures was posited as behavioral objectives, and criterion-referenced measures defined curriculum.

While the accountability/efficiency perspective had emerged earlier as a strand in the progressive educational movement, specific technologies appeared after World War II for interrelating the theories of curriculum with actual materials for organizing schools and classrooms. Outcome-defined curriculum was interrelated with specific curriculum content through the development of reading materials, such as Science Research Associates (SRA) kits. Textbooks focused on implementation strategies to meet specific behavioral objectives, experimentation in open-space schools, and large-scale organizational changes that introduced differentiated staffs to implement management schemes in the daily life of schooling.

Changes in Relations of Economy and Culture

A third dynamic of the 1960s curriculum reform movement was the changing economic base of society, a shift that required a labor force with the orientations and sensitivities needed for an economy based on science and technology. That is, it became structurally important that all citizens appreciate the social value of technology and science even if they did not need any specific technical or engineering know-how. While it was not necessary that everyone understand the technology behind a calculator or a computer, a consensus that such technologies were appropriate and useful in the conduct of daily life, and that they were part of the consumable elements of society, was essential. While the introduction of physics, sociology, and other expert knowledge was intended to make each individual more responsible and involved in modern society, it also tended to discipline the individual toward certain patterns of acting and "seeing" the world that were shaped and fashioned by the power relations that underlie professional knowledge.

In fact, when the curriculum reforms are examined, it becomes clear that the emphasis on scientific knowledge and reasoning—such as problem-solving and inquiry-and-discovery approaches—shared a particular character. Common to the actual curriculum designs was a functional notion of knowledge that defined individuals in relation to existing social and economic structures (Popkewitz, 1977a, 1977b). Further, a dominating psychological orientation responded to the commodifications of cultural objects by which people were to define self-worth and life styles. Instruction was meant to develop the discrete abilities, qualities, and states that were considered innate "properties" of every individual.

This view of individuals as proprietors of their own capabilities has been called "possessive individualism" (Macpherson, 1962). Intelligence, character, achievement, and morality are treated as "objective facts" that can be identified and measured independent of one's relationship to the community; to possess a quality is to own it as one would own property or commodity. The pedagogical implication of possessive individualism is that schooling is to provide opportunities for children to develop the appropriate traits they possess innately and to use them for their own social betterment.

A common theme of possessive individualism is that society is improved through the efforts of its individual members to better their positions through participation in the polity, through work, and through the exercise of the entrepreneurial spirit. Such a view is entirely consistent with a liberal democratic view of society and of the individual as free to gain materially without necessarily doing so at the expense of others. A different theme of the public discourse tied social progress to a conception of possessive individualism by stressing the importance of an egalitarian, merit-defined society. Advancement should be based on equal opportunities to develop individual ability, thus enabling all citizens to overcome inequities based on birth. Schooling was one of the several institutions that, when reformed, could lead to such a better society. Embedded in these arguments were social dreams and visions of human possibilities.

The Importance of a Millennial Vision

A fourth dynamic of the 1960s was a new spiritual and moral hope that accompanied the economic transformation. The United States, in contrast to other industrialized nations, maintained strong religious convictions that tied beliefs in a national manifest destiny to millennial visions (Greeley, 1985). The period following World War II was one of the most expansive economic periods in American history, with production and wealth exploding at an unprecedented rate. It was believed that the economy could sustain both a war in Vietnam and social-welfare policies that would eliminate poverty. One strategy tied social goals to the economy as a means of providing or fostering social mobility for the poor and minorities who had not enjoyed free access to the opportunities of the market. Training in the craft unions, for example, could be open to apprentices from minority groups without threatening those already employed in the occupations. The expansion of the universities enabled their faculties to assimilate many of the sons (and sometimes daughters) of the immigrants who came to America at the turn of the century. Prior to the 1960s, many major universities, such as the one in Wisconsin, were restrictive in their hiring of minorities, and anti-Semitism was common. The rapid expansion of academic positions coupled with a reaction against the atrocities of Germany enabled minorities, such as Jews, to move into professorships. Affirmative action to bring blacks, and later women, into industrial, government, and academic jobs eventually became formal policy and law.

The promise of a millennial vision was incorporated into the social activism of the 1960s. The school was to provide a means of achieving liberal democratic goals. Social activists looked at the spoils of the social system and found that certain groups were not participating. Social and educational reforms were coupled by Friedenberg (1963), Goodman (1966), and Illich (1971). Concerned with social justice, they saw the schools as one means by which a more just and equitable society could be developed. Their calls for school change rejected the human-engineering approaches and brought forth proposals that ranged from the development of progressive, open schools to the ending of formal schooling. These reforms emphasized commitment and community rather than a possessive individuality. Further, some observers viewed conflict as a progressive element of society. Students were to consider social issues, the moral dilemmas of political policy, and social action as a way of moving toward a more just and equitable society.

The curriculum reform movement of the 1960s provides a background against which to consider the continuities and discontinuities of the current reform movement. The reform tendencies to position curriculum around specific academic fields of knowledge had at least two consequences. First, they established these disciplines as authoritative sources of knowledge about society; and faith that social progress is defined through a positive science organized by observation, rigorous methodology, and a value neutrality became more pronounced in the curriculum. Second, professionalization came to be viewed as an epistemological category. It made the particular form and content of social scientific knowledge an authoritative source for considering the relation between individuals and society.

While there is significant evidence that the reform programs were implemented only intermittently in classroom practice, their greatest effects lay in their normalizing qualities. The new rules and obligations of professionalized knowledge provided finer distinctions for organizing the processes by which identity was formed in schools. Construction of knowledge about the disciplines incorporated definitions that were functional and pragmatic, with competence tied to a view of the self as possessing discrete and taxomonic qualities that could be ordered and regulated. While science in the curriculum was to make citizens more responsible and autonomous in an increasingly complex world, the abstract, depersonalized knowledge of the professions masked the social arrangements that made such knowledge possible.

Professionalized knowledge had *both* legitimating and identity-bestowing qualities. The self-examination of social relations presupposed by professional knowledge also had specific rules for disciplining the knowledge that a person was to hold.

THE PRESENT IN RELATION TO THE PAST: THE NEW CALLING

Current calls for school reform maintain the visions of the previous era but extend and redefine them in relation to contemporary transformations. While beliefs in possessive individualism, manifest destiny, and the importance of professionalization are maintained, the spiritual and moral problem today is to rekindle a desire and motivation that many believe have been lost. The debate about priorities has emerged in both liberal and New Right discussions, although the general tone of public debate has shifted since the 1960s to the political center and the Right. At some junctures, there is a religious undertone to the new nationalism that draws on the rhetoric of the New Right. It rejects the liberal notions of professionalism that focused on providing institutional help for the poor and redefines a self-help agenda without refuting the functional, pragmatic strategies of professionalization. As exemplified by the reform documents, the moral tone that emerged in the 1980s combines a particular economic agenda for scientific and technological knowledge (Westbury, 1984) with a cultural emphasis related to certain conservative issues (Hunter, 1988); by the end of the decade, concerns with the poor and socially disadvantaged were framed by the general rules of the discourse about reform, as exemplified in the slogan of choice that privatizes social institutions. These interests are presented as a policy expression for society as a whole.

To understand these visions and their tensions, we need to recognize important elements of change in our social, cultural, and economic situation. The calls for school reforms are intricately linked to these historical elements. Let me pursue three themes introduced in the previous chapter.

One dynamic of the current reform is the continual influence of economic transformations on schooling. The economy has moved from traditional industry to a mixed structure of services, information, technology, and more sophisticated manufacturing. Foreign industrial development following World War II increased economic competition and the demand for improved quality in productivity in the United States. A major export of the United States is expertise related to its scientific information and technological know-how. Control of technology through U.S. patent laws and export licenses in trade has become an important part of American foreign policy, used to reward friends and alter other governments' policies.

The "new" curriculum of the 1960s, emphasizing science, mathematics, and technology, has become a tacit assumption in the 1980s. The scientific orientation of schooling is not challenged, although it is often expressed as a vocationalism—"a key to opportunities and careers" (National Research Council, 1989, p. 3). Today, reformers call for consistency and standardization of content as the avenue to excellence and achievement. The science posited in the reform proposals is one that focuses on the neutral technology important to production processes. The state support of science education in schools is extended on a cultural and political level (Dickson, 1984), intended to develop a consensus of the growing functional and ideological role of science in society. Further, while expressed in language that promotes excellence for all, state investment is directed at the education of the few who will enter scientific or technological occupations. During the 1980s, numerous specialized schools were created to focus on students talented in science, mathematics, and, in a few places, the arts.

A second dynamic of current reform involves a shift in the work of science. The new international importance of science represents certain fundamental transformations in the nature of science itself. The ongoing relationship between the material and ideological roles of science contributes to a view that science is an economic commodity in which the value of private commerce sets the priorities of public knowledge (Dickson, 1984). In part, this is highlighted by the massive expenditures on research and development by industry and the military since 1978. Renewed relationships among university faculty, industry, and the military; university participation in partnerships with business through joint enterprises and high-tech parks; as well as changes in patent laws that increase private control over discoveries made with public monies—

all contribute to pressure for private profit from scientific research. The revived relationship among public policy, social progress, and business gives a particular legitimacy to the collaborations between business and schools in the 1980s—a sharp contrast to the decades of the 1960s and 1970s. Though contested, there is also a centering of a political discourse on peace as an issue of more technologically sophisticated weapons; domestic prosperity as a problem of developing technological innovations; and science and mathematics as providing authoritative interpretations of various claims and data surrounding social issues (National Research Council, 1989).

The changing context of science embodies specific notions of science and technology. The new expansiveness of the American economy is built on an economy that is regulated by certain types of commodities and industries. Spring (1984) argues that decreases in the labor pool have prompted business to maximize the number of available workers by focusing on a common training in schools. Increased graduation requirements in mathematics, science, and technology can be seen as related to this demand for a new labor pool, despite debate about whether the new economy will produce technical or nontechnical jobs.

It would be incorrect, however, to link scientific knowledge directly with the economy and vocationalism. The 19th-century emergence of social science discourses into projects that plan for progress also had implications for social regulation as the discourse practices related to the modern state. The current placement of science in reform programs entails a reconstitution of the state as new patterns of social regulation are constructed.

Whereas much of the 1960s reform focused on introducing professional knowledge into the curriculum, the current concern assumes that knowledge and seeks a more rigorous organization and evaluation to effect curricular change. Standards are developed to provide specific guidelines for teaching and evaluation. Reform proposals focus on the work of teachers, recognizing that the new curriculum requires a change in the patterns of school expectations. Part of the reform proposals contain strategies found in the demands for labor outside the school in which work patterns are conceived as flexible but requiring greater inner discipline to produce standardized outcomes. Under the label of professionalism, a more hierarchical organization is sought to better use expert skills (Holmes Group, 1986; National Commission on Excellence, 1983). The labor force is to be not only trained but also, as current discussions emphasize, motivated. But to see the reform strategies as only a borrowing of business technologies is to lose site of the debates in business as well as the specific dynamics of schooling in which a number of practices converge.

A new emphasis on motivation reveals a characteristic particular to the current climate of reform. The direction and values that have emerged in the past 20 years have created suspicion, especially among the New Right and other conservative groups. For many, the material improvements of the last few decades have not produced a similar spiritual betterment or generosity. Middle- and upper-class Americans see crime, social-welfare programs, and a lack of social and religious commitment as a reflection of a deep moral malaise in American society. The rise in evangelical religion, the organization of ''right-to-life'' groups to protest abortion, the efforts to amend the Constitution to allow prayer in schools, and the belief that juveniles are not motivated and disciplined reflect the general feeling of social disintegration, the need for a new sense of ''nationalism,'' and the need for tighter control to produce more consistent values and cultural homogeneity. The skepticism and angst can be compared to the America of the 1960s, a nation that recognized in itself the moral and technological know-how to fulfill its longtime spiritual dream. Important segments of today's American middle and upper classes see themselves as fighting to maintain the nation's traditional visions; the problem has become one of asserting a consensus and national harmony.

These changes are best evidenced in the educational sciences. The 1960s' view that science would contribute to social equality has been transformed; today, the improvement of education is to occur through social efficiency that produces excellence tied to market forces. With the talk of multiple paradigms and approaches come particular research strategies; functional perspectives in a cognitive psychology emerge to draw on artificial intelligence to study teacher thinking; and sociology is turned to as a way of finding improved grading systems to better motivate students or increase participation in order to reduce dropout rates (Wells, 1989). Further, the metaphor of choice is used to describe school policy, joining political discussions about privatization with research agendas to articulate an economic concept of market forces in social institutions. There is a parallel assumption in the deregulation of telephone service, airlines, and interstate transportation to produce increased efficiency and the ''choice'' of parents in placing their children in schools.

Within this context, current calls for school reform are highly moralistic in tone. They are religious and millennial, as if to respond directly to feelings of spiritual crisis. There is a new nationalism. The greatness of America is to be restored and revitalized by the schools, which will provide the moral and economic inspiration. Increased efficiency and improved administration are to produce this regeneration. The basis of the efficiency, it will be argued later, depends on the development of the "possessive individual." The public discourse situates schooling as related to other social issues and institutions; however, the professional discourse often transforms those problems into pragmatic ones of increasing productivity.

SCHOOLING AND A MILLENNIAL VISION

While the school has long been viewed as an essential element in the millennial vision of the United States (Tyack & Hansot, 1982), current proposals give further credence to the notion of schools as redemptive institutions. The goodness, sanctity, and progress of American life is now seen as tied to the process of schooling. The language of reform often has a particular U.S. Protestant character: The concerted good works in schools are to establish those conditions and spiritual values that can shape a heaven-on-earth. The dreams of democracy, material abundance, and spiritual contentment—visions that underpin the nation's belief in itself—depend on the success and progress of schooling. The future is a future that is to be fulfilled through the accomplishments of society's children.

There is a sense of prophecy, urgency, and possibility. The urgency is phrased in unequivocal, highly charged language: National survival is at stake! The Educational Commission of the States' Task Force (1983), for example, is convinced "that a real emergency is upon us; a conviction that we must *act* now, individually and together, and a passionate optimistic conviction that action, soon enough and in the right directions, can succeed" (p. 4). The National Commission on Excellence in Education's *A Nation at Risk* (1983) defines the current situation as a genuine fall from grace in all significant areas of American life. A challenge to American commercial and industrial preeminence in world competition is combined with dire warnings of the decline of individual intellectual, moral, and spiritual strength essential "to competently participate in a free, democratic society" (p. 7). John Goodlad's (1984) study of high schools reasserts this theme, reiterating a lack of faith and a need for renewal. The current criticism of schooling, Goodlad suggests, "is in part psychologically motivated—a product of a general lack of faith in ourselves and our institutions" (p. 21). The weakening of the home and the church, the faltering economics of the country, and the increased specialization that underlies recent social changes, as well as a division within education about purposes and goals, are seen as related to the current crisis of schooling.

The reports' authors appear to feel little doubt as to the existence of a consensus about what is morally and intellectually appropriate; the task of school reform is to introduce a coherence and standardization of school programs in a world believed to have one true set of values, priorities, and interests. The reports' recommendations tend to range from a set of national standards to outlines of a general core curriculum for all students. In an intellectually sophisticated report for reform in mathematics education, the National Research Council (1989) asserts that mathematics education can be "a powerful instrument for understanding the world we live in" and proposes elaborate strategies for implementing national standards (p. 4).

The assertion of a consensus, however, ignores the interests that underlie knowledge and the conflict within the social disciplines about what knowledge is appropriate. Educators, politicians, and other thoughtful observers bring multiple perspectives and different worldviews to the discussion; nor do mathematicians, scientists, or educators agree upon what content or epistemology should direct teaching. By ignoring these conflicting values and traditions in selecting curriculum, the proposals obscure the political and social origins of the spiritual malaise to which they bear witness.

In place of analysis, these reports offer exhortation and prophecy. Their language bemoans the nation's fall from grace and holds out righteous action as the means by which redemption is possible. The National Commission on Excellence in Education states that "the educational foundations of our society are presently being eroded by a rising tide of mediocrity that threatens our future as a Nation and a people" (p. 5). Adler's *The Paideia Proposal* (1982) offers the millennial belief that a properly educated people can unite politics, government, economics, and culture into a progressive and cohesive whole:

> Achieving peace, prosperity and plenty could put this country on the edge of becoming an earthly paradise, but only a much better educational system than now exists can carry us across the threshold. Without it, a poorly schooled population will not be able to put to use the opportunities afforded by the achievement of the general welfare. Those who are not schooled to enjoy the blessing of a good society can only despoil its institutions and corrupt themselves. (p. 79)

These general concerns about the nation's moral and economic revitalization come in to focus through the processes of schooling, which are viewed as preparation for an earthly paradise that has spiritual and material bounty. The president of the Carnegie Foundation in a report on the high school suggests that "the time for renewing education has arrived" (Boyer, 1983, p. 1). He asserts that the current era provides the best opportunity to improve schools because there is a "growing national consensus that the future depends upon public education, that previous resources cannot be wasted and an eagerness to 'rebuild,' with a new and more compelling vision of education is required to meet the challenge" (p. 1).

The current reforms emphasize that social progress is dependent on the nation's children and the system that educates them. Their religious and moral tone heightens the expectation of reform while, at the same time, it removes from scrutiny the conditions that limit social transformation. While the reports recognize that schooling involves more than what is learned as subject matter, their focus on a national consensus negates the conflicts of social groupings that pervade both schooling and society. The premise of the millennial dream is that schooling must become more efficient and rational in developing that which is already a fundamental social theme, the possessive individual.

There have been instances in the plethora of reform reports where the impact of social cultural differentiation on schooling is recognized. The reevaluation of mathematics education (National Research Council, 1989), for example, contains arguments that teaching should "transcend the cultural diversity of our nation" (p. 32) and that mathematics tends to be a preserve of upper- and middle-class males. The report asserts that although these differences occur, mathematics "has few links to issues of belief" (p. 32) and need not be embroiled in such distinctions. Yet the report's examples of the uses of mathematics belie its own assertions: Mathematics is related to consumer practices that are part of the market economy and the interpretation of socially constructed data, such as statistics about crime. In practical application, the National Research Council calls for universality while it narrows its discussion to conform to socially derived and culturally distinguishable patterns.

Possessive Individualism

The reform reports assume that the nation's spiritual, economic, and intellectual revitalization is to result from the good works of individuals. In this context, the function of social institutions is to stimulate the presumably innate abilities, personal qualities, and individual desires that, once formed, will provide the driving energy necessary to rebuild America. This individualistic view of social reform is rooted in liberal ideology about the nature of society and people. It assumes that society is composed of free, equal individuals who are related to one another as proprietors of their own capabilities. Their successes and acquisitions are the products of their own initiatives, and it is the role of institutions to foster and support their personal development.

The centrality of the possessive individual in the moral uplifting of society is articulated in *The Paideia Proposal*. It is argued that the challenge of reform is to bring out what is innate in the individual, to provide opportunities for "the full development of the country's human potential . . . to bring progress towards fulfillment of democracy" (Adler, 1982, p. 6).

The individualist vision produces a contradiction in the manner in which reforms are to be developed. There is a belief in a common, neutral core of knowledge and skills that exists in the formation of individuality. This assumption ignores a substantial literature that suggests that our social and cultural conditions are not equal, that the selection and organization of school knowledge contains dispositions and values that handicap certain groups while they benefit others. To suggest that the challenge of reform is to stimulate the "innate" capabilities of every citizen is to ignore the relationship of individuality to socialization and of pedagogy to broader structural relations. Possessive individualism, however, does reinforce the ideology of the new science that holds that knowledge is a commodity that generates a return.

By the end of the 1980s, the ideology of possessive individualism appeared as part of a constructivist psychology. The National Research Council (1989) defined excellence in mathematics as demanding "results that unfold fully every person's potential" (p. 29). That innate potential is realized when individuals construct their own understandings, since "each individual's knowledge is uniquely personal" (p. 6). Group work is important to individual construction in that it provides a motivating device by which personal knowledge appears. The council suggests that there is "compelling evidence that students learn mathematics well only when they *construct* their own mathematical understanding" (p. 58). While the view that knowledge is personal is contradicted by statements that mathematics has its own "inner logic" (p. 3) separate from the person and that mathematics provides scientific patterns, teaching reforms are proposed "to motivate students as they struggle with their own learning" (p. 58).

The National Commission on Excellence in Education's *A Nation at Risk* (1983) also defines the problem as one of individual effort. The school is seen as a carefully calculated system for the maintenance of an orderly relation of exchanges. All students are to be treated equally, and the task of instruction is to provide those competitive conditions that will enable them to develop their innate capabilities:

> Part of what is at risk is the promise first made on this continent: All, regardless of race or class or economic status, are entitled to a fair chance and to the tools for developing their individual powers of mind

and spirit to the utmost. This promise means that all children, by virtue of their own efforts, competently guided, can hope to attain the mature and informed judgment needed to secure gainful employment and to manage their own lives, thereby serving not only their own interests but also the progress of society itself. (p. 9)

The ideology of the "possessive individual," however, is masked when individualism is treated as a technical problem resulting from individual differences in learning. Despite social differences, Adler (1982) argues, all people are thought to be the same in their "human nature," all people have the same inherent tendencies, powers, and capacities. "In our democratic society, moreover, all children can look forward to a future that is the same in a number of essential respects" (p. 43). Denying issues that underlie and define American society, Adler asserts that these similarities are the results of equal suffrage, political liberties, and civil rights. Differences in experience and outcome result from variations in teaching styles, from the rates at which children learn, and from the availability of remedial programs to overcome specific deficiencies.

A Nation at Risk warns that failure to provide the social and educational conditions under which all individuals can reach their full potential will take a major toll on the nation's progress and development. The individual's responsibility for the coming of the millennium is a common theme; the commission asserts its belief in "the persistent and authentic American dream that superior performance can raise one's state in life and shape one's own future" (p. 15).

Individualism, the "New" Federalism, and Decentralization

Possessive individualism underlies the political theories of a federalism of the 1980s in which progress is defined as the sum of individual local political bodies. Inherent in the federalist principle is a distrust of centralized authority, which limits the free development of the individual. Instead, local decision making is viewed as the most direct and effective way to institute change. In Chapter 4, I spoke about current federal strategies to steer local practice through moral persuasion and statistical data gathering. Here I will discuss the tie of decentralization strategies to possessive individualism.

In some of the current reform proposals, the implementation of change is to occur at the district and building levels (site management). There is an effort to ease central or bureaucratic controls, both by reducing federal control and by transferring more authority to the district or local school system (Boyer, 1983). The National Association of State Boards of Education (1988) calls for new partnerships in local "agencies and informal networks in the community" (p. 1). Goodlad (1984) argues that the process must be one of improving instruction on a school-by-school basis; it is the individual school "where all things come together" (p. 129). "Improvement is enlightened by the degree to which those associated with each school and trying to improve it have the data required for building a useful agenda" (p. 19). For Boyer (1983), involvement is a process that should draw on industry to make curriculum more relevant to students and to the community. Mathematics reforms to implement national standards at the local level call for "grassroots" activities that are coordinated and evaluated through a national steering committee (National Research Council, 1989).

Decentralization incorporates the assumptions of individualism into a policy of social organization. As society depends on the stipulations of social contracts, so social organization must foster the processes by which individuals are afforded the opportunity to engage in appropriate decision making. The development of social affairs depends on ample opportunities to stimulate the innate capabilities and qualities of the individual. While there is an appeal to the classical notion of democracy in which social and individual development are related to participation in institutional life, the current reforms define participation as a technical notion of individuality and democracy (see, e.g., Popkewitz, 1983a). In this context the term *technical* refers to two conditions of the current discourse.

First, the notion of participation is related to a particular liberal interest-group theory that assumes that society is based on a social contract of individuals, the sum of whose actions produces the social structure. In complex modern societies, it is believed that various associations (or interest groups) negotiate to produce the common good. It is the responsibility of an effective school system to create opportunities in which all groups can be involved in decision making, including parents, teachers, administrators, and state educational officers.

This stance about participation fails to examine or recognize the decisions that become part of the public discourse and the power arrangement in which those decisions are made (Popkewitz, 1979). The rules of participation maintain a market metaphor that benefits those with education, flexible working time, and dispositions associated with these social and economic advantages. Further, the current discourse about decentralization is part of a state steering practice. As discussed in Chapter 4, centrally defined criteria and categories of the state are positioned within educational fields to provide boundaries for local practice. The issues of power and the structured relations in the current discourse remain unexamined and unchallenged, with local participation defined in terms of process rather than substance (see Chapter 7; see also Hamilton, 1980; Popkewitz, 1976a).

Second, the reform reports bring a particular bias to bear on the negotiations that shape schooling practice. As argued in this chapter, certain types of problems and solutions are structured into the reforms, such as possessive individualism. Inherent in the catch words—*community participation* and *decentralization*—are certain distinctions and categor ical hierarchies that constitute power relations that relate to state steering (see Weiler, 1989). Further, the practices of participation tend to favor particular segments and strata of society who have both the free time and the social and cultural dispositions that foster involvement (see Popkewitz, 1978).

The reform rhetoric about decentralization embodies fundamental contradictions. Decentralization is a state steering strategy, while the assumption of social consensus is related to calls for increased standardization. The current reform reports emphasize measures of student achievement and teacher competence. In response, more than 30 states have instituted some form of student testing as a prerequisite to high school graduation, and most other states are at various stages in the consideration of such programs. Further, high school graduation requirements have become much narrower in terms of the range of acceptable courses. This, in combination with increased state-mandated testing, has reduced or altered the quality of teacher and community participation in school planning and organization (see, e.g., Chapter 7). Further possessive individualism concerns abstract aggregate qualities that are externally defined and can function to discipline the person by saying "here are the things a person should do or be," thereby negating the notion of individuality as personal or unique expression of a self. Individuality, instead, is that which is defined by the "experts" who determine specific characteristics and abilities as universal, aggregated qualities.

Instrumental Rationality

To this point, it has been argued that the professionalization of knowledge, a millennial vision, possessive individualism, and decentralization as state steering combine to provide the rules of discourse. These rules, however, embody tensions and contradictions as they confront the multiplicity of social relations present in schools. The millennial vision and the belief in possessive individualism assume that a common framework of experience exists for all people and that this experience involves fixed goals (see, e.g., Habermas, 1971). The challenge of reform is to identify the most appropriate means by which to attain those given ends, as well as strategies to increase the effectiveness and coordination of programs. We call this focus an *instrumental* concern of reform. In part, this emphasis on the effectiveness of means relates to the notion of possessive individualism: Reform is to create procedures that promote the individual's self-confirmation. The emphasis on efficiency has its own irony: The reform discourse has little to do with relating means to ends but has instead become a moral domain in which the means have *become* the ends. In this context, the view of centralization as decentralization can be viewed as a triumph of instrumental reasoning.

The instrumental quality of contemporary reasoning is so pervasive a part of the public language that its values and assumptions are taken for granted. In some ways, the emphasis on quantity *as* quality is the most explicit way in which reason is made instrumental; more subtle are the categories that create distinctions in school practice. *A Nation at Risk* defines the existing secondary curriculum as a homogenized, delimited, diffused smorgasbord. Students have less homework, take less demanding courses, and meet lower standards. The remedy? Rationalization of school time, more testing and evaluation, longer hours, more coursework, new subjects, and upgraded texts. Quantity becomes quality, and reason is the process of coordinating means with ends.

Common distinctions of individualization and flexibility often are posited as means separate from ends. *The Paideia Proposal* focuses on the quality of learning as "the heart of the matter" and teaching at its best as "only an aid to learning" (Adler, 1982, pp. 49–50). Goodlad (1984) attends to the humanistic teacher who is a "facilitator" and to teaching as a source of "nurturing support." Boyer (1983) considers a teacher's role in counseling students "far more important than paperwork" (p. 157) but acknowledges that it is time consuming and calls for a significant expansion of guidance services. Instruction maintains this concern with procedures. Individualization often involves little more than the pacing of children through a common curriculum.

At least two distinct notions of individual differences appear in the reform reports. One is related to a deficiency view, the other to a vision of development; both assume a possessive individual. For Adler (1982), individual difference is acknowledged in strategies of remediation to overcome individual deficiencies in meeting requisite standards of performance. A report on early childhood education focuses on developmental psychology as a means to individualize and produce a pluralism that takes into account cultural and linguistic diversity (National Association of State Boards of Education, 1988).

Possessive individualism occurs in developmental psychology through a number of presuppositions. A discourse is produced about the early childhood "needs" of students, the use of "developmental or readiness tests" that are "to serve the needs of children," and "unique characteristics that children bring to school" (National Association of State Boards of Education, 1988). There is an underlying assumption that all children experience a set of essential, natural needs and that the task of schooling is to provide more efficient procedures to nurture what is already "owned" by the child. While the emphasis on development differs from the behaviorism of the effective schools research, they share a similar epistemology about the underlying natural qualities of individuals, differing only in terms of the routes to be used to increase school effectiveness. As the developmental "rules" are accepted to plan reform, the priorities and standards of human development fashion choice and establish direction for change. These tend to be instrumental techniques designed to "move children through the stages as rapidly as possible" (Shaver, 1979, p. 23; see also Montangero, 1985).

The technical aspects of reform are evident in the reports' promotion of and emphasis on the notion of flexibility. As with individualization, flexibility captures the tenor of the desires and aspirations of the middle class. The broad value commitment, however, is reduced to administrative concerns. Flexibility refers neither to the substantive ideas or values of schooling, nor to how those ideas are realized in the social processes of schooling. It focuses instead on an educational process that begins "where the student is ready to begin" (see, e.g., Goodlad, 1984; National Commission on Excellence in Education, 1983). Adler (1982) defines flexibility in terms of the size and length of the instructional period. The National Commission on Excellence in Education (1983) states that at all times, in all settings, it is necessary to make provisions for individual difference, for "equitable treatment of our diverse population" (p. 5). Flexibility is intended to enable all children to be paced differently but to meet one united set of objectives. Mathematics education reform calls for relevance to children "at risk," who typically do not complete courses, but, at the same time, maintains a belief in a common core of knowledge for all students (National Research Council, 1989).

The rituals of science give legitimacy to the instrumental quality of schooling. Research problems and findings focus on the procedural elements of schooling. The logic of science is to make the expectations and performances seen independent of social value. Learning, it is asserted, "appears to be enhanced when students understand what is expected of them, get recognition for their work, learn quickly about their errors, and receive guidance in improving their performance" (Goodlad, 1984, p. 111). Humanism is important because "no measure of students' relations with peers was as highly related to matters of student satisfaction in the classroom as were the measures of student-teacher relationships" (p. 19). Learning, motivation, and satisfaction become ends in themselves; what it is that should be learned, counseled, or satisfied remains vague and uncertain. To treat learning, individuality, or flexibility in a technical manner is to obscure the social interests that underlie pedagogical discourse. Learning also exists in relation to the principles of authority embodied in the social processes of teaching.

Toward the end of the 1980s, instrumental considerations became explicit in U.S. Department of Education publications. Reports such as *What Works* (U.S. Department of Education, 1986, 1987) focused on the direct relationship between research "results" and teaching strategies to produce higher achievement. The first report (1986) provided lists of specific activities that teachers and parents could do to improve children's success in school, such as articulating the school's and the parents' expectations clearly and explicitly requiring more homework. The simplistic cause-and-effect approach of *What Works* far exceeded the arguments and subtleties of the research it cited. When discussing the education of poor and minority populations, for example, *What Works* assumes that the problem is home motivation and that the solution involves increasing the effectiveness of the strategies already in use.

The categories of school reform reduce reasoning and intellectual initiative to issues of the administration of social affairs. The nexus of the value, purpose, and procedures that comprise our social conditions is lost, replaced by an increasing concern with training and motivation. In contrast, we can think of teaching and learning as interrelated elements of school patterns. Notions of learning and individuality always exist in the context of current community definitions and interpretations of the social world; in short, the impact and importance of background attitudes and dispositions of schooling that enable certain groups in society to compete more successfully are blurred in the face of the direct relations between specific practices and achievement (see Bourdieu, 1984).

Again, while the reform reports embody instrumental strategies, we can turn to the standards developed and presented by the National Council of Teachers of Mathematics (1989) as an example of a reform report that recognizes the relationship of means to ends. The report, which considers curriculum as a problem-solving activity of scientific mathematics, seeks to relate the curriculum issues about what is an appropriate epistemology to evaluation procedures. While the focus on the domain of scientific mathematics limits the range of content and forms in thinking about the discipline of mathematics, careful attention is given to the use of measurement schemes to correspond to the liberal- izing intent of the curriculum program. A warning about how choices in evaluation can drive curriculum is also found in the reform report of the National Research Council (1989; see also National Association of State Boards of Education, 1988). How practices emerge in relation to the mathematics standard remains to be seen, especially as measure- ment procedures are developed in a field that has historically focused on instrumental knowledge (see Kilpatrick, in press).

Political Uses of Symbols

The reform reports use a language of exhortation. The call is written and presented in such a way as to crystallize people's cherished hopes about American society in a manner that channels efforts toward the problem of schooling. The language of *A Nation at Risk* directs attention to the organization of a single social institution, schooling. While the language of exhortation may be potent, it is founded on questionable research and outdated data (Stedman & Smith, 1983). We need to ask, then, what accounts for this political hyperbole. The reports are instru- ments of persuasion, tools in the rhetorical exchange in which power relations and status in society are established.

The assumptions that inspired and influenced the format and focus of the reports have much to tell about the social goals and aspirations of the audience to which the reports are directed. It is a millennial world created and protected by a liberal democratic government. It is a world in which individuals have the ability to maximize their share of available goods, one in which individual initiative is rewarded, presumably not at the expense of others. In this ideal society, all citizens have the right— and the motivation—to participate in the polity. And there is national consensus about what is right, both legally and morally. Debate and conflict emerge only as means of determining the best avenue by which to achieve agreed-upon ends.

Social progress is seen as the transition from our present imperfect society, with its lack of purpose, pride, and coherence, to one of moral unity, wealth, and freedom. Perfection is constrained only by the limits of one's own capabilities, which can and must be developed to their maximum. Progress is the sum of individuals' accumulation of cultural properties and economic wealth. The reports define the schools as the sites at which the society will learn to increase the production of this personal capital. Schools are to provide the bridge from the imperfect City of Man to the ideal City of Social and Personal Fulfillment.

But there is a fundamental contradiction in this notion of progress. The millennial dream and the crisis of spirituality are bound to some concept of community. Possessive individualism, in contrast, celebrates personal relations and subjectivity as ends in themselves; consumption itself is a goal. Individuals' understanding of their own role in a system of productivity and culture is undermined, and they are left with little sense of belonging or commitment to the general good. The fragmentation and self-obsession that feeds possessive individualism, then, erodes each person's sense of the whole and his or her relation to that whole.

Perhaps as mystifying is the reports' focus on the school as the sole agency to bring about broader social change and transformation. Review of earlier eras suggests that the role of the school was viewed as an integral element of larger social trends and developments. School reform was a part of the modernization of society in the late 19th century, as well as a key component of the nation's efforts to launch a War on Poverty and to spur technological development in the 1960s. However, the current reforms eliminate consideration of other institutions, implying that a concerted effort in schools can right all of the larger wrongs.

The idea that social progress could be provided by children is an invention of the 20th century. Prior to this period, people looked to the organization of adult life for ways in which social and cultural life could be improved. The ideological origins of the American Revolution, for example, embodied the idealization of the newly founded democracy as a vehicle to bring perfection to humanity. Increasingly, though, the society's future has been defined in relation to its children (DeLone, 1979). Social, political, and economic progress is to come from the enlightenment and productive training of children. Children who learn rationality and morality will bring these virtues to bear to alleviate the depravities of contemporary society and to foster progress. The twin strands of equity and quality that run through the reports reflect a liberal democratic belief in the power of education to ameliorate social inequities and to guide the development of a better society.

The view that children are the key to social progress is not exclusively an American invention. Children are seen as the saviors of Japan, the Soviet Union, and many other countries of the world. It is easy to speculate about why this has come to be the case: As industrialization erodes cultural tradition and customs, as well as alters the relation of the rulers to the ruled, the relation of childhood to adulthood becomes more romanticized, and the importance of schooling in the problem of governing becomes more central. Custom, social solidarity, and tradition can be inculcated in children through the cultural sensitivities and social practices found in schools.

A secondary aspect of the focus on children involves the rationalization of educational affairs. The reductionism that projects or generalizes individual attributes or qualities to the society as a whole is a prevailing worldview in the milieu in which reform is sought. The future is tied to the ability of individuals, alone or collectively, to redefine the spiritual, moral, and economic well-being of a society. Finally, the suffering, disillusion and, in some instances, degradation that accompany industrialization make it psychologically appealing to place faith in children and the world in which they will live.

I cannot overemphasize the importance of the epistemologies that I have referred to as ''instrumental'' as practices. The language of the reports conveys a commitment to the public, a belief in equality as well as quality, a recognition of the limitations of knowledge and social diversity. Yet the manner in which these reports categorize social life dulls our sensitivity to the inevitable conflicts about the appropriate paths toward excellence, and obscures the visions and social interests that are historically embedded in our social patterns. Debates rage about the relation of individuality to society, the importance of power in social knowledge, and the role of history in the construction of identity—all central concerns of contemporary scholarship. And yet, the language of reform ignores these fundamental issues and, in their place, offers discourse that fragments reality and reifies social existence.

PROFESSIONALIZATION AS POLITICAL DISCOURSE AND ISSUES OF CONTROL

A central theme of the reform reports is that teaching should be made more professional through increased training, differentiation of staffing patterns, and more collegial work relations. The Carnegie Report regarding teaching as a profession (Carnegie Forum on Education and the Economy, 1986) proposes a national board on professional teaching standards, reduction of administrative rules to increase teacher autonomy and responsibility, making teacher education a graduate course of study, varying career patterns within teaching, and greater emphasis on scientific and practical knowledge. The Holmes Group's *Tomorrow's Teacher* (1986) makes similar recommendations concerning increased education, research, and differentiation of staffing patterns.

With this stratification of teaching come further specialization, sequential organization, and fragmentation of tasks, which, as I pointed out earlier, are associated with possessive individualism and utilitarian thought. Introduced into the organizational structure of school life, such stratification reinforces the tendencies toward increased regulation and decreased teacher responsibility.

The anomalies inherent in these reports are further exacerbated in that the reform efforts overlook the political and historical background of public schooling. As discussed earlier, attempts to reform teaching since the 1840s have introduced more hierarchical forms of control over a corps of mostly women teachers. Consider, for example, the development of reading textbooks from the 1920s to the present (Woodward, 1987). In the 1920s, teacher manuals were brief discussions of the problems and tasks associated with readings, with extended bibliographies for students. By the 1970s, teacher manuals offered completely scripted lesson plans with as many as four pages of detail per day to specify what teachers were to say, where they were to stand, how they were to organize the lesson, and how they were to evaluate students. These contemporary manuals subordinate reading to teaching specific skills. The status distinctions and power relations in the organization of schools that underlie these changes are ignored, since professional improvement is viewed as making teaching more scientific and requiring increased time spent in preparation.

The Holmes Group and Carnegie reports support their arguments by drawing on an idealized version of law and medicine. Altruistic ideals of professionals working for social betterment are portrayed, an approach that ignores the complex political, economic, and structural issues that underlie the cultural, social authority of professions. Whatever important social services are associated with professions, the publicly defined characteristics are myths that legitimate existing authority rather than illuminate the workings and contributions of the professions. Further, while the Holmes Group and Carnegie reports use law and medicine as exemplars of professionalism, the histories of these fields are not central to the occupational development of schooling. The interrelation of the university social sciences (and psychology) provides greater insight into the occupational dynamics shaping the social fabric of teaching. As discussed in Chapter 3, the discourse practices of these sciences embodied the regulatory strategies of schooling.

The current reports, like those of the educational psychologists of the turn of the century, argue the importance of an empirical functional knowledge to provide direction to educational progress. The Holmes Group Report (1986), for example, asserts that the reform of teacher education "depends upon engaging in the complex work of identifying the knowledge base for competent teaching and developing the content and strategies whereby it is imparted" (p. 49). In fundamental ways, the past ideologies of the expert and social control are reasserted and assigned a new vitality and institutional status under the rhetoric of professionalism.

LEGITIMATIONS AND MEDIATION: THE SOCIAL FUNCTIONS OF THE PUBLIC REPORTS

I have focused here on the assumptions of the reform reports as social practices. They emerged in a dynamic political arena defined by varied relations in which groups vie to establish or legitimate their position vis-à-vis the school. While establishing a political agenda for elites, the reports provide a symbolic canopy under which specific interest groups within schooling can pursue their particular ends by ascribing them to the society as a whole. In the context of policy formulation, coalitions are established among philanthropic foundations, professional associations, state research agencies (such as offices of educational research and development), university teacher educators and researchers, the testing industry, school administrators, teacher unions, and industries. Each group adopts stances to give direction to school programs, and their discourses mesh at various levels of institutional practice. The discourse of the reports makes the specific rules of practice seem consistent with the general good and public interest.

We can see the process of mediation occurring in many ways. The importance of computer instruction, for example, is argued. In part, it represents a particular scientific emphasis that occurs as military and industrial R&D commitment have dramatically increased since the Carter presidential years (Dickson, 1984). The introduction of the computer may have little to do with the "instructional potential" of computers themselves. As commercial text publishing houses have in the past, the computer companies consider schools a prime market. Apple and IBM have provided grants to schools and created foundations designed to increase school computer use. It is interesting to note that one of the economic competitors to which the current reports respond, the Japanese, have limited computer instruction to the high school.

The reports also provide an avenue by which to pursue professional issues of status and control. The reform proposals legitimate increased professional control over certification, further specialization of teacher's work, and more financial reward for educators. This occurs, however, in a context of increased state control through testing and restrictive graduation policies.

At another level of professional life, the reports reassert the importance of educational researchers and evaluators. Under the aegis of the federal Office of Educational Research and Development, experts have been called upon to develop reports and agendas for responding to the reform proposals. The agendas are self-aggrandizing, both for the experts who produced them and for the bureaucracies who have emerged to implement them. Mathematics education professors, for example, held a National Institute of Education conference in December 1983 that recommended that model programs be prepared and that ''the professional organizations associated with mathematics education should establish a continuing national steering committee for mathematics education to survey efforts of federal, state and local agencies to report on progress of the reform effort'' (Romberg & Stewart, 1985, p. vii).

The standards have, in fact, been produced (National Council of Teachers of Mathematics, 1989), and other reports have been developed to outline strategies for implementation (National Research Council, 1989). In 1990, a national ''summit'' of state governors and President Bush produced a call for national standards. The reform reports are central documents in the formulation of the arguments and the justification of the derived agendas.

A different process of mediation occurs in relation to the dual position of the state in the problem of governing. First, there is an emergent state discourse concerned with establishing and renewing the role of the school; that is, schools are to ascribe to the society as a whole the particular social and economic relations that define science and technology. We need to recognize that only particular segments of American society are directly associated with the production of knowledge in science or the engineering development of technology. Further, the science of the reform proposals is one that is important for the development of technological products and production processes. Second, the implications of the reforms, which are explored in Chapters 6 and 7, involve not only the problem of legitimating economic agendas but also of producing an identity that is related to the social arrangements.

The implications of the production of identity, however, are subtle and complex. The systematization of ideas and the authority that supports those ideas operate at multiple layers of the institutions. Agencies and publics establish their own territories related to the definition of schooling, explanations of progress, and the processes by which the steering of social affairs is to occur. The construction of a discourse about reform embodies the power relations that have set the parameters of reform; deciphering those power relations is particularly difficult in that the instrumental language that describes them makes the problems universal in application.

CONCLUSIONS

The reform reports of the 1980s share a strong nationalism, an unwavering millennial vision, a continuing assumption about possessive individualism, and a belief in the efficiency of the market. While philanthropic support continues to underwrite the calls and planning for reform, professional organizations and government have assumed a more active role. Some of the proposals recognize the limitations of planning and assessment; some pay explicit attention to the problems of diversity, but not to the point of questioning the viability of universal standards and curriculum. The decentralization of steering occurs while, at the same time, there is a centralization of strategies and epistemology.

The discourse at multiple levels of schooling intertwines the efforts and positions of governmental agencies, professional organizations, and philanthropic groups. The different and sometimes disparate proposals create the illusion that the problems and solutions occur in a "stateless" state. By the end of the 1980s, more specific arenas of action had been identified, such as the various curriculum content areas of schooling, teacher's work, and teacher education, a development that moves the discourse into the specific domains of teaching in schools. The diffusion of effort and multiple sites of concern have masked the power relations and dispositions that underlie the various proposals, thereby obscuring the merging of power relations of state, civil society, and secularized religious visions with the polity.

The cultural values that drive the construction of institutional practices contribute significantly to current reform proposals. Possessive individualism and instrumental rationality establish a belief in a meritocracy and a consensus of goals in a society that is, in fact, culturally, ethnically, and economically differentiated. The arguments for a decentralization of decision making are based on a liberal democratic stance that holds that those most closely associated with the daily problems of institutions should have responsibility for providing the solutions. But the arguments for decentralization represent conflicting interests. On one hand, decentralization is intended to make schooling more responsive to the requirements of the polity; it is to create a more effective mechanism for implementing a state-determined mandate. At the same time, flexibility, individuality, and critical thinking are emphasized, but positioned within an ecology of instrumental reason and possessive individualism. The discussion of universal standards juxtaposed against a local determination of strategies presupposes centralized definitions.

The reform reports legitimate the transformation occurring and are involved in the processes related to production. The policy formulations articulate particular interest-bound responses to social and economic transformations. The practices of implementation become legitimated by the symbolic canopies provided by the policy formulations. While the seeming consensus of purpose, linearity of movement, and administrative quality of strategy are a chimera, the state and professional discourses are part of the shaping and fashioning of institutional arrangements. The resulting practices are neither neutral, disinterested, nor without social consequences.

This framing of discourse patterns with institutional practices cannot be read as either a theory of conspiracy or the voluntary practices of a misguided people. The language that positions recommendations, cautionary tales, and assumptions about schools and children has evolved in a complex web of structured relations. We can view, for example, the authors of the National Association of State Boards of Education report (1988) as introducing important issues of equity absent in early documents, and as warning against teaching basic skills and testing without integrating these evaluations with criteria such as children's age and development. The concerns of educators who work with minority and poor groups are evident in the report. But this constituency interest is defined in relation to the interests posited in the discourse about development, a discourse dependent on current formulations of the truth, making it impossible to speak of will, intent, or determinism in a straightforward manner.

6

Cognitive Educational Sciences as Knowledge and Power

In this chapter, I return directly to the relation of the educational sciences to social movements and the state. The educational sciences have been an important factor in the production of state reforms since their creation in the 19th century. I focused on the mobilization of educational sciences as part of the management of teaching in Chapter 3 and as an important dimension of institutional relations and the discourse of contemporary reform in Chapters 4 and 5. In this chapter I want to pursue this relation by examining the epistemology of cognitive educational psychology, specifically considering recent studies of teacher thinking and the teaching of school subjects.

The research on teacher thinking is considered for three reasons. First, the study of teacher thinking is an important part of the educational reform movement. Its rhetorical claim is that it is derived from a "psychological revolution" associated with the shift to a "constructivist" epistemology. The new psychology is intended to better relate social and economic demands with pedagogical practices. Whatever the scientific value of the constructivist approach, we err if we "see" the science in isolation from the social field that sustains it and gives it credibility. Second, the constructivist approach maintains the social amelioration tradition in the social sciences at the turn of the century; progress is to be achieved by a practical, functional knowledge. Third, educational psychology provides an illustration of the more general problem of the relationships of science, social movements, and power. Because of psychology's intrusive strategies into individual lives, it brings to the fore the subtleties of power contained in modernity. The organization of knowledge at the very specific and practical level of the interactions of teachers and students is, I believe, most potent in the formation of social regulation.

I initially explore current interests in cognitive psychology as a problem of state management of schooling. I then proceed to outline the broader reform-related research program on teacher thinking. In each instance, I intend to show how the research brings together a variety of socially constructed rules and standards about power.

The discussion is not meant to be an exhaustive review of the literature. Its purpose is to consider how the governing of the state and the self-governing of the individual are intertwined in the knowledge of science. Power is related to ordering procedures for the production, regulation, distribution, circulation, and operation of knowledge (see Foucault, 1980). My concern here, as before, is with the social epistemology of research. The truth claims of science are not only the logical standards for interpretation and coherence; they are also social rules about truth. These rules have the potential to construct social identities and capabilities.

I draw again upon the contradictions of the Enlightenment. The Enlightenment traditions of reason and rationality are intended to produce social progress; science provides specific techniques that human beings constructed to understand themselves. Ironically, the desire to achieve some degree of human freedom through the social sciences led to the development of certain social technologies. These technologies regulate human life through a process of individualization. The governing of the self is through "regimes of truth" that are internalized to guide individual interactions, wants, and desires. For Foucault, the progressive and regulatory tendencies within social sciences are expressed by the transition from the epic, the main vehicle by which truth was communicated about the world, to the construction of the dossier. The dossier is to tell the truth about individuals by segmenting the person into discrete and taxonomical parts that can be ordered and governed. The truth-governing regimes are embodied in the record of the individual, with the social sciences and psychology giving form to the main recording devices.

TEACHER-THINKING RESEARCH AS STATE STEERING

The study of teacher thinking occurs at the intersection of at least three strands of practice in education. One is previous work on teaching effectiveness that originated with studies of correlational behavioral and experimental research. It is believed that the current focus on teachers' thought processes and planning is a significant advance in the study of classrooms. The research is thought to provide a more adequate portrayal of the complexities of the teacher's task than earlier behavior-based studies. In numerous instances, the turn to cognitive psychology is signaled as a "significant shift" in which researchers examine teachers' thought and decisions (see, e.g., Ball, 1988; Clark & Peterson, 1986; Clark & Yinger, 1979; Shulman, 1987). Second, the focus on teacher thinking is tied to state agendas to provide more effective teacher education and steering of classroom processes.

Current studies of teachers and teacher education interrelate multiple political strategies (Labarree, 1990b). It responds to a conservative climate within the United States, promoting excellence and standards through teacher training. Liberal interests are expressed about altering the bureaucratic nature of schooling and uplifting teachers who are considered the oppressed group of schools. The research also represents a professionalization strategy in which science is to improve the collective status and mobilization of teacher educators.

Research as an Instrument of Reform Policy

In a thorough review of teacher-thinking research in *The Handbook on Research on Teaching*, Clark and Peterson (1986) give attention to a 1975 National Institute of Education panel chaired by Lee Shulman, then a Michigan State University professor of educational psychology. The panel argued that central to classroom research is the study of teacher thinking. It is argued that such research is a more viable strategy for improving the quality of instruction than was realized in previous reform approaches. The federal panel stated that "it will be necessary for any innovation in the context, practices, and technology of teaching to be mediated through the minds and motives of teachers" (quoted in Clark & Peterson, 1986, p. 256).

The psychological research, Clark and Peterson (1986) indicate, is intended to stimulate reform and provide guidance for policy. The call for research initiated the first large federal program on teaching as clinical information processing. "To understand, predict, and influence what teachers do," according to the panel of the National Institute of Education, "researchers must study the psychological processes by which teachers perceive and define their professional responsibility and situations" (quoted in Clark & Peterson, 1986, p. 256).

Similar assumptions about research on the mental structures of teaching and social amelioration are contained in the models of pedagogical reasoning. In an article central to this research, Lee Shulman (1987), now at Stanford University, ties the study of teacher thinking to a recurring theme in the reform movement. This theme is to elevate "teaching to a more respected, more responsible, more rewarding and better rewarded occupation" (p. 3). The claim for professional status, the article continues, assumes a development of "standards by which education and the performance of teachers must be judged." Such standards occur through identifying a "'knowledge base for teaching'—a codified or codifiable aggregation of knowledge, skill, understanding, and technology of ethics and disposition, of collective responsibility—as well as a means for representing and communicating it" (pp. 3–4). To develop this knowledge base, it is important to observe carefully "how particular kinds of content knowledge and pedagogical strategies are necessarily interacted in the minds of teachers" (p. 5).

The research does capture general concerns of the reform movement. There is a belief that the quality of instruction is tied to the quality of teaching; this is to be addressed through strategies of professionalization. A central issue is recognizing the importance of the socially dynamic qualities of knowledge (see Shulman, 1986). Too much attention, it is argued, has been devoted to pedagogical practice without considering the different tasks of teaching across disciplines or content areas. Teaching different subjects of schooling also raises questions about the plural qualities of knowledge. One group of authors suggest, for example, the importance of asking what it means "to do mathematics, to consider the interpretation and argument about what is or isn't fact, and the relation of individuals to their disciplinary community" (McDiarmid, Ball, & Anderson, 1989, pp. 7–8). Further, it is recognized that disciplinary knowledge is represented poorly, promoting "conceptions or encouraging patterns of thought and action in pupils that do not correspond to the ways of thinking and knowing in history, mathematics, literature, or science" (p. 4). Different approaches to instruction, it is argued, are needed when teaching mathematics versus teaching history.

The call for research relates state steering priorities with a populist democratic belief. It is asserted that there is a direct link between the implementation of the reform programs and what the research on teacher thinking identifies as "the sources and suggested outlines of that knowledge base" (Shulman, 1986, p. 5). The professional development school, a major reform of the Holmes Group (1990) discussed earlier, is predicated on the incorporation of cognitive research findings into the organization of instruction. The new research group strategies contain a language of the expert in service of the democratic ideal: Professional knowledge is to elevate teachers and help them make decisions in their immediate environment. Research is to be anti-elitist and functional. Teachers' practices and reasoning are to be codified in order to improve the efficiency and quality of teaching. This faith in the person at the bottom of the institutional hierarchy is part of a populist tradition related to agrarian and later urban protest movements of the 19th century. In that prior context, social and political institutions were to be made responsive to their local and grass-roots constituencies. The revolt against expert knowledge, government, and bureaucracy was to democratically transform institutions by denying power to elites and bureaucrats. While the cognitive research maintains the populist rhetoric, this chapter will argue that the democratic intent is reversed. Status is given to expert knowledge and the decision-making processes within teachers' work are narrowed. The range of responsibility and autonomy is limited to technical concerns, with issues of power hidden behind a rhetoric of progress. A particular form of social regulation occurs as the study of the mind is separated from its social-historical context.

Continuities with Behaviorism

The Clark and Peterson (1986) article presents a clear and coherent presentation of the research on teacher thinking and, for my purposes, on the relation of educational psychology to the problems of social amelioration discussed in Chapter 3. I choose this article because I find it a thoughtful and extensive exposition of an influential style of thought in educational research. At the same time, the exposition can enable us to consider the relation of social movements, power, and scientific knowledge. As before, my concern is with the social epistemology of the research practices rather than with the intent or purpose of individual researchers.

The summary and interpretation of research in this article can be read as having two interrelated but different layers (these are explored further in Popkewitz & St. Maurice, 1991). First, there is an argument about the contribution of the study of teaching to improving classroom management. The purpose of research is to develop a useful knowledge based upon teachers' mental constructs. "The ultimate goal of research on teachers' thought processes is to construct a portrayal of the cognitive psychology of teaching for use by educational theorists, researchers, policy makers, curriculum designers, teacher educators, school administrators, and by teachers themselves" (Clark & Peterson, 1986, p. 225).

Research on teacher thinking is intended to provide more adequate explanations of teaching and curriculum than it had previously. It produces "potential sources of *hypotheses* about and *explanation* of some of the puzzling and contradictory findings of process-product research on teaching and of curriculum change implementation research" (Clark & Peterson, 1986, p. 292, emphasis added). The goal of this research is "to understand, predict and influence what teachers do," tying research to educational policy and school administration (see pp. 255–256).

Second, the Clark and Peterson article can be read as embodying certain rules and standards about social life. The chapter on teacher thinking continually gives reference to this incremental quality of knowledge: The ultimate goal is "a systematic and cumulative body of research" (Clark & Peterson, 1986, p. 292) and a comprehensive combining and aggregating of all elements and information (see pp. 256, 292).

Classifying and codifying the actions of teachers involves utilizing a particular functional U.S. psychology. Teacher thinking is seen as a mechanism for adapting to existing purposes and structures (such as those mandated by curriculum designers). Teachers' thought processes constitute "a more or less adaptive array of responses to perceived task demands of the profession" (Clark & Peterson, 1986, p. 292). Priority is given to useful knowledge about what is concrete and observable, such as what teachers report as decisions or beliefs. A concern of Clark and Peterson (1986), for example, is to make the implicit beliefs into the explicit theories of a teacher; for example, declaring as "mature" teachers who can articulate *their* thought so that it can be recorded and ordered. Change is defined as rationalized and verbalized actions, reported by teachers and nonetheless stable within existing social patterns.

While rhetorically positing a break with behaviorism, the form of the argument ties the cognitive science of teaching to the epistemology that it was to supersede. This occurs, in part, through the incremental view of knowledge. The belief in science as hypothesis testing and the view that data explain phenomena are residues of positivism (see Popkewitz & St. Maurice, 1991). The socially constructed qualities of theoretical statements are removed from their contexts in social struggles. History is limited to those events that sanction its specific methods. It is to these assumptions in research that I now turn my attention. I focus on the denial of a social history by considering three problems of scientific knowledge. These are

1. Reification, by which the socially constructed world is made to seem natural and inevitable
2. Decontextualization/reformulation of knowledge, by which the

complexities of social practices are reduced to a one-dimensional plane of administrative practice

3. Social regulation through the production of knowledge, by which the issue of power is raised as circulating in the knowledge teachers have of "self" and others

My concern here is to put aside the rhetorical claims about producing more professional and competent teachers and to give attention to the form of reasoning constructed by research practices.

REIFICATION OF SCHOOL SUBJECTS

As a philosophical concept, reification refers to the tendency to deny the role of human constructions and history in social phenomena. Categories and classifications formulate social affairs as having universal attributes, qualities, or stages for human development. Taxonomies of cognition and talk about a child as *the* learner, *the* African-American, *the* at-risk child are each instances of reification. They homogenize differences and make social, historically derived practices seem independent of time and space. Reification is a conservative element: What exists is made to seem natural and inevitable—enduring without multiple interpretations, social/cultural conflict, or social interest.

Reification in research about teacher thinking occurs in the dualism that separates content from teaching, a practice I focus on below. While the research agenda is to tie teaching to some curriculum content, the cognitive methodology separates the two. Discussed in the following section, is a problem related to reification—the decontextualization of the lived experiences and historical location of teachers' "thoughts." What teachers say and do are reconceptualized into universal qualities of logical and psychological categories. In this account about thinking, the immediate present is emphasized. Obscured are how the words of teachers are a part of a social field that maintains particular social values and particular social interests.

Representation and Misrepresentation: The Search for Truth

The cognitive research strategy takes for granted the selection of curriculum knowledge. The logic in which this occurs can be expressed as follows: Each of the school subjects involves different types of thought and practice. These differences are expressed in the representations of content found in textbooks, course syllabi, or the materials brought into the classrooms. Problems of instruction focus on how teachers and students re-present the concepts, generalizations, and facts taken from the various cognate fields. This entails identifying what schemata are introduced to order phenomena; what misrepresentations of the schema are found; and what flexibility in instruction is available to teach the correct representations. The research is limited to strategies of representing what is already assumed as fact.

A central element in subject-related pedagogy is to provide more effective and flexible teaching strategies to represent the content of the school subjects. Researchers make a distinction between representation in the subfields of psychology and those of instructional research. Psychology relates representation to schemata. It is concerned with how knowledge is selected and actively modified to arrive at a coherent, unified representation, such as how reading a menu in a restaurant entails a ''script'' of expectations and ordering of phenomena in which the menu is made understandable to the individual (see Abelson, 1981; see also Alba & Hasher, 1983). The epistemology of this psychology is a mixture of British empiricism borrowed from American behaviorism, and continental philosophy in which a whole is not reducible to isolated and individually distinct parts (Brewer & Nakamura, 1984). When brought into instructional research, the focus is problem solving. How do people look for cues that define a relevant context in which to decode appropriate strategies and practices? (Bransford, Sherwood, Hasselbring, Kinzer, & Williams, no date).[1]

The discussion of improving teaching provides a more specific reference to representation. Representation entails the identification of stable elements in the curriculum. Once identified, the instructional problem is how that content is mediated by teachers and students. Representation is defined as providing examples, analogies, and metaphors that ''fit'' the discipline. One such ''fit'' is the analogy that plants are ''factories.'' The pedagogical question about representation is to identify what materials are available for classrooms and ''how well it fits the context. . . . Is money a good model for helping fifth graders understanding decimals?'' (McDiarmid et al., 1989, p. 9).

Teaching uses the given representation to interweave ''a specific academic discipline with knowledge of learners, learning and the context.'' Here, a psychological underpinning returns. Understanding subject matter entails being ''able to view the subject matter through the eyes of the learner, as well as interpreting the learners' comments, questions and activities through the lenses of the subject'' (McDiarmid et al., 1989, p. 3). Researchers ask what activities, examples, analogies, and materials can bring the content to the learner. How can an idea ''be represented verbally, symbolically, graphically, or concretely" (p. 4)? Does representation entail "an equation in mathematics *or* verbal definitions, analogies, or dramatizations in literature" (p. 5)? The object of instruction is to tie teachers' and children's conceptions of knowledge to instructional representations.

Teachers' responsibility is functional and technically defined. It is the teacher's task to judge the appropriateness of representations (activities, examples, analogies, and materials). Representation is intended to produce a "repertoire and capacity to invent and select . . . [to] fit the multiple opportunities for pupils from diverse backgrounds to understand" (McDiarmid et al., 1989, p. 13); it is to introduce a "tighter connection between what teachers know and what they do" (p. 11).

A particular view of school knowledge is made apparent through examining the relation of the subject matter and cognition. The focus is on processes of the mind; this leaves concepts and generalizations as objects that have a constancy and stability.[2] Cognitive psychology gives attention to the mediations among teachers and students that define content, even though the explicit purpose of the research is to probe the dynamic relation between teaching and school content. The knowledge of school subjects is rendered as formal structures of concepts and methods that have fixed properties. Disciplinary knowledge comprises the "properties" or "syntactic structures" in which the words contain determinant meanings and permanent qualities.

At this point, epistemological limitations of cognitive psychology as a pedagogical lens can be located. There is a distinction between the rhetorical claims and the specific research practices. The literature about pedagogical knowledge acknowledges truth as fragile and tied to history. This acknowledgment, however, remains a formality that is separated from the ongoing discourse that defines representation. Flexibility is limited to the diverse activities of the teacher and the repertoire of teachers as they have pupils learn a subject matter. To develop, for example, a content-specific pedagogy, McDiarmid and colleagues (1989) suggest a broad approach in which teachers need to know relationships "within and across disciplines, what specialists in a field do, how knowledge is generated, and how disciplinary knowledge relates to the environment of classrooms" (p. 6; see also, e.g., Ball, 1988). The specific text examples leave these interests aside. Context is stable; strategies of learning content are flexible.

The reification of content is illustrated with the psychological concept of misrecognition. There is talk about the misrepresentation of scientific conceptions by children and a concern with understanding teachers' and children's conceptualizations. Misrecognition imposes a dualism formed through the relations established. The opposite, recognition, imposes an assumption of finite qualities to the school content. Subject matter has a true, absolute, and universal quality. The dualism may be appropriate for lower-order skills. But when a statement such as "Columbus discovered America" is made, the problem of its adequacy is not one of recognition/misrecognition but of social, cultural, and political adequacy. To posit uncritically that Columbus "discovered" America marginalizes those who already lived in the Americas at that time and justifies (tacitly) European dominance.

A similar difficulty occurs in identifying curriculum concepts or standards in the sciences and humanities. For example, there are continual debates in the cognate fields about the assumptions and presuppositions of change in research, an issue taken up in the first chapter of this book. Other commonplaces in education, such as the meaning of literacy or learning, can be considered not as clear-cut but as filled with analytical and social ambiguities. Philosophers of science have argued that the meaning of science is found in the manner in which ideas are formed and the conditions in which debate occurs. Educational researchers' focus on subject-matter teaching ignores the multiple interpretations that exist about concepts and obscures the substantive debate that shapes and fashions intellectual life. Recognition is a semiotic problem in which the constructions of language rules and contexts of use interrelate without any absolute definitions, a consideration to which I will return.

A certain functional orientation is maintained. In prior behavioral research, this disposition toward knowledge was called "concept attainment." In constructivism, the mind is a mediating instrument of what is objectively defined as certain. The truth is contained in the instructional representations of the disciplinary concepts. Research focuses on efficiency in reorganizing the teachers' thought strategies to eliminate misrepresentations.

My concern here is not to deny that the problem of representation in the curriculum is profound and important. Temporal visions of worth and nonworth are memorialized and are given authoritative intention through the forms of representation found in the curriculum. The notion of representation is a central problem in social theory. Earlier, in Chapter 1, I focused on the shift from a representational view of knowledge to that posed in the Enlightenment. According to the latter, knowledge is conceived of as humanly constructed. Progress was perceived as rationally understanding and planning for social betterment—early roots to the interest in cognitive psychology. In this current research agenda, an Enlightenment image is maintained, but with an emphasis on established and fixed categories that lead to a reorganization of experience. Representation and recognition are recast into their classical epistemology: There is presumed to be a direct relation between the words being taught and the real world. The role of research is to eliminate misconceptions and bring to the learners (teachers and children) an undistorted knowledge. In the world of cognitive research, reification trivializes that problem of representation. Representations become objects of curriculum that are given to teachers or children

Teaching Flexibility and the Loss of History

The psychology of pedagogy pays homage to discussions about pluralism in scientific communities, debate in the construction of knowledge, and the importance of an interdisciplinary approach in pedagogical research. Declarations about the interrelating of disciplines are remarkably similar to Gardner's (1985) celebration of the new cognitive science as a historical revolution. Gardner sees cognitive science as drawing on many social and physical sciences that will someday yield a "single, unified science" (p. 7). This dream of unity has a long history in American empiricism. It is consistent with the unity-of-science movement and logical positivism in the 1920s. Advocates of the behavioral sciences sought universal social laws in the 1960s. In his dream Gardner puts aside social and historical considerations, as do the researchers on teacher thinking. Gardner (1985) argues for "deemphasizing certain factors which may be important for cognitive functioning but whose inclusions at this point *would unnecessarily complicate the cognitive scientific enterprise*" (p. 6, emphasis added).

The complications occur as a consequence of Gardner's purging of social and historical considerations. A one-dimensionality is produced that distorts the problem of representation and of thought itself. To illustrate, let me return to the pedagogical discussion that relates representation to a corollary notion of instructional flexibility.

Curriculum representations, it is argued, should be taught with a "flexible" understanding of subject matter. The focus is on flexibility in the tasks of instruction. Here we return to the problem of flexibility raised in the reform reports discussed in the previous chapter, but given a particular content in the constructivist research. Flexibility "consists of topic-level knowledge of learners, of learning and of the most useful forms of representation of [particular] ideas, the most powerful analogies, illustrations, examples, explanations, and demonstrations—in a word, the ways of representing and formulating the subject that make it comprehensible to others" (Shulman, 1986, p. 6; quoted in McDiarmid et al., 1989, p. 3).

This view of representation and flexibility can be contrasted to much recent scholarship that focuses on pluralism and the social construction of the knowledge of science and philosophy. Work in the philosophy and sociology of science has helped us understand that the concepts of physics, biology, and sociology change over time. This occurs not in an evolutionary manner but through breaks in the epistemology of science itself (see Kuhn, 1970; Lecourt, 1975; Tiles, 1984). From this scholarship, we can understand that changes in concepts entail relating the work of science to the social fields in which it operates. The development of applied physics, for example, occurred after World War I and in relation to *both* the technological inventions related to the war and to changes in the industrial base of Western European countries. If we move to the current acceptance of a cognitive science, it was prefigured by Bartlett's schema theory in 1932 but not fully developed until the 1970s. Contemporary development cannot be understood without considering the social consequences of the computer. This includes the complexities of new industrial situations and of military hardware that require different types of psychology to manage the individuals who function in high-tech contexts (Noble, 1989).

The Loss of a Social Epistemology in School Subjects

The research on teacher thinking has an epistemological flaw in its construction: Mind is separated from material conditions and thought, from the objective world. School content is viewed as objective and stable. What is in flux and being debated in mathematics and history is treated as natural and unyielding knowledge. As such, the research strategy on teacher thinking is bound by prior epistemological commitments from which it cannot extricate itself. The psychology cannot accommodate the intricacies of the relation of curriculum to teaching. Let me explore this through a specific research report about subject teaching in a high school.

The discussion examines how undergraduate training influences the teaching of history among three teachers. Each had a different undergraduate major: political science, anthropology, and history (Wilson & Wineburg, 1988). Different emphases in teaching styles are found. One teacher emphasizes "the role of facts" (the political science major); another focuses on the relation of "interpretation and evidence" (anthropology); and the third places value on "chronology and continuity" (history) (pp. 527–532). These differences are described as the result of the particular "stamp" of each individual's undergraduate education; for example, the political science and anthropology majors' "*lack* of (historical) knowledge was most decisive in their instruction" (p. 535, emphasis in original).

The diversity, debate, and conflict among historians about knowledge and truth are reduced to a single, uncontested standard. The idea of historical inquiry is made into a positive set of rules and standards by which to judge each teacher. Wilson and Wineburg (1988) accept the comments of the historian R. G. Collingwood that there is "no difference between what happened and discovering why it happened," but they do not then consider or seem to be aware that Collingwood wrote in a phenomenological tradition that emphasizes intent and purpose in historical studies. To consider Collingwood's statement as an epistemological commitment is, I believe, also to recognize that there is debate within history (as well as in anthropology and political science). Argumentation is continual about the ways in which theoretical understandings influence what is made into "facts" and about the different and conflicting assumptions that exist about interpretation. For example, historians have debated the notion of causation. Some, such as Collingwood, define historical causes through a chronology that relates events and peoples' thoughts. This can be contrasted to definitions of Marxist and institutional historians. They may focus on structural patterns of economy and bureaucracy as the cause of events. Causes are not necessarily chronological or logical. A different strand, taken in this book, considers history as the interplay of epistemological breaks and continuities from which the present is constructed. Cause as an explanatory concept is severely reduced in this brand of history, since there are no grand explanatory systems or linear processes.

A crystallization of history occurs in the accounts of teaching school subject matter. The language given to the problem of teaching history is revealing. It is "assessing, reconfiguring and interpreting the historical record" (Wilson & Wineburg, 1988, p. 15). To assume that there is an unyielding record of the past is to suggest that history has one, true version to be identified. Research assumes that questions of valid evidence are resolved through an unrestricted empiricism; truth occurs as a result of "historians continually sifting through historical records" (p. 15). Obscured are the struggles of historians over what should be determined as "fact," issues about causation and the varying conception of time and space in historical study.

My purpose in signaling the different epistemological commitments in historical paradigms is not to claim which is most appropriate in curriculum designs. Rather, it is to illustrate that disciplines are not conceptually monolithic and universal phenomena. To treat academic disciplines as such is to misrecognize disciplinary practices.[3] To bring these misrecognitions into pedagogy is to accept as given those explanatory systems that political scientists, anthropologists, and historians, among others, debate. There is no monolithic "stamp" associated with any one academic field. To assume so is to fix and trivialize complex disciplinary knowledge and pedagogical practices.

To summarize the argument to this point: The style of reasoning employed to study teacher thinking typifies the problem of reification in educational research. Knowledge is converted into the information given by teachers and then mediated as it is given to children. The essential qualities or "structures" of knowledge require only efficient practices by which teachers represent information and skills to children. The concern is not with an epistemology of knowledge but with how teachers rationalize knowledge. But if the purpose of such research is to interrelate the complexity of disciplinary practices with teacher practices, the research processes result in educational thought that is inadequate for its own intellectual purposes.

The problem of reification in educational cognitive psychology occurs because it is not a science designed to deal with the complex relations found in the constructions of science, mathematics, the social sciences, or literature. It has more limited boundaries and pretensions. If we take Gardner's assertion seriously, it is a science for examining the mind as an entity in and by itself. The science is without recourse for exploring the sets of social and historical relations in which the mind works. As psychology reaches to questions of teaching and curriculum, it is a discipline whose field has extended beyond its range of competence. What was a useful analogy of the relation of the computer to the mind is now applied to a range of complex phenomena and institutional contexts that it cannot handle epistemologically. The research emphasis has little to do with the implications of the social, historical, and psychological patterns associated with disciplinary work. Further, to treat content in pedagogy as fixed is also to reify the knowledge of teaching. Reason and action are removed from history. A refocusing occurs upon one narrow dimension of the profound and complex problem of the selection, organization, and evaluation of school knowledge. Representations is the given content. Teaching is to be effective and flexible in conveying that content. To treat disciplinary knowledge solely as representation of a stable content is to ignore the social construction and social relations in which individuals locate themselves and their world, denying historical responsibility and autonomy.

Thought in Social/Institutional Contexts

The research on teacher thinking posits a need for a contextual knowledge of teaching, yet the research obscures the conditions of teaching. A universal language is constructed that hides the manner in which thought is not just what an individual teacher brings into a context. The social and historical construction of teaching can be focused through an examination of mathematics teaching. I use mathematics education because it is generally assumed to be unaffected by social criteria. In contrast, I will argue that teacher reasoning about mathematics education is socially constructed and institutionally bound (see Popkewitz, 1988b).

In most countries, pupils are taught mathematics in ways that suggest a homogeneity of practice and a consensus of purpose. Theories and organization of school mathematics imply that there is a unified, universal pattern of behavior to guide experience. In recent reform reports, there is the assumption that everyone is treated equally in learning school subject matter. If differentiation occurs, it is the result of merit rather than ascribed characteristics of individuals. The problem of teaching is related to a homogeneity of content that is to be effectively organized with appropriate technologies, such as use of calculators or computers "to insure that every student becomes familiar with these important processes" (Conference Board of Mathematical Sciences, quoted in Romberg & Stewart, 1987, p. 117).

While the language creates an illusion of homogeneity, the actual social transactions in schools differentiate what is taught and learned (Bernstein, 1977; DeLone, 1979; McLaren, 1986). Rather than one common type of school, there are different forms of schooling for different people. The different forms of schooling emphasize different ways of considering ideas, contain different social values, and maintain different principles of legitimacy and social regulation.

What gets brought into school as mathematics has as much to do with the social conditions of schooling as with considerations of the logic of knowledge. In Chapter 1, I considered Stanic's (1987) discussion of the emergence of mathematics education in U.S. schools at the turn of the century. It placed two types of instruction at the center of the debate on the construction of a curriculum language. The strands of mathematics education contained different views of the probable destination of the child, the type of harmonious society that the school was to produce, and conceptions of labor socialization. One was elitist and related to those who would go to college; a second provided skills for managing everyday life, such as using arithmetic for household budgets. The different views of mathematics pedagogy also contained competing views that emerged within the Protestant middle and upper classes about how to provide for social amelioration, discussed in Chapter 2 as part of the social gospel movement. Each type of instruction involved research programs that justified and organized teaching; in the process, issues of social differentiation were obscured as the problems of instruction were made to seem scientific questions of individual development and learning.

A consideration of institutional patterns in mathematics education can further explore the relation of thought to social conditions (Popkewitz, 1988b). The mathematics curriculum is not only about the abstractions of numbers or logical structure. Mathematics is realized with school patterns that frame what is taught. The importance of routines and conversations has little to do with *mathematics* education. The topic, the organization, and the social messages reflect assumptions about the nature of knowledge defined within schooling. These assumptions are not necessarily those of a mathematics discipline or understood as activities of the mind alone (Donovan, 1983; Stephens, 1982). The sequences given to lessons, the examples used to explain a concept, and the social/ psychological theories of children's growth embody epistemological and political theories about our world.

We can begin to understand from the urban elementary school mathematics lesson that the form and content of teaching are interrelated. The lesson was observed as part of a study of schools in which a national program of educational reform was being realized (Popkewitz et al., 1982). As part of a study of the culture of elementary schools, one school with students from black families of the industrial poor and unemployed was observed.[4] The specific teaching processes can be viewed as part of longer-term patterns that establish capabilities for the individual; the lesson observed is part of institutional patterns and culture. The stated and ostensible purpose of the mathematics lesson was to help students learn subtraction; the teacher wrote a lesson plan, constructed materials, and evaluated according to the previously stated objectives. The lesson was justified for different reasons: Subtraction is an important element of a mathematics curriculum, and future lessons depend on acquiring the presented knowledge. The teacher explained elements of subtraction during the lesson, and students read their textbooks and wrote on worksheets.

Subject matter, however, was only one part of a lesson's content; the lesson carried social messages that were as important as any overt information. The introduction to the teacher's lesson involved a discussion that focused on the children's academic failures. The teacher talked to the observer about how the students lacked the behavioral and attitudinal characteristics necessary for success in school. The teacher's comments during the lesson reflected assumptions that tied students' work to undesirable traits related to their welfare status. These were defined as poor work habits that needed to be overcome before any achievement could be obtained. The teacher talked after the class about the welfare psychology of the children's families. The teacher perceived the children as having no discipline, work ethic, or value for school learning as a result of being on the dole. Much of the classroom interaction and the teacher's reasoning carried background assumptions about social stratification, cultural distinctions, and power relations. These assumptions were hidden in the discussions about multiculturalism, learning theories, and student achievement.

While one possible explanation for this situation is inadequate teacher reasoning and the need for more effective teacher training, we can also consider the organization of thought and its assumptions. Pedagogy is not only a system of information or subjects that are organized for students but also an ordering of social fields. The organization of school knowledge defines categories and distinctions that decontextualize social relations. In this deeper sense, the markers of social distinction and aspirations bestowed through pedagogy are structured out of any examination in current research. To develop a research strategy that assumes existing distinctions and categories as the ordering principles gives legitimacy to the social fields in which schooling is realized.

Pedagogical Knowledge as a Site of Contesting Views of Society and Polity

The mathematics lesson can help unravel more profound and complex relations in the social organization and reasoning of classroom life. We can view teachers' conversations about their work as visions of society and polity and juxtapose them to other, different views of cognition (Popkewitz, 1983a). As discussed in Chapters 2 and 3, different conceptions of pedagogy emerged as part of the transformations that occurred in the 19th century. To treat a child as having a deficit is to define knowledge atomistically; the individual is an essentially receptive, reflective organism whose qualities are shaped by the environment over time. The epistemology entails a political theory in which the individual is likened to a machine that is to function efficiently. Social life is defined as fixed and unyielding to intervention. The individual is denied the role of actor in the creation of history and culture. In contrast, a focus on negotiation in classroom practices, found in different schools of the study, gives value to community and self as integrally related and mutually reinforcing.

Differing views of cognition, society, and childhood allow us to understand different layers of the relationships among pedagogy, psychology, and political theory in classroom practices. What seem simple acts of classroom planning or management in fact contain profound and complex principles of authority, legitimacy, and power relations. The "commonsense" view of pedagogy as imparting learning is itself historically constructed and tied to problems of the institutional development of American education (O'Donnell, 1985). The language of learning is drawn from the economic and political theories of the British in the 18th and 19th centuries and recast as a way to provide practical solutions for the socialization of children. The focus on the attributes of mind emerged with earlier associationist psychologists who related "learning" to liberal political theories about the duties, obligations, and rights of individuals. What counted was the present; the ideology was that society is composed of free and equal individuals who enter into a social contract. What behaviorism of the 1930s socially assumed in its associationism, cognitive psychology recasts as the order of society negotiated according to some base that is harmonized by natural market forces. Knowledge and people are treated as "things" or commodities manipulated in an orderly and efficient manner as the marketplace.

The importance of the different curriculum approaches has at least two dimensions that reach into contemporary discourses about content representation. First, the representations brought into schooling are not universally appropriated. There is no general, abstract "learner" who modifies, adopts, or adapts concepts. The representations are placed in social contexts in which there are differentiations in the work and knowledge of schooling. The social organization of schooling contains different sensibilities and awarenesses necessary for access to positions of privilege and status in society (Popkewitz et al., 1982). The social distinctions in pedagogy are made invisible by a language that makes curriculum choices seem problems of universal reasoning.

Second, any field of knowledge contains the multiple values and visions of society. Recent work in gender analysis, for example, points to the way in which democratic conceptions of participation are based upon distinctions between public and private. Female spheres are separated from the rational qualities associated with the manly political involvement of the 18th century (see, e.g., Pateman, 1988). Further, certain "rational" assumptions that underlie the selection of school subjects posit a social and political bias related to gender (Beechey & Donald, 1985; Gilligan, 1982; Sherman & Beck, 1979). These and other sources consistently direct attention to the selection of school knowledge as driven by social struggles and transformations in which schooling is implicated.

DECONTEXTUALIZATION AND
REFORMULATION OF KNOWLEDGE

The spacial and temporal differences in schooling are obscured through a decontextualized language. The categories and distinctions of school research have no clear relation to people, events, or human struggles. The everyday experiences and communications of diverse groups are decontextualized and reformulated to a set of rules, obligations, and values of the cognitive sciences. The problem is to identify common errors or misconceptions and strategies to overcome the deficit (see Ball, 1988). Individual perceptions, cognitions, and interpretations are reencoded into stages of learning, attributes, or skills of learning, or models of reasoning separate from social or historical processes. The reconceptualized knowledge about schooling and children makes existing relations seen "natural."

The principles of codification can be traced in the language about teacher thinking. There is a curious mixture of words that, at one end, posit a mediated, active, and purposeful understanding. There is the rhetorical focus on negotiated knowledge of teaching that occurs through interactions of teachers' understandings with disciplinary content. At the other end are assumptions that there is a true foundation or essential quality to teachers' reasoning. Pedagogy is thought to have "stages," a "knowledge base," and a "body" of knowledge. The knowledge is expressed as "a codified or codifiable aggregation" that can be identified and that directly informs teaching practice. The notions of base, stages, and body treat knowledge as given objects. These objects are to be relayed like messages on a machine—there are "particular kinds of content knowledge and pedagogical strategies which are necessarily interacted in the minds of teachers" (Shulman, 1987, p. 5). The knowledge about teaching is brought to teachers as "categories that might be organized into a handbook, an encyclopedia, or some other format for arraying knowledge" (Shulman, 1987, p. 8). In Clark and Peterson (1986), the "ultimate" goal of research is "to describe fully the mental lives of teachers" that can guide school improvement (p. 225). Reform is to occur through sciences that identify the content, character, and sources for a knowledge base (Shulman, 1987, p. 4).

Notwithstanding the difficult philosophical tensions between words such as *base* and *body* with those such as *growth* and *stages*, the words imply that knowledge has physical attributes. Here, I believe, is an example of how discourse patterns work to structure thought rather than thought structuring discourse. The words exist in a pattern of relations that suggest an inert, unyielding quality to schooling or the disciplinary knowledge of school subjects. The physical language naturalizes the curriculum. What is portrayed as a descriptive system becomes, upon examination, a moral one that posits a world of functional distinctions and priorities.

The psychological discourse of pedagogy crystallizes a particular structure of thought through its linguistic forms and makes it seem universal and appropriate for all. The problems of teaching are formulated into concepts that stress a rational, individualized, and sequential development detached from social contexts and historical roots. Models of teaching and learning build upon a conception of progress as linear, social relations as atomistic, and individuality as exploiting differences among populations. The view of progress builds upon a conception of whole as the sum of the parts; it is similar to the political theory of John Locke, in which society is seen as organized and progressing through the sum of individual social contracts. These are evolutionary assumptions functionally bound to the ordered relations and hierarchies that are linguistically postulated.

The research that I examine in this chapter generalizes and categorizes in a way that distances objects from their cultural and social context. The patterns of communication are transformed and experiences refocused in ways that embody power relations. This transformation occurs through the linguistic forms used to talk about the distinctions and the classifications of teachers' thought. Procedures and efficiency become goals as the historical setting and social constructions of institutional life are ignored. (For discussion of the assumptions and implications of models for change, see Popkewitz, 1984, Chapter 6.) But when offered as a reform strategy, the particular decontextualizations and reformulations can have an impact on those who were studied, producing a form of social regulation through the legitimacy as the science interrelates with diverse institutional patterns.

SOCIAL REGULATION

The research program on teacher thinking has significant implications for schooling and the work of teachers. The reforms contain commitments to the production of a more benevolent social organization.

The sciences of pedagogical thinking make possible refined methods of regulating and disciplining the individual. The individualization has a particular focus. It is not for the purpose of understanding the thought, actions, and practices of the solitary person. It defines people as part of an aggregate population and assigns rational categories to thought as a method of monitoring individuals. The individualization occurs through the application of the models of reasoning for the supervision, observation, and evaluation of a particular teacher's work.

This potential for social regulation occurs in at least two ways. First, the discourse about science hides the source of knowledge. Models of pedagogy in teacher-thinking research are said to be taken "from the point of view of the teacher, which is presented with the challenge of taking what he or she already understands and making it ready for effective instruction" (Shulman, 1987, p. 14). But the talk about the activities of teaching and reflection decontextualizes teachers' talk and reconceptualizes without social or historical reference. To do this is to make it more difficult for people to locate the interests that are speaking and the values according to which the knowledge is organized. The pedagogical constructions further distance people from the source of their own thoughts, thus normalizing a particular functional idea of progress and development.

Time and space have no consequence in these mediations. Time is defined as rational and functional. It has discrete parts that are logically ordered and involve sequential developments. Problem solving is tied to linear relation, taxonomic categories, and universal sequences. C. Wright Mills (1959) spoke of this science as a concern of people who administer individual cases and focus on a series of immediate and surface "causes."

Second, the technology of research also becomes a technology of power in the productive sense. The rationalization is a technique of social administration. The concern is to rationalize teachers' thought as a regulatory template. Pedagogical research breaks social interactions into more detailed, discrete tasks. Individual teachers are monitored through external evaluations and through the distinctions applied to determine their personal competence. The purpose of the regulatory systems is to guide the individual in determining needs, satisfaction, and further knowledge. Teachers are encouraged "to monitor their own thought." By making private thought publicly available, the psychology of reasoning makes individual teachers more open to scrutiny and regulation.

A different layer of power is the adoption of "clinical" perspectives as a guide to research and reform. Much of the current literature adopts a language of teaching as "clinical informational processes." According to Foucault's (1975) study of the birth of the medical clinic, the clinical gaze rendered the body a visible entity. The bodily parts were made reducible in quality and amenable to rationally structured discourses about individuals. With the clinical gaze, the object of the discourse becomes the individual who is made into a subject whose intentions are revealed and ordered by empiricism (St. Maurice, 1987).

The logic of research involved is not only a description of activities; it also acts as a particular form of social regulation. It assumes there are hierarchies and taxonomies of development, notions that contain 18th-century cosmologies about social development as cyclical and social regulation as administrative. In our current reform era, the cosmology includes managing the teacher, who is often female.

CONCLUSIONS

The language of cognitive research is one of pluralism and of a social construction of knowledge. It is also a language of consensus and stabilizing of the concepts and information brought into teaching, thus tying the epistemological rules of research to the governmental administrative rules discussed in Chapter 7 and those policies of the Holmes Group reports (see Chapter 5). The Holmes reports (1986, 1990) and the research on pedagogical knowledge recognize truth as fragile and tied to history. This acknowledgment, however, remains a formality that is separated from the ongoing discourse that defines teacher cognition and school reform. Discussion is limited to identifying strategies for representing what is already assumed as fact.

What, then, can the previous analysis suggest about the linkages of educational research to the complex relations and regulation in schooling? First, research about school knowledge has the potential to shape not only what is represented but also the space in which identity and esteem are formed. The significance lies in its producing boundaries to organize thought, perception, feeling, and practice.

Second, when we evoke images of stages and hierarchies of thought solely as logical entities, we reconceptualize teacher talk. That reconceptualization involves the serious omission of the particular institutional arrangements that make those conversations plausible. Cultural competence presupposes interpretative stances that emerge as part of a social space and systems of dispositions found in schooling. While rhetorically centering on the value of the work of the teacher, the pedagogical reasoning neutralizes the social distinctions in which language, thought, and action are realized. Thus, ironically, there is a dehumanizing of the world in which schools exist and teachers work.

Third, educational research consecrates a social order that school systems reinforce behind a mask of neutrality. The technical explanation of teachers' thought processes refers to a timeless quality of teaching and a unidimensional space. As I argued in previous chapters, the systems of classification in scientific knowledge embody relations that are productive in the work of teachers through their distinctions and logics of order and ability. The use of research to remake the commonsense of schooling has the potential to both translate and transform the contexts in which individuals act. An achievement of research is not in the empirical relations identified but in the forming of practices that direct social thought and the formation of intelligence in which actions occur in schools.

Fourth, the work of the educational sciences is positioned with the institutional conditions, changing structural relations, and actors that were discussed in previous chapters. In the current situation, there is an increased mobilization of educational research as part of the steering processes of schooling. The mobilization draws upon a longstanding belief that social science can bring progress. The progress of the cognitive educational sciences is tied to a functional knowledge that additively produces social amelioration. Legitimacy is gained through rhetoric of a practical knowledge that will improve the life of teachers. This positioning of expert knowledge in the service of the common person is a residue of 19th-century Populism. The social sciences were to make institutions more accessible and responsive to people through a rationalization of social patterns.

The strategy of teacher reform is argued as a new insight produced by the shift from a behavioral to a cognitive science of teaching. The new cognitive sciences, it is believed, open up the "black box" of teaching to allow understanding of intermediary processes. The recently declared revolutions in cognitive science are based on elaborations and extensions of behavioral methodologies designed to supervise and regulate individuals (see O'Donnell, 1985). Further, the methods of study contain prior commitments to positivism.[5] People and organizations are defined through taxonomic schemes, classified in ways that are based on subsumption, hierarchy, and universality of application.

The contemporary development of a science of teaching is part of its own historical relations. It entails strategies for mobility by teacher educators. Academic status within schools of education has been held by educational psychology faculties who could draw on the experimental science of its parent discipline; educational administration faculty dominated the schools organizationally. Within this context, teacher educators had low status (Schneider, 1987). In recent years, this situation has changed. Many of the deans of schools of education in major universities have come with a background in teaching and teacher education. Further, many educational psychologists have moved the focus of their research to teacher education and teaching. The research in teacher education as a science is intended to raise "the status of the status raisers; and it does so by promoting the development of a science of teaching, which both affirms the academic professionalism of teacher educators and legitimizes the professional authority of teachers" (Labaree, 1990b, p. 13).

To consider the mobilizations of a research field is also to focus on the relations of alternative and oppositional traditions that work beside and are part of the processes of intellectual production. While this chapter has considered a dominant research practice, others are offered as a way of opening up practice and making us more conscious of the degrees of freedom that exist (see Cherryholmes, 1990; Lather, 1990). That is the hope! To understand research practices is to be reflective about who is given authority to speak and those who vie for that authority. All intellectual work is implicated in the trajectories being formed. The struggles over symbols and the person who can speak with public authority are never without challenge.

The prescriptive/descriptive, formative/reformative qualities of science are ones we rarely consider, but they reveal an irony that linguistic and semiotic scholars have continually brought to our attention. Science is an abstraction of reality through the use of language; the languages of science enable us to categorize and classify events in ways that involve predispositions toward those solutions seen as appropriate. Strategies for collecting data about children's or teachers' performance, for example, create boundaries about what is important and how it should be considered. These abstractions, however, are not just linguistic. They embody power relations and are material practices. Our rules of classification contain distinctions that normalize and regulate hopes, desires, and needs. The implications of science for understanding, as well as the limitations of the boundaries created for considering human possibilities, are always with us.

7

Teaching, Teacher Education, and Professionalism

Power Made Invisible

In this chapter, I focus on two dimensions of contemporary reforms to improve teaching and teacher education.[1] One is the changing role of state government in monitoring and altering university teacher education programs. In particular, I examine the state of Wisconsin's administrative rules for credentialing teachers, a reform introduced in 1986 that reflects the general principles of contemporary reform efforts. The administrative texts are considered in the first part of this chapter as a significant mechanism of social regulation not only through the use of overt sanctions but also through the epistemology established for structuring intent and purpose into the events of schooling. State government reform practices "impose and inculcate a vision of divisions, that is, the power to make visible and explicit social divisions that are implicit, is political power par excellence" (Bourdieu, 1989b, p. 23). The second part of the chapter focuses on efforts to introduce sets of incentives to produce a more professional and rewarding workplace for teachers. To provide empirical specificity, I draw on an ethnography of a state of Wisconsin experimental project that introduced mentor teaching, differentiated staffing, and staff development programs to improve the quality of teaching in three school districts (Popkewitz & Lind, 1989).

In examining these two layers of the current reforms, my concern is to pursue in more detail the reconstitution of power relations occurring in schooling. Previously, I examined the public discourse of reforms and the epistemological relations embodied in educational research. At this point, I move to a particular setting to locate the categories, schemata of classification, and practices that guide, sanction, and produce school relations. Placing administrative authority and school district practices together involves reintroducing a notion of state as an arena in which various institutional coalitions produce school governance. I explore how a disciplinary organization is formed through a formal text while, at the same time, it is part of the ongoing lived practices of schooling.

As in the previous chapters, I am concerned with the systems of perceptions, appreciation of practices, and social patterns produced in school reforms. The relation of institutional practices and epistemologies organizes the perception of the world and, under certain conditions, organizes the world itself. As before, I am not concerned with words or language in and of themselves but with the forms of language that are part of power relations produced and embodied in the social practices. It is in the world-making effects of power that the significance of reform lies. The analysis explores how a field of power is codified and constituted in writing, speech, and institutional practices. In the last section, I consider the ways in which the reconstituting of regulation in schooling embodies power relations and a restricted meaning for democracy.

CERTIFICATION TO CREDENTIALING: STRUCTURING OF DISPOSITIONS IN TEACHER EDUCATION

The certification of teachers in the United States is determined by state governmental agencies. Typically, state governments have established general guidelines for programs that are located in colleges and universities. A central avenue of teacher reform in the last two decades has become changing the rules, procedures, and categories of teacher certification. Many state governments in the early 1970s moved toward more uniform certification for teachers (Di Sibrio, 1973). By the 1980s, more significant changes were occurring in the focus and substance of regulation. Legislative and administrative rules shifted from a focus of certifying approved programs to credential procedures that specify individual traits, experiences, and information, affecting a number of teaching categories that previously had not required separate regulation or credentials. Life certification is no longer granted in many states. Many of the changes are argued to be a strategy of professionalization intended to make the selection, training, and retention of teachers more rigorous.

A reconstitution of governing has been experienced differently by different states, yet the responses to the focus on teacher education have many features in common. Wisconsin, for example, has teacher standards that are among the highest according to national comparisons. Wisconsin standards for entry into schools of education are comparable to those for other fields, including engineering and the liberal arts. Yet the Wisconsin Department of Public Instruction has followed the general trend toward more certification control. The certification changes are said to make existing policies about teacher training more effective. In fact, rules produce new technologies of regulation through the strategies adopted.

To consider the regulation of teacher education, I will look at the Wisconsin Department of Public Instruction administrative changes in the regulation of teacher education. After much debate with the university system about the new requirements in 1985–1986 (Prestine, 1989), the Wisconsin Department of Public Instruction published a 71-page book on the rules and standards for teacher education, revised in 1988.

The shift in the governing of university teacher education has been from certification to credentialing. Prior to the new administrative rules, state education agencies set broad guidelines according to which universities could establish their own teacher education programs. The state emphasis was on approval of a training program. A certificate was given to individuals who successfully completed the course of study. Now, the governing strategy details the specific tasks, time elements, and relations that are to constitute teaching. In this sense, the movement has been from certifying teachers' competence through participation in university programs to a credentialing of teachers by measures of outcomes that are administratively mandated through governmental regulations. In certain ways, the move to credentials can be viewed as altering the university's role in the setting of agendas vis-à-vis schooling; yet the more subtle changes may be occurring in the manner by which regulation is articulated and in the coalitions that steer practice.

Movement from certification to credentialing extends control through the very processes used for generating text as well as in requiring compliance to the form and content of the texts themselves.[2] The administrative texts are pervasive not merely through the alliances established with sanctionary powers of legislation or through more subtle forms of coercion associated with accrediting procedures. The epistemology of credentialing provides a focus for action and disagreement. The government is the supreme classifier. "The legal consecration of symbolic capital confers upon a perspective an absolute, universal value, thus snatching it from a relativity that is by definition inherent in every point of view, as a view taken from a particular point in social space" (Bourdieu, 1989b, p. 23). It is the naming and world-producing quality that is significant in the administrative rules, although the production and impositions of legitimate visions of the world contain conflict.

The Language of Regulation as a Means of Control

To consider the assumptions and implications of the Wisconsin regulations, the content of only one section of the 1988 standards will be examined. It provides "General and Professional Education Rules: Common Rules" for elementary, secondary, and early childhood education. Within this subchapter IV, section PI 4.08 covers 14 items. The section requires that all professional education programs contain specified standards for certification. I will use this section of the regulations as a basis for excavating their social epistemology.

In this small part of the current text of regulation, we find four elements that redefine control of teacher education. First, there is a proliferation of regulation. There are 13 requirements that focus on provisions for every teacher education program. Every program is to have students *study, develop,* and *understand,* among other standards, "the historical, philosophical, and social foundations" that underlie "the development and purpose of" schools; "the diverse family, cultural and socioeconomic backgrounds of pupils"; competencies "to each critical thinking"; "issues related to children at risk" and laws "about child abuse and neglect"; pupil services available in schooling; psychological "principles and theories of learning"; "methods of creating a positive physical, psychological, and social teaching and learning environment"; "development, administration, scoring, interpretation and validation of teacher developed and standardized tests"; "educational research and practice related to classroom management and classroom organization"; and use of the library (Wisconsin Department of Public Instruction, 1988, pp. 70.8–70.9).

These administrative guidelines establish the role of the State Department of Public Instruction as providing particular rules and standards across a range of activities that previously were not the direct concern of the agency. More than 300 rules applicable across a variety of university programs are similar in form to those quoted above. A subsequently proposed administrative licensure added another 31 pages that define credentials for school administrators, distance education, and curriculum coordinators, as well as defining a university course ("at least 2 semester credits related to the topic of study") (Wisconsin Department of Public Instruction, 1990, p. 4).

Second, each standard contains multiple readings in defining social interests that are to be recognized in government actions toward teacher education. There are social reforming elements by which the school is to reconstruct society—expressed as protecting the child from abuse and establishing a curriculum for a multicultural society. There is joining of constituencies in a call for critical thinking in schools. This standard responds to groups that tie schools to economic priorities as well as those interested in cultural agendas of progressive education. These diverse interests will be considered later. Developing standardized tests that are valid and calling for effective teaching strategies that provide equal opportunities are goals that resonate with conservative and liberal interests. The standards embody the longstanding and cherished desire for a utopian institution where success is built upon merit; yet at the same time they perceive schooling as an objective, rational, and modern enterprise devoted to the "basics."

The multiple readings of the standards do point to contradictions (e.g., social reconstruction vs. individual responsibility in school processes). But the symbolic power of the standards is that they express diverse hopes and desires through their rhetorical form, while at the same time the actual distinctions and relations of categories produce subtle forms of social regulation. For example, while the different social interests are topically represented, these interests are, importantly, recast in a universal language of schooling that speaks of learning, competencies, and measurement.

Here lies a third element in the rules: The universal language homogenizes social distinctions and conflict by casting them as procedural categories. Policy is articulated through an instrumental language that makes the problems seem administrative in focus and universal in application. For example, one standard is that a program should have "study methods of identifying and evaluating the social, emotional, psychological, and physical behaviors of pupils as these behaviors may affect learning" (Wisconsin Department of Public Instruction, 1988, P.I. 4.08; p. 70.8). Standardized and routinized procedures are stressed, as consensus and stability are made central to discussions. There is no discussion of the moral, ethical, and political debate that surrounds the categories of psychology that focus solely on behaviors. The rationality of reform pays no attention to new goals but takes for granted the goals of the existing institutional relations. Human ends are no longer conceived as ends in themselves or as subjects of philosophic discourse.

A fourth element is the specificity with which the particular credential items are outlined. This provides significance to what is specified but, at the same time, creates silence about the social arrangements implicit in the organization of schooling. The assumption is that there is a common school for all and equity is only a matter of equalizing the effectiveness of "delivery systems." Teachers are to learn how to use multimedia centers, to apply research, to make tests valid, and to learn the proper procedures for scoring, administering, and interpreting tests.

Eliminated from scrutiny are the social differentiations that exist among urban, suburban, and rural schools among students who are black, Hispanic, Asian, and white (as well as within different ethnic groups within the label of Caucasian), male and female, poor and wealthy, and so on. These distinction are obscured by the universal quality of teacher education program rules: "Creating a positive . . . learning environment" seems to involve no temporal and spacial dimensions.

The rules are domains of practice that are seemingly neutral and transcend social values and conflict. The universality of the requirements makes it more difficult to identify the particular values or assumptions about society that are to give purpose and direction to schooling. The seeming universality and its consequences require further elaboration to consider the world-producing quality and power relations embodied in this text.

Social Transformations and Issues of Control

In previous chapters, I explored the post–World War II social tensions that interrelated with the changes in schooling. These tensions are found in the credentialing procedures but given shape through an administrative language that has implications and consequences for the production of social regulation.

The diversity of interests can be identified by focusing on one of the administrative regulations that appears in the Wisconsin codes. There is a rule that all professional programs must contain "study and experiences specifically designed to develop the competencies needed to teach critical thinking" (P.I. 4.08, pp. 70.8). The regulation can be read in multiple ways.

Critical thinking can be seen as a humanist project to develop a broadly educated teacher and to promote greater flexibility, innovation, and imagination in classrooms. The text can also be read as part of debate concerning teaching performance. Some groups support critical thinking as a functional skill for people working in situations where parameters are defined but flexibility is needed. A priority deriving from contemporary work situations, for example, is to train workers not for the assembly line but for a bound reasoning that requires individual judgment and responsibility, such as in the service or computer industries, where adaptability is important. Others "see" critical thinking as existing within social contexts where issues are ill defined and constantly shifting. The form of the administrative code, however, renders the varied foci for critical thinking devoid of any tension, contradictions, or intellectual content.

While different constituencies can be identified as supporting critical thinking, when placed in relation to the other elements of the administrative code, a more restricted interpretation occurs. The credentials are oriented to psychology, a discipline in education that, I argued previously, has historically been functional in purpose. Typically the meaning of critical thinking in educational practice is behaviorally or cognitively defined. It is not concerned with an understanding of the relations of self and society, nor with unmasking the facades of daily life to understand the pretensions, deceptions, and self-deceptions that organize individuals' lives. Rather, critical thinking concerns problem solving in which the parameters of relations are already established and flexibility in settings have limited degrees of ambiguity. Thinking occurs in a world of harmony, stability, and rationally ordered change. It is a notion that is appropriate for middle-level bureaucracy and business; critical thinking does not mean creating questions that are systemic or historical.

The epistemologies and strategies of reform homogenize and universalize social phenomena. The problem is one of administrative intervention in, and control over, the school world. There is a movement toward the production of regimented, isolated, and self-policing subjects; it is to this element of the administrative rules that I now turn. Here through references to psychology, research, testing, and measurement, the administrative categories of teacher education reform interface with other institutional practices and discourses. The distinctions and categories relate governmental standards with what I examined previously as a research and university discourses about reform (see Chapters 4–6). We can begin to understand at this point the interrelation of various and seemingly distinct institutional practices through scrutiny of discourse.

Organizing the Control of the Socially Disadvantaged

The focus on administrative efficiency in the governmental rules is a strategy to bring "deviant" interest claims and sociopolitical orientations under control. Debates in the wider community and within the educational arena become translated into technical and semiotic disputes, removed from their structural relations and activist purposes. In this process, the power relations of those engaged in the debate are defused and the issues transmogrified into a naturalized language of administration. The exercise of power becomes invisible through a discourse that obscures the politics of the pronouncements.

The neutralizing of social conflict is evident in the language and tone of the teacher education standards. The directives represent the program rules as necessary for certification of all teachers. The standards imply that the pupil makeup of all schools is such that all schools are in need of teachers who know the specified topics. Remediation, "at-risk" children, juvenile justice and delinquency are topics placed beside learning about child development and school services. As everything is given the same surface priority, then all must be equal. However, the specific language, ordering, and content focus of these standards allow a different message to emerge. The control to be exerted is clearly intended for those individuals and groups who diverge from the norm.

One example of the logic of the ordering of the 1988 Wisconsin regulations (items 4.08-3 to 4.08-10) will suffice. Student teachers are required to study the diverse backgrounds of pupils (item 3), then (in the order of the regulation text) children "at risk," the welfare system (5), and special pupil services (6). Following this, they are asked to study educational psychology and learning theories (7), and immediately afterwards to study methods of identifying and evaluating behaviors as they affect learning (8).

The sequence incorporates its own messages about how these groups (which, by inference, are expected to pose most problems for schools) are to be dealt with. It may be that the particular sequence is accidental; if so, it could not have been calculated to demonstrate more clearly the groups that are deemed in need of a "positive physical, psychological and social teaching and learning environment" (item 9) and that require the application of good classroom management and organizational skills (item 10), not to mention those for whom testing will be seen to be most necessary. That which appears to be a set of minimum prescriptions for all merely disguises a particular form of regulation for those who are socially and economically at a disadvantage.

Promoting equality in schools has a paradoxical effect through these regulations. It makes it possible to consider narrow, social-engineering technologies without much public outcry. This production of social categories and technologies is part of longer-term processes in which the Wisconsin standards are defined. Years of federal funding for small-scale projects have redefined marginal groups by introducing classification systems that make them subject to greater supervision under the label of "at risk." The mobilization of a discourse about "at-risk" children is assisted by professional literature and research that uses the category as descriptions of school failures and remediation. The state teacher education regulations draw on this "common sense" of schooling.

Officially set categories make it possible to assist groups through mechanisms channeling demands into language and practices that re-contextualize and reformulate the issues. Sociologically significant, the fight by blacks, Hispanics, and other "minorities" for proper acknowl-edgment of their children's educational plight and for better funding for their schools is produced within processes that normalize their strug-gle into systems of remediation. These systems introduce new forms of observation, supervision, and control. These implications of the regula-tions are obscured, since the issues of learning, teaching, success, or failure appear as procedural problems rather than social issues.

While the language of the new requirements is meant to diffuse tensions, that is not always the case. In California in the last ten years, the arguments responding to the growth of non-English-speaking eth-nic groups produced regulations governing the credentialing of teachers that include an English-language competence test as a prerequisite for teaching certification. The new subject-matter inclusions in Wisconsin point to the contradictory location of academics. While language study, reading, and mathematics have received more space in the new creden-tialing, the instrumental language has produced criticism within these fields. The requirements undermine the social position of other academ-ics. The effort to include specific social agendas to mute criticism has, in some instances, increased debate, as in the California bilingual require-ments.

State Universities and the New Expertise

The sanctioned effects of the administrative categories are found in the form dissent takes at the university. Legislative and administrative meetings held prior to the passage of the administrative rules focused attention on the specifics of the promulgated rules rather than on the assumptions and implications of the discourse itself. Once passed, fac-ulty agendas in teacher education were framed by the administrative rules. For four years since the initial regulations were passed (1986–1990), meetings about teacher education on the Madison campus con-cerned creating new courses and rewriting course syllabi to contain the language of the administrative rules in order to verify the coursework in case of a state audit.

More important are the implications of the governmental adminis-trative rules for the social field and power relations within the univer-sity. Rules about the curriculum and experiences mandated for teacher education reposition academic power. The rules give legitimacy to a particular expertise and hiring priorities within educational departments. These have potential to modify the internal power relations of schools of education. The rules for instruction in testing, measurement of competencies, counseling, and reading skills sanction disciplinary agendas that exist in schools of education agendas and that have a strong constituency within schools. The institutional appeal of the taxonomies of reform is that they fit existing networks of resource allocation although recasting and giving a privileged position to particular networks that previously were not strong within teacher education programs.[3]

The instrumental discourse of reform assigns greater credibility to university experts who have mastered the new codes of administration. The "new" faculty leader is one who attends all hearings and committee meetings on teacher education. It is the task of the expert to decipher the administrative codes for colleagues, organize committees to audit the implementation processes, and travel to meetings to discuss the codes with other faculty. The code interpreters occupy an administrative space within schools of education that previously were the domain of faculty from educational administration departments. The concerns are programmatic and related to working with state government departments.

The subtle result of the current reforms is the particular coalitions that emerge with authority to speak and the right to be heard. Teacher education is positioned in schools of education with increased legitimacy. University schools of education have been academically organized by departments of educational administration and intellectually defined by departments of educational psychology (see, e.g., Labaree, 1990b; Schneider, 1987). The new coalitions tend to blur these distinctions as teacher education becomes a priority in research and program development. At the same time, academic capital is obtained for governance of schools of education by faculty in previously marginal departments of curriculum, special education, and teacher education.

Structures of Power Relations and the Production of Texts

One way to understand the changing power relations in the current reforms is to historically consider the emergence of texts as a steering mechanism for social policy. Until recently, formal texts have not been an important element in the construction of a U.S. society. At a very general level, one could point to documents that are significant as symbols of the history of the country and its folklore. Texts such as the Constitution provide only a general mantle under which the tensions of change, demands, and struggles within society are considered.

Most U.S. social institutions have been structured without the invention of formal steering texts, their functions or purposes defined in a manner that seems similar to the development of common law. This role of the text is evident in the behavioral methodology of modern political science. Political science was originally concerned with legislative texts to describe the political process. Behavioral studies, in contrast, focused on the conditions, group interactions, and social interests that influenced the production and implementation of policy (Dahl, 1961). This was viewed as a methodological revolution. We can compare this to Western European state systems. The merging of religion and government into a highly centralized and strong state made the formulation of official texts an important element in studies of political processes.

The particular U.S. state formations have implications for the processes of schooling. U.S. schooling had, until recently, no significant national documents about purpose or direction. There has been no ministry of education and only occasional legislation to serve as landmarks. Prominent texts in schooling were, to a large extent, nonexistent, with historians turning to Horace Mann's reports to the Massachusetts State Legislature in the 1840s, the nongovernmental Committees of Ten or Eight recommendations, and post hoc explanations about formal texts in the emergence of school curriculum. School practice was given legitimacy and direction through a generalized faith about an educated citizenry and local control, rather than through explicit governmental or administrative statements. Non-state-directed negotiations in communities served to interpret and direct school practices within general parameters that in fact did relate to national discourses about schooling (see Tlusty, 1986).

The lack of texts to establish social solidarity is expressed in the focus of school pedagogy. Emphasis has been on "upbringing" throughout public schooling, making socialization patterns a central concern. There emerged in high school strong sports programs and extracurricular activities, which exist as club activities outside of schools in European continental countries, and in elementary schools "child-centered" pedagogy. For the most part, the focus on interactional processes is legitimated by 19th-century lore about face-to-face interactions and communicative qualities that are to establish the requisites of social solidarity and national identity.

As I have argued, the nonformal mechanisms of social regulation served well in education until the post–World War II period. The older mechanisms of control lost their ability to mobilize and give direction, requiring new institutional formations to steer schooling. The importance given to classroom interaction research, qualitative methods, and microcultural anthropologies of schooling are indications of changing patterns of social regulation (Popkewitz, 1981). Field methods begin to compete for academic legitimacy in curriculum and learning research during the 1970s. In-depth accounts and interpretations of teachers' and children's practices provide more intrusive mechanisms for guiding everyday policy. (See also James's 1986 account of anthropology as part of the social regulation of schools during the Depression.) Rising concerns about urban disruption, changing values of students who go to schools, and new economic priorities encompass expectations, attitudes, and demands that are different from those found in the existing curriculum. These changes sanction the utilization of field methods (Popkewitz, 1984, ch. 4).

Formal texts about school policy, regulation, and administration provide a different form by which a definition of social agendas is articulated. The language of regulation is cast as a universal one, full of mythic imagery and religious calling. There is a moral and passionate language about culture, global economic competition, and the social cohesion needed to unite a nation. At a different layer, a current concern of subject-matter teaching is to reverse the international focus and to make the formal texts in schooling more significant.

The Wisconsin administrative texts over the past decade can be viewed as a microcosm in which specific practices interrelate and broader trends are formed and articulated. Governmental texts exist in relation to the development of greater executive regulation and the cultural authority of educational sciences in establishing categories of differentiation. The style of presentation and categories indicate priorities and specific strategies in the reconstitution of regulation discussed earlier. The divisions, categories, and distinctions in the regulations become the common sense about schools.

I can summarize the implications of the administrative texts in the following way. The official discourse of the texts signifies a direction, a sense of will and purpose that organizes educational practice in at least three ways, independent of the authors' intended effects (see, e.g., Bourdieu, 1989b, p. 23). These are

1. The texts comprise a diagnostic that asserts recognition of what a person is and what every person is universally due. They assign an identity. Fixed in the administrative practices and detailed procedures are rules and obligations about the differentiations of behavior that separate, rank, and organize individuals.
2. Administrative discourses indicate what people have to do, who and what they are. The texts contain a system of rules that govern what talk about education is possible and who are to be

regarded as serious talkers. The public texts define which knowledge about current affairs is selected (or suppressed), shaped, and presented as interpretations of human experience.

3. The texts establish what people have done, as exemplified in certification programs. The credentialing rules are seen as the repository of the common sense about teaching and schooling.

TEACHER INCENTIVES AND SOCIAL REGULATION

At a different layer of governance are the school practices concerned with changing the work of teachers. Since 1980, school reforms have been initiated by almost every state in the nation to improve the quality of teaching. A central theme in the reforms is to make teachers more professional and, therefore, more qualified and more satisfied. The use of the word *professionalism*, however, is produced within a set of relations that have continuity and, at the same time, breaks with occurrences in the 19th century. It is these distinctions that I would like to explore in the realization of the state of Wisconsin's experimental projects concerned with improving teachers' working conditions. The Wisconsin Incentive Program maintains a generalized focus found in the national reform reports, research categories, and administrative rules, although it is realized in particular social relations.

After submitting plans to a state advisory committee, eight school districts were given matching state funds for pilot programs that could serve as the basis of eventual state regulations. In 1986–1987, three districts were selected by researchers for in-depth case studies to investigate the manner in which incentives were realized (for a report of this study, see Popkewitz and Lind, 1989). The school districts contained a mixture of suburban and rural populations; two were bedroom communities near a large Wisconsin city, while the third was located in a rural area but near a college. Teaching staff, administrators, and laypeople were involved in the construction of the program in each district.

The incentive programs varied in their organization and focus. One district was to experiment with a staff development program, experienced "mentor" teachers to help first-year teachers, and a career ladder that divided teaching into different levels of competence. Each level was accompanied by a differential salary schedule. A second district adopted a performance assessment of teachers, a professional staff development program, and a recognition-and-reward system for teachers that incorporated a career ladder. The third focused on an incentive program that provided a differentiated salary schedule for its teachers. While the reform's rhetoric spoke of improving teachers' working conditions, the daily practices, organizations, and epistemological rules produced particular technologies of regulation.

Discussions in the various school districts about improving teachers' work reasserted the more general rhetoric about the professional quality of teaching, at points drawing on arguments found in national reports about school reform. Teachers and administrators described the tension and stress inherent in their jobs. These included demands that teachers confront multiple levels of achievement in large classes of students, limitations of available materials, and pressures of maintainence and control during an eight-hour day.

Initial district discussions about the reforms focused on the conditions of teachers' work. One district formed an "Our Nation-At-Risk Committee" to consider how school conditions could be altered to respond to the issues raised in numerous national reports. In another school, teachers talked about the Holmes Group (1986) report to improve teaching and teacher education and the Carnegie Forum on Education and the Economy (1986) report to describe more adequate plans for the way teachers spend their time. Original project proposals included programs designed to improve the conditions of teachers' work. Release time for teachers, sabbaticals, reorganization of the school day, team-teaching arrangements, and exchange programs where teachers worked in other districts for a year were to be part of the reform practices.

The specific set of power relations produced through the reform strategies adopted can be examined by considering four elements. First is the assumption that a common framework of experience and goals existed. A second is the intensification of teachers' work. Third is increased monitoring through new evaluation schemes. Fourth is the limiting of teacher autonomy; the public rhetoric about professionalism was transformed to questions of motivation, efficiency, and self-management. These transformations occurred in each of the three school districts, although differences were reflected in the local organization of the reform programs.

Assumptions of a Common Framework
of Experience and Goals

The reform practices assumed that a common framework of experience existed for all and that the goal of the reform was to identify the most appropriate strategies for rewarding teachers for increased work. In defining district projects, discussions focused on broad statements of purpose that were juxtaposed with the specific details and procedures related to problems of implementation. Practice was organized as though there were agreed-upon rules and regulations that needed only to be operationalized, such as whether teacher preparation time or travel time for a conference should apply toward career ladder advancement.

Let me provide an example. At a meeting to discuss the viability of a career ladder, the committee listed the purposes of the project: A career ladder should foster "encouragement, enrichment, enhancement of growth; flexibility to advance opportunity; better teaching, improved staff; fairness in evaluation; accountability." (Popkewitz & Lind, 1989, p. 580). These statements are slogans—emotional appeals to elicit interest, cooperation, and possibly commitment. The slogans, however, did not represent any sustained public discussion about the work of teaching; they were systematically ambiguous, leaving the nature of the district's plan of action unclarified. Procedures developed around a broad language of consensus that served as a symbolic canopy. It enabled the committee to take for granted the patterns of regulation that organized teaching, even though individual teachers did express reservations.

Far from being mere technicalities, the operational choices carried substantive implications for the values and patterns of teachers' work. While teachers viewed the standardization with uneasiness, their efforts to find alternatives often were channeled in ways that produced new forms of regulation, since they included more work-related routines and evaluation procedures.

Intensification of Work

Certain assumptions about the organization of reform emerged in the ongoing practices across school districts: Teachers should do more work than they are doing; increased monitoring would improve teachers' competence; monitoring should be objective so as to eliminate judgments and biases; the increased work and monitoring should be systematically organized to provide a new hierarchy for teachers to allocate financial reward. These assumptions were common to each site despite the fact that each of the three school districts had different incentive projects.

Different strategies increased the work of teachers. One approach was monetary rewards for projects thought to improve teaching. Teachers would write a proposal and explain what its specific outcome would be. At the end of the project, teachers submitted evidence of outcomes to receive the stipend. While intended to recognize special teacher projects, projects simply rewarded teachers for new, more specific record-keeping of what many said they were already doing: attending conferences and workshops or planning special activities, such as taking children on outings. A second approach was a career ladder, which involved evaluating teachers four times each year. The results were to increase their salary levels by enabling them to apply for master teacher or teacher specialist positions. Model/mentor teachers provided a third incentive strategy. Some teachers were chosen to receive a monetary reward and release time to work with new teachers. The model/mentor teachers had to complete 20 activity units each semester to receive the monetary reward. Each activity unit required a teacher to conduct either a one-hour faculty seminar during afterschool hours or to observe instruction by another district teacher for one hour. District teachers received a $15 stipend each time they attended a topical seminar.

In one community the practice of accounting for teachers' time to receive extra money was related to the conservative political climate of the community. It was the administrators' perception that the school board elections had indicated a need for fiscal constraint and a reaction to any programs that might seem too liberal. These administrators sought to counterbalance that public pressure by producing new record-keeping that would assure the public that the school district workforce was efficient, professionally competent, and fiscally responsible.

Monitoring as a Discourse of Power

Each incentive program linked increased teacher rewards with evaluation. The form taken in the evaluation procedures provided routinized procedures by which actions were to be standardized and judged. This ties issues of power and gender to concerns for a differentiated staff and increased teacher monitoring, an issue discussed below.

Reform practices assumed that the problem of teaching was a momentary weakness in planning that evaluation could overcome through more intelligent ordering of lessons and organization. The evaluations assumed (1) the existence of agreed-upon standards that can demonstrate effective teaching and (2) planned performance criteria in which teaching is dissected into subparts to be measured. These measurements, usually identified by some specific behavioral attribute, were assumed to be evidence of good teaching.

The mentor program, for example, required that each teacher have exemplary evaluations. These evaluations were based on performance criteria that listed specific behaviors that were to occur in each lesson. These performance criteria would, in turn, be used to supervise first-year teachers or veteran teachers who requested assistance. The purpose of this practice was to standardize teaching as new teachers were inducted into the school system.

Teacher lesson planning was seen as important in determining competence. Lessons for each part of the day were prepared and made available to supervisors as part of the new evaluation. Administrators reasoned that the new rating system would make teachers more conscious of the value of systematic planning and thus improve their teaching.

Yet for many teachers and administrators, the demand for systematic lesson planning produced a ritualized performance that had little to do with issues of teacher creativity, professional competence, or the actual conditions of instruction. Teachers perceived the planning as a prescribed pattern in which they identified the problem and recorded a recipe for its solution to satisfy an administrator. The lesson planning required them to reproduce and gather materials to be available during the week. This entailed weekend work that previously had been done during the school day. The incentive rewards and evaluations eliminated consideration of longer-range concerns of practice in favor of those that were more capable of producing an immediate outcome.

A project committee in a different school district invited the head of a commercial company to discuss its teacher evaluation kit. In opening remarks to the school staff, a professor, who directed the company, said the national discussions about schools required outsiders to construct objective, rational evaluation measures because teachers could not do it, as they "wear their hearts on their sleeves" (Popkewitz & Lind, 1989, p. 588). Administrators, board members, and teachers were told that the evaluation observation scheme provides a simple administrative organization that any person can use to evaluate a teacher. Evaluations assign "word descriptors"—from a long list such as *purposeful, expressive,* and *scholarly*—to the teaching they watch. Each of the words has a designated point value that, when summarized through simple addition, defines a teacher's strengths and weaknesses.

While the evaluation procedure was viewed as administrative and not normative, the procedures and words embodied particular values and ideologies. These biases can be illustrated by focusing on the evaluation's descriptors of *purposeful, expressive,* and *scholarly*. In the context of the evaluation, *purpose* in a lesson referred to direct instruction in which a set of precise objectives is articulated and practices are directly related to achieved outcomes; that is, frontal teaching. Purpose as a directly observable outcome was assigned a higher point value than the characteristics labeled *expressive* or *scholarly*. The procedure valued knowledge that is directly useful, and, in turn, devalued reflective or contemplative knowledge for which there may be no immediate application.

We can begin to focus here on the subtle implications of gender, social regulation, and teaching. Expressive knowledge is culturally associated with female qualities, behaviors not rewarded in this evaluation scheme. The comment about "teachers wearing their hearts on their sleeves" can be linked with the devaluing of expressive elements of teaching. This issue of gender is not straightforward but is intermingled with the historical situations of teachers, such that it impacts on all—male and female—who work in school situations.

Anti-intellectualism is another aspect of the evaluation. Scholarly work, associated with an intellectual playfulness of ideas, was to be replaced with a style of thought that emphasized predictability and criteria of controllability. The evaluation defined teaching as discrete and fragmented segments that could be managed more efficiently. The systems of selecting and ordering "fit" the management style associated with the bureaucracy of schooling. Judgments about the worth, direction, and appropriateness of the work tasks were made by experts outside the workplace. The values that underlie the evaluation, however, were never debated but were assumed to be procedures proclaiming the efficacy of science, research, and objectivity.

Redefining of teacher behaviors in these monitoring schemes is an important part of the normalization of control. There is evidence in the study that the new criteria of administration were incorporated into the discourse teachers used to discuss their work. The incentives and career ladder embodied strategies that objectively separated individuals by rank through various systems of ordering, reporting, and evaluating their work. In this context, the individual in the school emerged as an object of political and scientific concern, but the issues of power were muted in the discourse of reform. The evaluation procedures made the exercise of power invisible as new forms to rationalize attributes and behaviors were created and then opened to scrutiny and manipulation.

Professionalism as a Common Language

Acceptance of increased monitoring and work intensification are elements of a more general rhetoric about professionalization. Much of the teaching literature maintains a view of professionalism as the development of autonomy and responsibility. The discussion is based on a number of ideal characteristics, such as control over entry, professional ethics, and a scientific/technical language. In the incentive program, the scientific/technical language assumed importance for achieving professional status. Teachers viewed increased evaluation and record-keeping as part of the complicated process of being professional. It was perceived as a means by which teachers demonstrate the knowledge and skill that they possess.

One project slogan, "Confidence in Our Competence," was related to teachers' beliefs that a common, technical language would enable them to think of their teaching as a science, offering an analogy to medicine. The management language of behavioral objectives and performance measurements used in lesson planning provided a feeling of commonality, community, and objectivity.

Yet the language created a poverty of expression about teachers' knowledge. As one examines the common language, its unidimensionality becomes apparent. Priorities transformed teachers' work into actions that can be defined in explicit, hierarchical, linear, and sequential ways. The importance of aesthetics, the playfulness of experience, and the use of intuition were lost. The "common" language of the reforms refocused teachers' understanding on a narrow range of communicative competencies.

The strategies in the reform program and the language of professionalism embedded in them represent a fundamental contradiction. They called for teachers to be more responsible yet defined a world that called for less competence. The reform practices focused attention on extra work and more monitoring that turned teaching into questions of efficiency and evaluation. This occurred in all three sites, although there were local variations in the responses.

The reform practices focused on sets of procedures that condensed complex interactions and events in a manner that made their recitation seem comprehensible and coherent. The public discourse about teacher incentives became a language that teachers used to express their hopes and aspirations. Many teachers and teacher educators recognized negative implications of elements of the incentive programs but were unable to speak in a collective voice to protest the transformation of work issues into administrative problems. The writing of lesson plans and of the administrative rules themselves projected images of competence, responsibility, and efficiency that helped some teachers feel a sense of accomplishment; yet the symbolic manipulation had little to do with objective conditions or long-term changes in the teachers' work. The symbols and performances of the reform programs were a dramatic enactment of affiliation, while the reform patterns were an element in the redesign of the regulatory patterns for teachers' work.

We might ask at this juncture why teachers accepted the need for greater monitoring of their work. This "need" can be related to the language of professionalization in the social-political contexts of schooling and teaching. In the different districts, evaluations were intended to improve teaching and prove to the public that teachers were professionally competent. The teachers' acceptance of evaluation schemes involved multiple factors. Teachers perceived them as important for achieving greater status and financial reward—evaluations would establish criteria of worth. The participants (teachers, school board members, and administrators) thought that evaluation procedures would make it easier to ask for higher teacher salaries, arguing that teacher performance was being improved. Teachers thought the evaluations would also provide the opportunity for peer interaction and therefore a way to overcome feelings of isolation.

RECONSTITUTING THE GOVERNING AND REGULATION OF SCHOOLING: THE CIRCULATION AND EFFECTS OF POWER IN REWORKING DEMOCRACY

The social significance of the Wisconsin reforms lies in bringing into practice certain generative sets of rules and resources by which performance and competence are to be determined. In the following section I would like to explore certain themes about power raised throughout the book but given a particular focus in the current discussion. These are

1. There is an increased focus on the executive interventions of government.
2. The instrumental discourse of reform refocuses and reformulates social issues into procedural and administrative tasks. Various social and cultural interests are deconceptualized and reformulated into problems of efficiency and effectiveness.
3. The rhetoric of participation replaces practices of democratic participation.
4. Power relations are made invisible through the epistemology and the institutional relations established.

An implication of these different elements is a redesigning and narrowing of the notion of democracy.

The Executive Interventions

The Wisconsin teacher education and teacher reforms are part of a larger process in which the executive branch of government has assumed a greater role in formulating and realizing policy. While public discussion still contains residues of the mythologies of local control of schooling, the fiscal and cognitive steering has become more centralized and less responsive to local concerns. This regulation, as I indicated in earlier chapters, is contained in the epistemological practices by which distinctions are made authoritative in schooling. It is also related to who is authorized to speak. In Chapter 4, the emergent position of state governors and administrative agencies in education was initially explored.

The shift in governance is only partially explained by considering legislative acts or overt social actors. Credentialing in Wisconsin teacher education occurred through the construction of administrative rules for teacher education that did not entail legislative action. In the promulgation of the administrative rules, the Department of Public Instruction argued that the rules were not policy and did not entail increased financial commitments, arguments that the legislative oversight committee accepted.[4] The legislature did allocate funds for the teacher incentive project, but those funds were part of the administrative budget initiated by the state agency.

These instances illustrate how social policy can be made through an administrative agency, with only minor involvement of the legislative branch of government. The pattern of governing through administrative agencies follows, in certain ways, practices established as the modern state formed during the Progressive Era. At that time, to counter the authority of local political parties and the judiciary, centralization of governmental control was achieved through the construction of administrative agencies. These agencies had legal authority to legislate in particular domains, such as interstate commerce and, later, banking. In the current reforms, regulation is formulated through administrative agencies whose official functions are related to carrying out policy. In this instance, as well as in the case of the creation of a national board for developing a teacher certification examination, formulation and realization of policy occur within the administrative agencies.

To criticize this development, however, is not to criticize centralization or standardization per se. I say this because there are numerous examples in highly centralized Scandinavian states of pursuing goals of equality and justice through national policy, sometimes having to overcome local parochialism that runs counter to national purposes (see, e.g., Granheim, Kogan, & Lundgren, 1990). The actions of the federal government in fighting segregation in the southern United States is another example of central power that promoted the common good. The problem of governance is also not one of standards (vs. standardization). Standards that reflect and respond to ethical, epistemological, and political commitments of schooling, for example, are feasible, and there is a long curriculum history in which examples of standards have been considered, from John Dewey and Charles Rugg to the work of Arnold Bellack. My concern is that the social and epistemological assumptions circulating as current reform standards mystify the problems of schooling and decontextualize the profound and complex issues of curriculum.

The formation of an executive government needs to be placed within contexts of the relations in which factions coalesce across institutional boundaries. Governmental administrative rules and participatory arrangements of the incentive program combine with and relate to other institutional patterns. Earlier, I identified factions coalescing in response to calls for reform and the selection of research problems to define schooling. The governmental administrative rules produce factions within the university that seek more administrative control, professional reading teacher associations that aspire to have all future teachers take extra courses in reading, and unions who want control over who enters the field. The incentive program, at a different layer, combines interests of teacher unions, school administrators, and state agency planners.

The coincidence of events across institutions produces a conjunction of different social fields. There is a realignment within and across institutions as new coalitions assume dominant positions in the negotiations undertaken. Certain types of expertise come to dominate, creating a particular form and content in participation. The relative strength of the coalitions within the institutions and their self-evaluating patterns are altered. The changes that occur are not merely in the production of new regulations or the production of particular work arrangements.

This trend in the United States toward centralization of governance seems in opposition to the direction of countries that have strong centralized traditions of governing. In Sweden and Spain, for example, the parliaments are creating stronger regional and communal authorities. The centralized government's new role is to set policy guidelines and outcome measures. The results of these practices and those in the United States, however, may be a mixture of centralized and decentralized practices of school governing.

Instrumental Rationality and
the Construction of a School Common Sense

It is in the multiple and regional patterns of the reforms that the effects of power are understood. State educational agencies actively sought to reform schools through long-range planning and anticipating problems in teacher education and teachers' work conditions. The instrumental vision posited a common framework of experience and a consensus about goals. At a daily level, the common sense of schooling was defined by standardized and routinized procedures. In both school and university settings, discussion focused on the sanctioned categories and distinctions. When debate and dissent entered into the public arena, it was either marginalized or structured out of consideration. The refocusing and reformulation of educational and social issues obscured the various social and cultural interests that compete for social space in schooling.

A technicalization of work further eroded teacher autonomy and responsibility in the immediate control of the teacher environment.[5] Reform practices moved from redesigning the conditions of labor to confronting psychological problems. Incentives were intended to improve teachers' motivation within existing patterns and power relations. While the public rhetoric spoke of empowering teachers through professional practices, the strategies adopted limited reflection to the development of techniques. Procedures came to be considered devoid of reference to specific purposes and goals. Purposeful, rational discourse is a form of regulation that emerges as a consequence of the strategy applied.

An irony of current strategies is that the standardization involved a further incorporation of bureaucratic structures. The organizing of teacher education courses and the hiring of staff at the university to fulfill new requirements were directed by the priorities and distinctions posed in the credentialing rules. The talk of school district meetings about incentives assumed that increased monitoring was of value—focusing on performance criteria that separated elements of teachers' work from a consideration of the intellectual or social dimension of teaching. A consequence has been to reduce teacher autonomy and redefine responsibility. The particular instrumental interpretations are related and embodied in the particular coalitions established across institutions.

The Rhetoric of Participation and the Practices of Democracy

Defining of teaching and teacher education as an administrative province occurs under the rhetoric of democratic control. Public discussions focus on making teacher education and teaching more accountable and more professional—goals that at face value have conflicting tendencies. Teacher education is to demonstrate its responsiveness to the wider community by being subject to accountability measures in the form of (and interpreted through) administrative regulation. Through

words like *professionalism* and *accountability*, teachers and teacher educators are to rationalize their work and provide indicators that define
performance and competence. The creation of differential staffing patterns is intended to provide teachers with more autonomy and responsibility.

The rhetoric of participation and professional accountability provides a way to connect administrative values with larger social beliefs.
Credential systems are made to seem a reflection of changing priorities
in the community, with changes open to public debate via legislative
and administrative hearings prior to the passage of a new code. The
teacher incentive program was meant to respond to the particular local
needs and school organization. Participation was sought from various
actors in the local community—school board members, teacher unions,
and administrators.

The categories and distinctions within participation are given legitimacy by political interest group theory. It is assumed that progress
and the general good are achieved through the individual pursuit of
self-interest. The sum of these interests produces a social contract that
maximizes both individual and collective good. In modern societies, it
is argued, the complexities of ruling require that individual interests be
articulated through associations and groups that compete in the public
space for the allocation of values. The question of who rules is posed as
the competing of multiple groups in which the outcome of negotiation
produces public policy.

In this version of democracy, the criterion of participation is inclusion of interest as defined by group or role. Thus one considers equity
as participation of role groups—that is, whether community members,
teachers, administrators, students, or constituent groups are involved
in planning. A notion of "community" assumes negotiations among
the various groups who have equal power. For example, the governance
in the incentive programs was assumed to be participatory since board
members, teachers, laypeople, and administrators were represented.
Democracy becomes a form of role theory that defines participation as
representation of different groups in the processes of decision making.

Ignored was the bias that made certain types of solutions and proposals more "relevant" than others. The role of staff in framing the
agenda for participatory settings in the state credential program, for
example, is not considered in developing teacher education certification
practices. Nor are the epistemologies of schooling that sanction certain
types of speech and actors as authoritative considered in the incentive
program. Rather, the form of participation is emphasized and lauded as
a form of democratic control, while the generation of administrative

work undercuts that democratic impulse. In these instances, issues of schooling and teachers' work are narrowly defined in relation to procedural issues.

Participation formed within an instrumental rationality contains two seemingly different implications for social regulation. The administrative rules distance participants from the sources of interest involved through the distinctions and categories formed. Attention is not directed to specific people who form the rules, but to the regulations that focus attention on what the *program requires*. No person or agency seems in control. Responsibility for the quality of teaching and teacher education becomes diffused through the symbolic rituals of democracy, while various patterns of social regulation proliferate ostensibly to ensure accountability. Further, distinctions of a political interest group theory make the categories of groups, not epistemology, the criteria of legitimacy. The standards of truth and the criteria of individual competence remain unscrutinized.

Proliferation of practices make it difficult to argue about the style of argument presented. Opposition to the administrative rules is marginalized or framed in relation to publicly sanctioned categories and distinctions. The rituals of reform make its structural relations as a matter of assumption.

Making Power Invisible: Formal Texts and State Practices

Strategies for educational change contain their own relations of power, not only representing existing structures but also articulating power arrangements themselves. The reforms link social changes with people's knowledge of the world in a manner that can enable individuals to feel satisfied that the processes will effectively serve personal as well as social ends. There is a blurring of the boundaries between our own thoughts and actions and those that are given to us in the practices that form our collective efforts. The rules and standards provide ways in which individuals are to monitor their conception of "self" within institutional relations. In this manner, the reform discourse provides self-regulation and monitoring.

In this instance, we can talk about the effects of power. Teacher practices embody epistemological rules and, at the same time, contribute to the production of rules and standards that are to monitor their work. Within the school system, for example, the new work of teachers to develop "grant" proposals is lauded, but this practice typically means learning an instrumental language and style of thinking associated with writing grants and proposals. At the university as well, the university's own "self"-management is bound to long-range changes in which administrative and budgeting controls are brought into the internal organization, including the gradual replacement of the "older" cultural orientations of university officers. This is an irony of the modern university. While it is structurally positioned at the intersection of social, cultural, and economic arenas, its leaders have tended to be tied to the older humanist traditions of the academy. The past few decades have altered that pattern of leadership; greater stress is now placed on business skills rather than academic legitimacy. The new University of Wisconsin president and the chancellor of the Madison campus are, for the first time, appointed people who see themselves as administrators, not as academics who are working in administration.

The changing internal power relations tend to make certain kinds of expertise dominant within the university. There is a need for people who understand and can negotiate with the state agencies and legislature, emphasizing administration, political negotiation, and monitoring of regulation compliance. These experts with instrumental reasoning assume academic, if not intellectual, power.

Reformulations of the relations of power impose new interpretations of the state in schooling. Older notions of the state as a composite of the governmental agencies that issue rules and regulations in civil society are no longer a viable way to understand how power is exercised, values allocated, and choices made. The emerging relations are not merely the product of a corporatist state, in that dominant interests assign the implementation of policy to other nonstate coalitions within society. The notion of state involves more than the issuance of regulations, the role of governmental agencies, or the traditional problem of who makes decisions about educational programs or course content. Elements within government and civil society, such as universities and professional groups, interrelate in forming patterns of social regulation. The changes impose a redefinition of the meaning of democracy. Not only have the interests represented been narrowed; participation exists within a restricted range of problems and possibilities.

CONCLUSIONS

The concerns about the narrowing of democracy are the conclusions of this chapter and a summary of previous chapters. The limiting of the conditions of and the manner in which people participate in schooling is not the outcome of macrorelations that produce a progression of domination by those who rule. Rather, the narrowing of democracy results from a variety of institutional relations and epistemological rules. There is a conjunction through the formation of public policy and the construction of school practices.

The administrative rules and the teacher incentive programs discussed in this chapter, like the public policy statements of reform and educational research programs, are expressed in the most humanistic and progressive terms. They are to bring democracy to all, to provide for economic growth and cultural revival, and to foster individual development. But with the millennial dreams and progressive rhetoric comes the creation of technologies that enter into and organize daily life and its hopes and desires. In focusing on the interrelations and effects of power, however, I recognize that the embodiment of power in the knowledge and institutional patterns is not without resistance and oppositional practices.

There is a literature in education which holds that instrumental practices can be viewed as rituals of accountability and public legitimation in institutions; those rituals are different from the everyday practices of organizational life. This literature about organizations, as loosely coupled, argues that the rationality of rules and procedures helps to make the school seem modern, advanced, and fulfilling its tasks—and thus deserving continual public faith (e.g., Weick, 1976). The formal organization is viewed as having little to do with the actual interactions and norms of daily life in schools. It would be an error, however, to accept this distinction between public face and everyday interactions of schooling. The epistemologies of reform are embodied in and are a dynamic element in the ongoing relations and formation of identity in schooling. Under the labels of professionalism and accountability, a practical discourse defines possibilities of the teaching situation. New rules that routinize teachers' work have become plausible, since status is to be gained through performance tied to a notion of "science." These practices have been served by a professional literature and national reform reports that focus on strategies and procedures of implementation. To separate discourse and institutional practices is to misconstrue how power circulates at multiple and interweaving layers.

Contemporary reform practices contain words of professionalism and science that have been a part of the vocabulary of schooling since the 19th century. They have been and are elements of social regulation in schooling. Their assumptions and implications changed as the ecology of the epistemologies and institutional patterns contained new social relations. It is with a social and historical method that I sought to understand the social relations established.

8

The Problem of Change and Educational Sciences

Notes on the Relations of Knowledge, Intellectuals, and Social Movements

In this final chapter, I return to the conceptual themes raised about change in Chapter 1. My purpose here is to outline a theory of educational change. I emphasize a social epistemology in which the concepts and practices of schooling are presented as historically formed social patterns. Central to this conceptualization is change as ruptures in the epistemological and institutional practices of schooling. The intent of this conceptual focus is to deny notions of progress, intent, or teleology in the formulation of educational theories. The view of change, however, is political as well as conceptual. It decenters intellectual claims about progress, the concern of the second part of the chapter. Here, I question the ideas of progress as tied to the social amelioration tradition through utilitarian focus and the acceptance of the progressive role of the state. In the Hegelian traditions of critical sciences, progress is also an inherent principle. History is the progressive fulfillment of people's moral and spiritual destiny. Both, I argue, contain visions of progress that view the intellectual as an authoritative figure in social affairs.

Since the 19th century, science and progress have been bound as a dynamic force with historical development. Reason is located in science, producing the engine of progress in the United States (Ross, 1984). In 19th-century social science, progress was a notion that gave secular authority and political power to the gentry, reversing their exclusion from the various forms of popular democracy that were developing. In contemporary reforms, the idea of progress is retained and legitimates new spokespeople as representing the wisdom of progressive projects.

It is in this context that I write this chapter. While I accept that all social research is a part of its social relations, I reject an epistemology of progress in science and place some pragmatic humility and sociological theory about intellectual work into the political discourse about a science of schooling. To foretell my biases, when claims are made about the future as the product of science, they are to be rejected as science and seen as part of the social position of educational scientists to gain cultural and social capital. I look on any claims of science (or scientists) to possess superior strategic knowledge about social change as containing dangerous ethical, moral, and political consequences for a democracy.[1] I believe an important element of intellectual work is to offer a self-critical stance toward social phenomena, including that of the social fields of intellectuals. This entails an analysis of the conditions that shape the intellectuals' fields of endeavor, their connections to larger systems, and their own internal conditions of engagement and autonomy.

Before proceeding, I recognize that some might object to calling social and educational scientists *intellectuals* or to my use of the word *science*, which is so heavily associated with positivism in the United States. The word *intellectual*, as I use it, attends to the institutional position and social relations of those who produce knowledge rather than to normative criteria about someone who has wisdom and insight. *Intellectual*, then, is a category concerned with the historical formations and social positions of knowledge-producing occupations.[2] For historical reasons described in earlier chapters, the particular intellectual that I am concerned with is one who is practiced in discourses of social science and education—the academic educational researcher. I also recognize that most people who occupy this position in the United States are trained in analytical traditions of science. They place priority on questioning the procedures rather than the rationality of science itself, accepting uncritically their role of explaining and reforming the world. The word *science*, as I discussed earlier, is concerned with the systematic questioning of social affairs that relates theoretical considerations to empirical phenomena. In the United States, positivism has so captured the discourse about social study that those who reject positivism see the word *science* as synonymous with its assumptions and limitations. That view of science is historically shortsighted and narrow.

CHANGE, SOCIAL EPISTEMOLOGY, AND HISTORY

I have focused on the study of change as a problem of social epistemology in this volume. As explained in Chapter 1, *epistemology* considers the rules and standards by which knowledge about the world is formed. The distinctions and categorizations that organize perceptions,

ways of acting, and conceptions of *self* are a central focus. *Social* epistemology places the objects constituted as the knowledge of schooling in
historically formed patterns and power relations. Statements and words
are not signs or signifiers that refer to and fix *things*, but are forms of
social practice. I considered, for example, the changing concepts of reform, professionalism, and educational science within sets of relations
that combined to express and produce the practices of schooling. In
this approach, the knowledge of schooling becomes a social practice
amenable to sociological inquiry.

In light of this strategy to understand change, I asked in this study
how and why it is possible to think about reform as we do. How does
reform as an object of power relations change over time? What are the
implications and consequences of educational reform as it is and has
been practiced in the United States? This political sociology of reform
concerns the kinds of rationality that come to prevail in defining schooling and the power relations they embody.

Toward a Study of Social Epistemology

I have juxtaposed 19th-century practices with contemporary school
reforms to explore how the past is brought into the present. Posing the
relation of the 19th century and the present is not to search for the
origins of phenomena or to trace a chronology, thus producing a linear
narrative of time and space. The 19th century provided certain social
and epistemological patterns that are embedded in contemporary practices. Yet when the present is juxtaposed with the past, there are breaks
as well as continuities. This conception of change can be likened to
Thomas Kuhn's (1970) discussion of the relation between normal and
revolutionary science. Whereas Kuhn gave attention only to the changes
in the ideas of science, my concern is with concepts that exist within
institutions and material practices. This approach, I suspect, will make
some historians, who look for a sequential narrative, feel uneasy. My
history is of the field of reform as social practices and social regulations:
the authorities who code and interpret social experiences, the grid that
gives specification and classification to categories, and institutional patterns that structure the rules of the possible.

We can understand history as breaks and ruptures by focusing on
words of schooling—such as *profession, educational research,* and *teacher
education*—that persist in creating an image of continuity and stability
from the late 19th century to the present. When these words are examined, they give reference to different social patterns at different times.
They embody the social regulations in which schooling is implicated.

Mass schooling in the 19th century was a social innovation that emerged from different movements within society that, at a certain level, worked autonomously from each other. With changes in classroom teaching and teacher education came the rise of the modern university and the formation of social science and psychology; this in turn interrelated with changes in economy, culture, religion, and arenas associated with the state.

The international realignments and national cultural redefinitions of the past few decades, in contrast, have produced different sets of social regulations and a reconstitution of the state as it relates to education. The reforms of the 1980s, as argued in previous chapters, are part of a long-term shift that began after World War II. The economy, professionalization of social institutions and knowledge, and the state have assumed different sets of relations in school steering and regulation than those that existed in preceding periods.[3] The redefinition of behavioral psychology into a cognitive science of instruction is one example of this subsequent reconstruction of the social patterns of regulation. The disciplinary shift is publicly signaled as progress, yet when scrutinized, it becomes clear that certain continuities with past practices are maintained. New configurations that tie knowledge to issues of social regulation are made visible.

The study of school reform can be likened to a thread made up of many fibers. Its strength does not reside in the fact that some fibers run through its whole length, but in the overlapping relations as the many fibers intertwine. Reform practices are not just the practices immediately available for inspection but a composite that transcends the lines of particular people and events as they interact over time.

My focus on epistemology and institutions maintains a relation between the workings of schooling and society. This is to recognize a continual interplay between the social world of which schooling is a part and the dynamics and priorities of the conditions of schooling itself. These include the concerns for school administration, the social differentiations of who comes into mass schooling, and the hierarchical and gendered quality of teaching, among others. But the social history of schooling in this study is different from many contemporary studies, which define purpose and progress in the story that unfolds. Let me briefly explore these differences.

Structural Relations and a Regional Study of Change

The term *regional*, a geographic concept, is helpful here in considering the structural relations that guide the analysis of this study.[4] The geographic term *regional* provides a metaphor for thinking about the detailed practices of institutions and how they interrelate in the production of power. The regionalization of study considers the multiplicity of social forms and power relations that occur in particular historical sites.

To study in a regional manner is, I believe, to avoid placing everything at the door of individual responsibility or deriving power from structural categories without modifying them to be sensitive to historical contingencies. Reform in the early 19th century, for example, was intended to eliminate the evil and sinning of the unfortunate; professionalism in teaching was the task of "professing" Christian sincerity. By the 20th century, reform had come to focus on issues of labor socialization, cultural upbringing, and, at times, problems of creating an enlightened citizenry. Changes in concepts stood not by themselves but within specific social, cultural, economic, and religious transformations. Further, at different layers of schooling and with different implications, there emerged instrumental forms of reasoning as part of the strategies of reform undertaken. What counts as reform, or professionalization if we use this example, has no essential properties or final causes; rather, it refers to objects produced within institutional patterns and power relations.

In its micro and specific context, the study of reform includes multiple events in which people act with purpose toward specific ends; yet the method of study recognizes that the net result of those actions may not be the intended consequences. Durkheim, among others, has helped us consider the infinite variety of thought and conditions in which people constitute their world. While I do not ascribe to Durkheim's functionalism, his search to understand the mutable forms in which social identity is constructed provides entrance into problems of modern social theory:

> For the immense wealth of what has been produced in the past is precisely what makes it illegitimate for us to assign a limit in advance to what man is capable of producing in the future; or to assume that a time will come when, man's capacity for creative innovation being exhausted, he will be doomed merely to repeat himself throughout all eternity. Thus we come to conceive of man not as an agglomeration of finite specifiable elements, but rather as an infinitely flexible, protean force, capable of appearing in innumerable guises, according to the perennially changing demands of his circumstances. (1938/1977, p. 328)

Power, Knowledge, and School Reform

Social epistemology relates to how knowledge is intertwined with institutional worlds to produce power relations. The goal of research is to understand how choice, speech, feeling, and thinking are regulated through a range of anonymous practices in which goals and motivations are inherent.

A study of schooling to interpret the productive quality of power becomes almost commonsensical as a starting point. Schooling is a major reform of modernity. It redefined the issues of upbringing and socialization as new patterns of relations occurred. The various practices of schooling contain systems of rules that govern what sort of talk about education is possible; who are to be taken as serious talkers; and how desire, want, and cognition are to be constructed (here I again draw on Foucault, 1980; Martin, Gutman, and Hutton, 1988; and Foucault's Afterword in Dreyfus and Rabinow, 1983). Pedagogy, as a part of that institutional setting, is a practice of social regulation that is to discipline, manage, and create social capabilities for the individual; whether that management is called a pedagogy of child development, learning, social engineering, or social reconstruction.

From this, we can think of power as having at least two conceptual dimensions. One relates to groups, "forces," or individuals that exercise power over others. These forces or actors articulate their interests as social, cultural, political, and economic transformations occur within society. They continually demand to regulate the pedagogical practices used to teach specific values or content, such as sex education or science and technology. Here, the notion of power is related to a concept of *sovereignty*: Someone makes and "owns" the decisions that produce a context of domination and subordination. This notion of power is found in much of the sociology of school knowledge that defines power as a structural concept about the totality of domination and subjugation in society. It is also found in much of the literature of the state in which domination produces rules that effect outcomes. The study of power is intended to identify the placeholders who prevent progress and others who are resisting or lying in wait to place the world correctly on its feet.

Power as sovereignty creates a dichotomous world in which there is the oppressor and oppressed, thus producing a dualism whose effect is to define particular social groups as monolithic entities. The story often unfolds as one group dominates and the other, perceived as socially righteous, lacks power. The dualism of oppressor/oppressed loses sight of the subtleties in which power operates in multiple sites and through the actions and practices of individuals (see Popkewitz, 1988a). Dichotomies do not enable an understanding of the multiple agendas that exist within social factions and movements and the multiplicity of relations that exist within and among groups at any one time. The seemingly dichotomous world produces homogeneous "others" that can deny intellectual work one of its major reasons for being—skepticism. Feminist scholarship has cautioned us against totalizing social grouping as well as making us aware of the multiple strands and dispositions that exist within the debates about the purposes and direction of theorizing (see, e.g., Lather, 1990; Nicholson, 1986).

A second notion of power concerns its *effects* as it circulates through institutional practices and the discourses of daily life. The effects of power are in the production of desire, dispositions, and sensitivities. Power is embodied in the ways that individuals construct boundaries for themselves, define categories of good/bad, and envision possibilities. Power, in this latter sense, is intricately bound to the rules, standards, and styles of reasoning by which individuals speak, think, and act in producing their everyday world. Power is relational and regional.

We can focus on this orientation to power through the two meanings of *discipline* used in this study. There are the social science disciplines, social actors in the production of social regulation. The disciplines of the social sciences are part of the social transformations that are identified with the Progressive Era reforms discussed in Chapters 2 and 3. At one level, the disciplines of social science were related to shifts in the material conditions that entailed breaks from earlier forms of social regulation. There were challenges to Protestant theology, family patterns of upbringing, forms of governing, and the political economy. In Chapters 4 and 6, I explored the reconstructed structural relations through the interplay of educational sciences, universities, and mass schooling through the 1980s.

The theories, strategies, and practices of the social sciences also produced new potentials for individual self-management. The distinctions, categories, and rules of educational sciences give individuals direction as they consider their roles as parents, reason about family relations, and plan to help children through their stages of adolescence. Here, epistemologies are placed within a social space in a manner that circulates power as rules and standards of truth.

Let me further illustrate the productive quality of power through examining the American Psychological Association's (APA) manual for reporting research. The APA manual was developed over a 50-year period to give regularity and consistency to research (Bazerman, 1987). It maintains, however, a behavioral assumption formulated in the 1920s as a canon for all contemporary psychological research: Knowledge is additive and developed in fragmented steps, as illustrated by the way citations are placed at the ends of sentences. Footnotes are discredited, thus structuring out ways to explore, discuss, and criticize the texts cited. The APA style is, for many U.S. educators, an authoritative index of research. Its canons give organization to the discipline of psychology (and educational psychology) through the styles and rules of interpretation. The APA style of reporting becomes an element in the production of relations as its rules circulate through research practices. As one conducts a research project or writes a graduate paper, the adoption of this stylized manner of expression is associated with the dispositions of science itself. The behavioral assumptions and visions are internalized into styles of writing and the constructions of educational problems.

The *macro* institutional relations of the social disciplines and *micro* patterns of discipline are not oppositional categories. They are part of the social relations in which the management of society occurs in specific arenas, although the weaving of institutional and epistemological practices is not linear, reductive, or evolutionary.

THE STATE AND THE EFFECTS OF POWER

Central to the power/knowledge relation is the analytic concept of the state. The state is empirically defined through the changing patterns and relations in which social regulation occurs. My concern with the state is to provide an orienting concept for describing change, as in school steering, regulation, and self-discipline. In posing the state in this manner, I alter the Weberian notion of the state as related to governmental agencies and the legal-administrative mechanism of modern societies (see, e.g., Carnoy, 1984; see also Torres, 1989). Instead, I pose a notion of the state as a historical concept that focuses on specific arenas that relate civil and political society. The arena in which I consider state patterns is schooling. What is appropriate, as I argued earlier, is to "see" the state as the interrelation of different layers of institutional patterns that cohere and secure a social body over time, and how these practices have an impact in forming pedagogy. This view of the state enables consideration of the relations of macro- and micropatterns of governing, which is more than government and which is obscured in Weberian concepts.

This concern for the state does not neglect the importance of structural thinking. I do recognize that patterned relations are part of the horizon in which we continually act and theorize. My concern, however, is to continually explore how power is regionally exercised, the mechanism by which it circulates, and how it traverses and produces social relations. This requires, at one level, sensitivity to the issue of the sovereignty of power, through making it into an historical problem. For example, religion, economy, culture, gender, and the problems of political governing are part of the structural relations in which schooling occurs. But at different times, different elements are important, such as religion as it combined with economic and social interest as the modern state formed in the 19th century. The combination of elements in a historical context produces complex social relations that would be obscured through a priori stipulations of concepts that make one element or parallel elements into an irreducible base, such as class, religion, gender, or race.

We can pursue the effects of power by examining the relations of professional knowledge to the changing meaning of the state in the United States. In the early 19th century, professional knowledge increasingly tied together scientific rationality and moral responsibility as the modern state assumed responsibility for social and economic progress. The last decades of the 19th century saw professionalism as having two related meanings in schooling—one structural and one epistemological. It referred to structural relations in which there were those at the top of institutional hierarchies—educational researchers, professors, and school administrators—who conceived of ways to rationalize and organize schooling. When the word was used for teachers, *professionalism* was defined in relation to administrative capabilities that limited responsibility and types of reasoning.

Epistemologically, the relations between power and knowledge were made invisible by distancing professional work from social interests through rhetoric about autonomy and responsibility. The distancing was sanctioned through the assumptions of theory making. Educational theories about teachers as professionals impose visions, divisions, and distinction onto empirical phenomena that have the effect of creating the categories as the reality itself (see Bourdieu, 1985). Current research that investigates degrees of implementation of professional ideal types assumes that the theoretical distinctions about professionalism are real phenomena. Research intends to prove the existence of professionalism among teachers and to identify the laws of its development. School reforms are intended to impose the images of professionals in the ideal types onto the work and subjectivities of teachers. The study of the teacher incentive program in Chapter 7 revealed how the discourse about professionalism circulated through everyday practices: One consequence was to produce greater observation and supervision of teachers.

I center this study on the "effects" of power with some sense of personal disquiet. I "see" racism, social distinctions, and privilege. I feel gendered politics and walk continually among class distinctions and anti-Semitism. Yet to be sensitive to them is not to say that we can locate a single or parallel set of causes or origins. Rather, it is to be concerned with how distinctions occur in particular institutional patterns and the practices by which "identities" are produced. Gender, class, and race, among others, are not neatly packaged "things" that are rooted out to be destroyed. They are historically structured and interact through multiple social relations.

But to focus on the construction of social regulation is also to recognize that the effect of power is often to produce possibility and capability. The medieval reform to teach dialectics had as its purpose the use of reason to accept church orthodoxy; people who were rational about their faith would have a better and stronger faith. The question-producing strategy, however, also produced questions that confronted the faith and helped to undermine the power of the church. While this book has focused on the production of social regulation, subsequent research will need to consider more thoroughly the relation of regulation and capability.

While my focus is on U.S. schooling, other work suggests that the dynamics in the redesigning of the state, the introduction of Anglo-American conceptions of professionalism, and the increasing role of social, psychological, and measurement sciences in the steering of schooling are not restricted to this national setting. Governments of strong centralized states, such as Sweden and Spain, are bringing about transformations of educational institutions through decentralized strategies (Granheim et al., 1990). These strategies are producing new mediating institutions and social relations. The circulation of discourses and power in these settings, however, needs a wider theoretical net than could be cast in this study. At a different layer, I recognize that the use of state physical force and the lack of a developed civil society still exist in many southern hemispheres and Eastern countries, and this situation requires a more explicit state theory concerned with brute force and the repressive elements of power. In contrast, the subtleties of the relation between macro and micro contexts in the United States make the productive elements of power important. The productive relation of knowledge, power, and social management reaches into the most intimate and minute corners of everyday life.

WHAT ARE SOME OPTIONS PROPOSED FOR CONSIDERING THE RELATION OF RESEARCHERS AND SOCIAL MOVEMENTS?

My interest in outlining a theory of change is multiple. I am concerned with methods to interpret the practices of schooling. But such a narrative does not stand by itself: Intellectual work has consequences beyond the particular narratives offered. The relation of power to knowledge production is a central theme in this study. In light of this, I want to pursue a second theme about knowledge. The strategies of educational research are also the work of people who have structural positions and are part of structural relations. Educational sciences exist in the twin institutional worlds of social science and schooling.

If we accept research and the researcher as responding to and embedded in social relations, what are options proposed for a relationship between the researcher and change in the world? I explore three strands here. One which emerges from positivism, says that research simply describes the world but that those descriptions can lead to progress through social amelioration. A second offers a critical stance to existing social institutions but maintains an epistemological assumption of progress in its interpretations. The assumption is expressed in a reading of Hegel through Marx that the problem of the intellectual is not to study the world but to change it. That strand of critical scholarship pays attention to two layers of social phenomena as simultaneously related. One is an interpretation of the social-political context of schooling. The other is that of praxis, claiming that social analysis can be directly tied to social movements and change—often under educational slogans such as empowerment, critical reflection, or progressive practice. The internal shift in texts from analysis to praxis is what I call a popularist discourse in traditions of critical U.S. educational research. My concern is that the close proximity of an interpretative discourse to the problem of immediate change privileges the researcher *as* the agent of change.

My intent is to raise political questions about social scientists in social movements. I produce through this confrontation a third position, which I think is consistent with the lines drawn earlier about a theory of change. Viewing change as historical and pragmatic denies progress in an absolute sense. The politics of the intellectual from this perspective is to be self-critical about its visions and distinctions and rejecting of an epistemology of progress in science. This is not to suggest, however, a "free-floating" intellectual. Rather the political position of the intellectual in a democracy is not privileged. Further, it is to argue that the political struggle of the intellectual lies in the tension between engagement in and autonomy from particular social movements.

This stance is offered as a cautionary tale. I view tendencies for a vanguard as potentially undermining democratic projects in the name of liberation. The intent of this discussion is to break with the familiar of my own field and, as Bourdieu (1988) suggests, to place the supreme classifiers in the net of their own classifications. In this sense, my stance is political. I believe that to focus on the dangers of the intellectual acting as a vanguard is to contribute to working for democracy itself.

The Positivist Claim to
Descriptive Knowledge and Social Progress

The practices of a social science concerned with social amelioration were discussed in previous chapters. The amelioration tradition of social science took shape during the Progressive Era (approximately 1880–1920). It was a reformulation of earlier agendas of Christian ethics and initially tied efforts toward social interpretations with improving urban conditions of the post–Civil War era. The claim of the new academic social sciences was that they would promote social and economic progress through the application of rational investigation and planning. These claims, as I illustrated, derived from internal struggles within different academic fields as well as from the type of resources available from various social, economic, and governmental institutions, such as schooling.

The social amelioration efforts of social science were supposed to be politically nonpartisan. The ideology of the social sciences was only supposed to describe how "things" work; that knowledge could be used by any group or interest to provide direction for social progress. Evolutionary and piecemeal change was emphasized. Functional qualities, individuality, and rational organization had priority. Planning was intended to promote social progress as well as to ward off radicalism. Conflict was channeled into concerns for administrative efficiency, effectiveness, and social engineering, as well as being used to communicate the plight of the poor and dispossessed to middle-class publics. This tradition of social science in the service of policy makers is still dominant in the educational sciences, including the current shift from behaviorism to a cognitive model of educational psychology (see, e.g., Chapters 3 and 6).

In part, this is a legacy of a distinctly formed positivism that occurred in the United States at the turn of the century. The rules and procedures were seen as the guarantors of scientific knowledge (see, e.g., Popkewitz & St. Maurice, 1991). The commitment to science as bound to logical rules of language and methods coincided with beliefs that knowledge should be useful and speculative knowledge disregarded. This positivism remains a residue in the teaching and writing of books about social and educational sciences. It is found in the canons that organize empirical dissertations by labeling statistics as a research method that is separate from theory.[5] Debate is about the proper scientific rules rather than the social production, distinctions, and power relations in science. Where social conflicts and interests are recognized, they are redefined as methodological problems to control values, as one does bias and prejudice.[6] Major ethical questions of research are quieted.

The belief in neutrally descriptive social science knowledge is analytically and historically untenable. Analytically, it ignores the large body of literature about language and representation as part of the embodiment of interest in the world (e.g., Clifford, 1988). It also ignores the historical relations in which problems are made into research and the fact that the categories, distinctions, and methodologies of science are a part of social fields and power relations (Popkewitz, 1984).

The chimera that educational researchers operate independent of issues of history and power relations is a part of the historical mythology of the American political arena. For most Europeans, the state is a clearcut actor in social research. Social and educational research is directly funded by governmental agencies and geared toward ministry and parliamentary acts. In the United States, where the state regulation is less apparent, the state is taken for granted. Practices of governing are diffused through multiple levels of government legislation, bureaucracies, universities, philanthropy, professional organizations, and scientific occupations. The image is of independent and disparate fields with no processes of governing. Educational theory carried this image through an emphasis on the particular and the immediate. Concepts of decentralization and the theories of negotiated order, for example, focus on experiences as contained in individualized contexts. The particular sets of events are removed from the social and political history by which they are constituted. Questions about social betterment are continually contextualized as concerns of instrumental progress.

The structuring out of the state creates the myth of the educational researcher as operating free from all restraints except those provided by the rules of science. Educational researchers become individuals who have no attachment to political movements or social values. This occurs even though their work is constructed by political agendas, such as in current reform proposals that tie educational research to perceived mandates for science, technology, and economic improvement. The issue of power in social science is marginalized and delegitimatized.

It is interesting to me as I read through the literature on cognitive research that it is continually related to federally organized panels and grants. To take that position, however, is to celebrate, not question— not even asking which science, what technology, or what conceptions of economy one is to use in organizing *functional* research agendas. A quick reading of the daily papers challenges the research position that a common purpose exists. The ongoing disputes occurring in business, government, and science are ignored; the "needs" of society are taken in the educational sciences as global "facts."

Before leaving this discussion about the social amelioration tendency of the intellectual, I must return to the idea that rules and standards of science do not simply hide the relations of power. They also produce power. The reforms to better people's lives are also practical technologies to define and discipline individuals as they construct what those lives are to be. The styles of reasoning explored in earlier chapters contain technologies to increase the supervision, observation, self-regulation, and self-administration of the teacher. In rhetoric, the social amelioration tradition symbolically ties its research agenda to 19th century radical rural and urban Populist beliefs, such as the teacher-thinking research discussed in Chapter 6. The promise is progress through identifying knowledge that is immediate, local, and helpful to individuals who want to improve their lives. The research practices, in contrast, reposition the work of teachers in a manner that denies their practical knowledge and reformulates it into a rational, instrumental knowledge that is organized by experts. Without a capacity to place individuality into history, the distinctions seem independent of social interests and power relations.

The Popularist Approach:
Taking the Intellectual to the People

To challenge the social amelioration tradition and its positivism, there has been much talk in education about critical pedagogy, action research, and empowerment. Symbolically, the popularist literature begins with a critical analysis of existing institutions and concludes with claims of a universal attachment and organic relations with oppositional social movements.[7] The ostensible concern of this literature is to bring the intellectual into direct battle to alter schooling. It is to consider the inequities that exist in society, and to offer practical solutions by which to contest these inequities though the production of particular courses of action. I view this strategy about liberation, emancipation, and empowerment as a popularist agenda within a tradition of critical scholarship. It is related to this 19th-century radical rural and urban Populist movement in the United States.

Popularism and a social epistemology exist within a broad band of social science that can be called critical science (Popkewitz, 1990). These intellectual traditions treat the criteria and standards of social life and "self" as problematic and perceive social practices as embodying power relations and, to varying degrees, as in continual evaluation and reappraisal. The concerns of critical sciences are to challenge the present as self-evident and undisputed, considering that the seeming inevitability of the present is historically constructed. Critical traditions are a part of Enlightenment movements in which reason and rationality are continual endeavors to remake social conditions. (Positivism was a part of that radical movement, concerned with challenging the received wisdom given by the priests or aristocracy. But from Comte came a distinction between a positive science that could help in planning and the older negative sciences that did not offer guides for the future.[8]

The popularist scholarship maintains particular characteristics within critical scholarship. It accepts global dualisms between the oppressor and the oppressed. There is a reaching to concerns about praxis that are postulated, post hoc, from an initial critical scholarship, asserting the researcher's direct attachment to all oppositional social movements. The category of progressive is assigned to the practices associated with oppressed groups. Most significant for this discussion, the popularist scholarship contains an epistemology that defines the knowledge of the critical researcher as producing progress. This images the popularist as possessing authority in social movements.

The literature draws on Antonio Gramsci (1971), an Italian Marxist theorist of the 1930s, who suggested the notion of organic intellectuals. The intellectual, it is believed, is tied to particular social movements and is charged with articulating their direction and will. In popularist discourses, the disinterested stance of social amelioration research is rejected. Scientific knowledge is positioned as related to the direct tasks of social praxis.[9] The popularist is to be the agent of teachers in the production of practice. A claim is made that the progressive disciplinary discourse is developmental and practical: All theory should speak to teachers; when it does not, theory and theorists are elitist.[10] It is assumed that intellectuals speak to and for social movements, with an ad hoc political acceptance that practices can be given to teachers about what educational programs and political action should organize their futures.

A Critique of Popularism's Epistemology of Progress and Its Social Space. The claims of progress in contemporary popularism occur in relation to at least three interweaving strands: a historical populism in the United States, the social space in which educational academics work, and the epistemological commitment to a universal concept of progress.

Populism is a part of historically longstanding strategies for equality in the New World. In the early part of the 19th century, populism was related to an agrarian revolution against business, professions, and experts. Populism sought to bring old-fashioned principles of religion and morality into the construction of social policy. Intellectuals were feared and resented in public life, defined as experts and as ideologues. "This preference for the wisdom of the common man flowered, in the most extreme statements of the democratic creed, into a kind of militant popular anti-intellectualism" (Hofstadter, 1962, p. 155). The progressive political movement of the late 1800s and early 1900s was an extension of the earlier populist movement, but part of its leadership was drawn from the urbanized middle classes. Populist parties in the late 19th century, symbolizing the discontent among workers and poverty-stricken farmers in the Midwest and South and containing radical platforms, were the political avant-garde of the times and produced strong showings in presidential elections. Contemporary critical popularism draws on the anti-elitist sentiments of populism. There is a rejection of the instrumental knowledge of social amelioration. The popularist discussion, however, picks up and reconstructs the distrust of certain types of expertise, entrenched classes, and bureaucracies, and in some cases, of the intellectuals themselves. The distrust is reformulated to make the intellectual the agent for helping teachers overcome the oppressions of schooling and society.

Sociologically, the popularist arguments are formed in and related to a social field of schooling where social amelioration has social and cultural authority. Dominating schooling is an anti-intellectualism that is tied, in part, to the administrative demands of constructing mass schooling. The amelioration tradition, I argued, utilizes the historic mistrust of the intellectual by making knowledge seem functional. The popularist seeks to claim the space of the social ameliorist by offering a practical, seemingly nonexpert knowledge about the reconstruction of teaching.

The positioning of the popularist, in fact, supports the status quo of the intellectual. Popularism, while posing an oppositional knowledge, also positions itself as a competitor by promising practical advice for the teacher.[11] The popularism of critical research and social amelioration traditions contain the appeal that teachers will become more autonomous and responsible, and, in the latest rhetoric, empowered—helping teachers to help themselves through the expertise of the intellectual (Gore, 1990). The offer of better ways to produce progress reestablishes the legitimacy of the particular intellectual as an authority in moral matters.

Epistemologically, the modern popularist is bound to a Hegelian conception of history as providing progress. There is an acceptance of a dialectics of negativity: Scholarship's unmasking and the elimination of social suffering produces direction and legitimation for moral action. The position connects individual and community into a whole that finds the good in universalist politics, morality, and aesthetics. (For arguments about the need for a concept of totality, see Grumley, 1989; Jay, 1984; Roth, 1988.) Moral responsibility is determined through the ordering of meaning and the giving of direction to history. Intellectuals are to exercise a collective critical consciousness for the oppressed. They are to alleviate oppression through moving toward some new and better universal good.

The Hegelian conception of progress needs to be considered within the particular social space that gives it historical specificity; that is, the epistemology is part of social practices that provide academic capital to particular academics in educational research. This strategy is underscored, since popularism is not attached to any particular social movement. The Hegelian conception of moral action assumes a certain universality in popularism, be it elimination of class distinctions, gender distinctions, or racial discrimination.

The Last Chapter on Organic Linkages.   The popularist strand is usually articulated in the last chapter of a book about the social, political, and cultural relations of schooling.[12] Preceded by a critical analysis of educational processes, there are calls for academic researchers to become spokespersons for social groups. Phrases such as *linkages* and *organic connections* appear to establish a relationship between the text, author, and "progressive" teachers, labor, women's groups, and people of color. There is an assertion that the academic task is to learn how to talk in ways that is deemed accessible for teachers. Specific examples of practices called progressive are given and are logically linked to critical scholarship. Language is used to tie critical scholarship to such universal political phrases such as *democratic socialism, democracy, radical democracy,* and *progressive politics.*

As a rhetorical stance, the call for accessibility and linkage is powerful among critical intellectuals, who have been historically without influence in the United States. However, when the notions of linkage, connections, and accessibility posited in the popularist strand are examined through their semiotic relations, there is a privileging of the researcher as the bearer of progress. This occurs in multiple ways.

Interspersed in the last chapter are examples of progressive school politics. These examples are of coalitions of people and practices to counter the prevailing utilitarian values in schools. Juxtaposing the academic work to practical endeavors makes these linkages seem natural, inevitable, and unproblematic. The placing of specific alternative practices after the scholarly narrative puts the researcher in privileged relation to social movements. The researcher is an arbiter in defining the irreducible principles of democratic practices.

The social relations established between researchers and social movements are not inevitable or natural, as the popularists assert. References to universally defined groups are distinctions that are real only as they relate to the visions that are established by the researcher. There are no global groups of people of color, women's groups, or classes, but rather different and multiple groups of people who are historically defined and who do not have the same internal agendas or liberation commitments. This includes the social field of intellectuals as well; radical scholarship, the literature on social and political movements, and contemporary feminist literature demonstrate multiple positions and heterogeneity (Altbach & Cohen, 1989; Nicholson, 1986). There are no fixed and firm classes or social groups but rather sets of relations among groups that are dynamic (Bourdieu, 1988). Nor does the idea of organic relations consider the tensions and contradictions that continually occur as intellectuals become involved in social planning. To perceive oneself as organically tied to something that has no empirical specificity is a strategy to gain social space for the critical academic.

An element in the popularist's last chapter is the call for researchers to speak to teachers. At one level, this claim is difficult to argue against: Writing should be crafted to be understandable. But the argument about language is complex because of the values and interests carried in discursive practices. Problems are inherent not only in achieving clarity but in engaging a language that has at least two qualities. Narratives should be constructed to reflect the interests being pursued. In the chapter on teacher thinking, for example, I gave attention to the tension between the claim of the social construction of knowledge and the reifications produced through the research methods. At a different layer, the language used to write about a science of schooling should challenge the commonsense systems of relevance and logic found in the official conversations of schooling. The problem, then, is more than making language accessible.

This requires that the rhetorical claims about making language accessible be scrutinized. Some critical writers do recognize the problematic quality of language and the difficulties in the argument about accessibility. Others make speaking to teachers into a pedagogical task— inverting the interpretative practices of research into one of explicitly guiding and organizing teacher practices. For example, prior chapters that promote historical skepticism are subsumed in the ending narrative that promotes the intellectual as someone else's agent. It is rhetorically asserted that research needs to be written for the teachers so the scholarship can function pedagogically. The function is expressed as an applied language that can enable the researcher to construct the audience for the democracy being built. When this talk about constructing audiences appears, questions can be raised about whose democracy is being constructed.

The positioning of the academic work as a pedagogical task is important. While all scholarship is pedagogical in the general sense of promoting an understanding of patterns and relations (see, e.g., Giroux, 1990), the use of pedagogy in populism is more restricted and focused. Previously, I explored pedagogy as a form of social regulation that imposes distinctions, visions, and practices. The skepticism of scholarship, however, is removed in this popularist version of research. The pedagogical function of popularist research is a project of the academic constructing audiences.

The Social Positioning of the Academic: Opposition Concepts of Resistance and Voice.   Populists are caught between their desire to be universal intellectuals who provide social interpretation *and* universal intellectuals who unravel the political exigencies of social movements through defining immediate, useful knowledge. Notions of resistance and voice are two examples of this tension: There is a merging of empirically warranted claims with ideological positions about futures produced by intellectual work.

The concept of resistance is a structural concept that explores the diversity of responses to a world of inequal power relations. Where a concept of resistance has theoretical focus, it defines a dualistic world of those who dominate and are dominated.[13] As an empirical concept, resistance explores the ways in which power is sustained, bestowed, and challenged. At other times, resistance is a political notion that points to places where intervention can be used to mobilize groups. The oppositional strategies are labeled progressive through the sets of distinctions posited by academics (with some having stronger views than others) that are to provide guidance and leadership for the mobilizations.

A more recent version of resistance is found in the notion of voice. It contains dual agendas of interpretation and redressing social privilege. As a theoretical problem, voice is offered as a way to "see" the relation of history, structures, and subjectivity. Here I draw upon the work of Britzman (1989) who provides one of the few populist arguments grounded in empirical research. She draws on the post-structural tradition to identify the conflict in student teaching between practices that structure meanings and a structuring as students practice teaching. The act of teaching is "a clash of polyphony of voices and contested realities" about "who has the floor" (p. 145).

A tension exists. There is the making of the individual as an epistemic figure, with speech viewed as historical property associated with the social space that a person occupies; *and* there is the political commitment to give suppressed peoples' voice in their immediate context.[11] The theoretical intent is expressed as "critical interrogation of the contradictions of how the classroom practices affects students and teachers during the immediacy of the felt encounter allows us to raise contextual questions such as, whose meanings are felt? And, what is encountered?" (Britzman, 1989, p. 144). But the "reclaiming" of the suppressed voice privileges power as ownership and a presentism: There is a call for "empowerment" that expresses power as sovereignty in that one can own, give, or take power. This produces a structural dualism. There are ideas of "mutuality" and "research subjects speaking for themselves," concepts that embody a nonhistorical present and give priority to the immediate.

Ultimate purpose and foundational values about truth and progress are established as voice is tied to the production of social practices. Finding of "one's own voice" establishes an end to history in the speech of the research subjects. The student teacher, for example, is positioned in the text as a volitional individual who can "own" language to make one's "own voice" (Britzman, 1989, pp. 159–160). There is a "local knowledge, or the specific experiences and theories of specific teachers" that present "the perspectives of those who are experiencing educational life" (p. 146). Presupposed is a basic reality that is found in individual expressions. *Truth* lies in the interpretations of experience by those who participate in schooling, thus obscuring history in the subject's voice.

The stance about knowledge tied to progress produces a contradiction. Theory is posited as organically related to progressive practices, but theory and theorists are made superordinate. This notion of voice presumes the intellectual authority of the researcher. Implicit in the notion of empowerment is that power is something given by those who have power—a commodity to be bartered. The experience expressed through "voice" is theoretically defined and given ultimate purpose through intellectual practices. Yet experience is not a category about the reality of life. It is itself a theoretical concept that presents the relevancies of conversation and thought as "fact." In the instance of voice, the researcher reclaims, defines, and categorizes the voices that are given as the language to be owned by others. This authority to reclaim is not the statistics of positivism but "the methodology of ethnography [to] empower prospective teachers in the critical re-reading of their experiences in order to transform it" (Britzman, 1989, p. 160).

My concern here is not to diminish the political project undertaken to develop more appropriate social institutions. It is to make problematic the universal claims for practice associated with an epistemology of progress in critical scholarship. A difficulty with popularist reasoning is that it oversimplifies the problem of social action and knowledge and follows indirectly the utilitarian rules of knowledge that are, at the outset, rejected within this view of intellectual work.

Belles-Lettres and an Arrogance of Intellectuals.   The popularist position capitalizes on a historical positioning of the intellectual as producing transcendental knowledge and rejecting the particularistic. Intellectual practices are historically defined through the ambitions of intellectuals to constitute themselves as functionaries of humanity. This model of the universal intellectual, according to Bourdieu (1989a),

> implies duties, or at least the acceptance of sacrifices, which, like hypocrisy, are the homage vice pays to virtue. More precisely, the appearance of a universe such as the intellectual field, where the defense of universal cause (illustrated by the petitions) is traditionally rewarded, creates a situation in which it is possible to rely on the symbolic profits associated with these actions to mobilize intellectuals in favor of the universal. (p. 110)

Those "profits" are reflected in popularism. The popularist collapse of science into a concern for programs for "others" loses the critical edge of science (again, I consider science in a broader manner rather than its narrow, positivistic concerns). There is a difference between the ephemeral qualities of particular events and the self-reflectivity central for scientific work, the latter requiring autonomy from the demands of the immediate. Focusing on the initial interpretation of the May 1968 student revolt in France, for example, Bourdieu (1988) argues that there are political profits for the intellectual from the "topicality" of the events. The present interpretations are cultural products destined for sale to markets for the reputation of the authors. But social science, "constantly threatened with regression into *belles-lettres* (p. 160), must move away in time from the object studied because of the time necessary for scientific work.

> The researcher can only arrive after the show, when the lamps are doused and the trestles stacked away, with a performance which has lost all the charms of an improvisation. The scientific report, constructed in counterpoint to the questions arising from the immediacy of the event, which are riddles rather than problems, and call for integral and definitive action rather than necessarily partial and arguable analyses, lacks the advantage of the fine clarity of the discourse of good sense, which has no difficulty in being simple, since its premise is to simplify. (p. 160)

Bourdieu argues that to pay attention to the instance is to be drowned in the events and emotions of the particular and to perceive the specific movements as the totality of history and explanation. In contrast, a scientific interest (again in its nonpositivist sense) is to insert the particular into a series of events that locates the singularity as a part of a historical phenomenon that is more than a continuous addition of ordinary events. Those constraints and restraints are obscured in popularism.

In the politics of social movements, such concern for pragmatic strategies is essential—in science it is dangerous and arrogant. The paradox of science is that to reinsert the critical moments into the series in which their intelligibility resides is "to understand the unique as part of a critical situation in which there is an opening of time and an intrusion of the possibility of novelty" (p. 162). To do so is to make all theoretical questions and their intersection with the empirical as historical, thus neutralizing the effects of simple description and pure rationalization.

This point is partially taken up by the branch of feminist literature called post-structural and socialist-critical (see, e.g., Alcoff, 1988; Fraser, 1989; Nicholson, 1986; Weedon, 1987). These theorists are directly attached to a social movement and explicitly concerned with the merging of the project of a critical science with the tasks of social transformation.[15] In contrast to the popularism that claims a universal attachment to those who are oppressed, this feminist literature maintains an uneasy "truce" between a theoretical epistemology that rejects progress and the intellectual as a prime actor in social movements. Weedon (1987) argues that the distinct role of the intellectual is to focus on power, control, and social relations in their historical and structural relations. Theory helps to explicate the formation of experience and the relation of the objective and subjective. The relation of experience and theory, as well as access to knowledge and the patriarchal structure and content of knowledge—issues of central importance to feminism—are still being contested. Fraser (1989) points to "the knot of genuine tensions and contradictions that are endemic" to the academy that seeks to combine activism and scholarship (p. 1). The social role and political function of the intellectual, she asserts, is critique, drawing on Marx's definition of critique as "the self-clarification of the struggles and wishes of the age" (p. 2).

To recognize the relation of theory to social movements is not to reduce one to the other, as occurs in populist literature. There is a simultaneous move toward autonomy and engagement. Fraser argues that there is a need to keep "simultaneously in view the distinct standpoints of the theorist and of the political agent, not to reduce one to the other" (p. 2). The role for intellectuals in social movements is a "non-Leninist, non-vanguardist conception of the role of the intellectual." She worries, at the same time, that intellectuals comprise a social group that can easily become mesmerized by its position in power relations. The intellectual is "mightily subject to delusions of grandeur" and needs "to remain in close contact with her political comrades who are not intellectuals by profession in order to remain sane, level-headed and honest" (p. 108).

The practical value of a critical theory in feminist literature is to make "social movements as the subject of critique" and to ensure that "in the crucible of political practice that critical theories meet the ultimate test of viability" (Fraser, 1989, p. 2). Where the populist needs to construct a global audience through declarations about universal struggles, these feminists argue for a particular involvement in actual or possible political practices. Fraser continues that this involvement is not an academic issue, highlighting how social theory and the changing social and working conditions of women have combined to produce new political arenas of debate and conflict about social policy that influence women's lives.

In what follows, I explore the relation of autonomy and commitment, but in a manner that focuses more on the relation of these two dimensions than occurs in feminist literature. My cautionary tale recognizes the politics of knowledge and the intellectual as located in structural relations. The tensions and dangers of an epistemology of progress drive this discussion. Thus I am proposing not that intellectuals retreat from politics but that they take politics more seriously.

Science as/and Social Practice

The purpose of my discussion of populism and my juxtaposing it with feminist scholarship is to point to the complexities of the relation between science, scientists, and social movements. While I cannot resolve this Gordian knot, I provide some direction toward that relation in the following discussion. First, I explore the sociological importances of a bidimensionality of autonomy and commitment in the work of educational research that is ignored in social amelioration and popular-ist traditions. Here, I distinguish the intellectual struggle for autonomy from the direct demands of specific social movements. Second, I argue that the problem of change is not one of science alone, although the scientist is an actor in that process. This entails, I believe, focusing on the relation of the intellectual to the pragmatic projects in a democracy.

The Enlightenment Project Without the Intellectuals' Project of Prog-ress. While I accept the general commitments of the Enlightenment, my argument takes a more limited and restricted view of the work of intellectuals than is found in positivism or in popularism. In part, the differences revolve around the concept of history in social interpreta-tion. I reject any notion of global progress inhering in the work of re-search. At a time when so much authority is invested in scientific dis-course and professional expertise in the United States, I worry about the social implications of conceptions of universal progress.

My concern is with the productive effects of academic discourses as they circulate in social arenas. Privileging progress also privileges the intellectual as part of a vanguard in producing change. These ef-fects have little to do with the academics' intent or purpose, no matter how noble or progressive we believe the arguments to be. (I recognize that the particular epistemological assumptions of populism are not "merely" of knowledge but part of a peculiar social space in which U.S. academics work.)

Removing the presuppositions of progress does not mean that sci-entists ignore issues concerning the reconstruction of more appropriate social conditions. Commitment is always bound into the work of educa-tional sciences. The problems, issues, and conceptualizations of the hu-man sciences are responses to and part of the varied and multiple social movements that constitute a particular time and space. Giddens (1987) argues, for example, that social movements are of prime significance in stimulating intellectual work. Commitment is also found as intellectuals act in the world. As the social histories of Chapters 3 and 6 indicate, links between intellectuals and social movements are continually pres-ent. The intellectual needs to speak out, and these acts occur in many specific ways—the production of academic texts, the battles in faculty meetings in which choices are constructed, and in particular protests against injustices and oppressions in and outside the university. I recog-nize, for example, the multiple roles of the university of transmitting, interpreting, and developing cultural traditions in society; I also recognize that the academy politically "influences the action-orienting self understanding of students and publics" (Habermas, 1970, p. 4). I reject, as does Habermas, reducing the university to the narrow concerns of technological education.

Here, though, lie central tensions in the articulation of commitment. Commitments are not universal and totalizing as the positivists and popularists posit. They are historically situated, provisional, and tied to the regional practices in which social life is being structured. Commitment, then, has no absolute principles to define social practices. Commitments and visions are, in fact, pragmatically bound through paying attention to the power arrangements that exist at particular sites and in particular historical moments.

Further, the engagement of the intellectual is continually juxtaposed with the struggle for autonomy. The important historical battles of intellectuals have been in the productive elements of power—the control of the symbol, that is, the distinctions, categories, and rules embodied in the constructions of social relations and identity. Both Bourdieu and Foucault, for example, with different foci and emphases, argue that the political power par excellence of scientific work is to uncover the effects of categorization and the struggles to produce and impose legitimate visions in the world. The reflective quality of intellectual work is also one of self-reflectivity. There is a continuous destabilization of the inherited rhetoric that gives authority to the world-making images of the intellectual.

The challenge of the politics of world-making requires an autonomy from existing social movements through a self-critical stance. In part, there is a recognition of how pressures for state planning, legitimation of social movements through the construction of symbols, as well as the intellectual's own search for social and cultural capital, produce epistemic drift as concepts and standards are closely allied with particular social interests (see, e.g., Elzinga, 1985).[16] The work of intellectuals is to confront the new mandarins of cultural production. This occurs through challenges to the instrumental reasoning in which choices become administrative, technical, and related to the decisions of the modern expert. It also entails a self-critical stance toward the bearers of an epistemology that positions intellectuals as agents of others.

This paradox of commitment and autonomy calls for "a more modest redimensioning of [the intellectual's] mission" (Bourdieu, 1989a, p. 109). The particular historical task lies in exploring the practices in which truth is made and battling those efforts to subsume the relation of intellectuals to social movements. It is to be aware of the tendency to position intellectuals as the "celebrated universal class . . . who designated themselves as the ultimate judges of universality in their designation of the 'universal class'" (p. 109). It also requires a recognition that the myth of the organic intellectual, as Bourdieu argues, reduces the intellectual's role to some "fellow traveler" (p. 109) of others' interest— "a situation which leads them to feel solidarity with any and all the dominated, despite the fact that, being in possession of one of the major means of domination, cultural capital, they partake of the dominant order" (p. 109). The self reflectively recognizes that what is made into the possibilities of community is itself a regime of truth. The notion of community contains an ensemble of rules that separate the true and false and the specific effects of power attached to the true. To struggle for autonomy is to provide the historical conditions that enable suspicion when people speak of a general will to which the intellectual can be attached.

An important intellectual strategy is to take up the defense of their own autonomy and to focus on the most effective means to struggle on behalf of social commitments. Bourdieu (1989a) presents this battle as a continual animosity between engagement and autonomy, with any ethical or political action "grounded in a rigorous understanding of how the intellectual world operates" (p. 99). Autonomy entails the development of corporate traditions that guarantee "*the social conditions for the possibility of rational thought* against the transcendent illusion which tends to confirm the universal structure of reason in the consciousness of language" (p. 103; emphasis in original). To maintain this autonomy entails a struggle to guarantee economic and social conditions but, at the same time, to be free from the temptation of building an ivory tower. In the modern political economy of the intellectual, it is autonomy that constitutes one of the main battles, one that has been evident in the formation of the social sciences, during the McCarthy period, and in current attacks against the academy as a left-wing institution.

The place of autonomy in intellectual work should not be viewed in the naive sense that permeates contemporary educational literature: the teacher or researcher as a professional who acts in solitude, without history, power relations, or social location. Nor is it an old-style intellectual prophesying or a notion of the intellectual as "free-floating" class. Autonomy and engagement must be simultaneously extended in a manner that maintains the autonomy of the intellectual without its crude elements of disenchantment. A predominant battle of intellectuals is to maintain (or create) autonomy to challenge the regimes of truth and world-making images, including that of the intellectual.[17] It is an irony that the popularists, who have secured some autonomy within the academy, have tended to be nonreflective about their social location.

I realize that one could see this stance as that of someone in the university who is simply out to protect his privileged position. I hope not. To understand and maintain autonomy does not exonerate one from moral responsibility.

Pragmatic Actions and Democracy.   By focusing on the tensions of commitment and autonomy, I position the problem of social reconstructions in a larger public space in which the intellectual has no privileged space. A problem of a democracy entails a constant dialogue in which provisional constructions of informed guesses occur to enable us to do practical things. Where intellectuals do engage in debates and struggles in public arenas, it is without an epistemological privileging. Engagement is not an absolute and totalizing concept but always accepted with a humility and skepticism toward the social position and historical constructions of truth and community.

This sense of humility is tied, I believe, to a pragmatism which allows political debate to occur and makes reconstructions possible. Cherryholmes (1988) has called this a critical pragmatism in which "our texts and discourses-practices continuously require interpretation and reconstruction" (p. 150). Attention is given to the interrelation of ethics, morality, and politics in questions about daily existence and its communicative practices. Here I would add that this reconstructing entails a historical sense of society and individual that allows one to recognize the dangers in intellectual practices.

The social task of constructing more appropriate social conditions entails a broadening of specific and multiple public spheres for political thinking and moral identity. This involves argument among particular people in specific situations, dealing with concrete cases, and with different things at stake (see, e.g., Rorty, 1988; Toulmin, 1988; and, in education, Giroux, 1990; Rizvi, 1989a, 1989b; Walker, 1987). There are no final truths or fixed moral foundations that serve as guides. There are continuous interpretation and reconstruction that are, in fact, responses to the situations in which we find ourselves and "based on *visions* of what is beautiful, good, and true instead of fixed, structured, moral, or objective certainties" (Cherryholmes, 1988, p. 151; emphasis in original).

Here, the Enlightenment traditions merge with and are reconstructed by postmodern and neopragmatic discussions.[18] There is a need to come collectively to terms with ourselves and our world and to confront the various ways power affects social relations. The idea of progress enters into the practices of social reconstruction, but in a context of provisional choices made in public debate. The human sciences are a part of the dialogue about democratic conditions in which skepticism and commitment are pragmatically located. The intellectual can help in the expansion of cultural reason by examining the historical conditions in which truth is formed. Theory or theorists entail no prescriptive tasks. Foucault (1980), who adopts a critical pragmatic stance, argues:

> Political analysis and criticism have in a large measure still to be invented—so too have the strategies which will make it possible to modify the relations of force, to co-ordinate them in such a way that such a modification is possible and can be inscribed in reality. That is to say, the problem is not so much that of defining a political "position" (which is to choose from a pre-existing set of possibilities) but to imagine and to bring into being new schemes of politicization. If "politicization" means falling back on ready-made choices and institutions, then the efforts of analysis involved in uncovering the relations of force and mechanisms of power are not worthwhile. (p. 190)

These public processes entail no epistemology that authorizes the intellectual as the agent for others. Structuring out such visions, as best as possible, from the sciences of schooling is not to imply that visions are unavailable. Rather, it is to place the legitimate context for the construction of visions in the debate formed in public arenas. Engagement becomes a part of the strategic actions in particular practices.

CONCLUSIONS

My concern with a social epistemology in this book is twofold. First, it is to understand reform as an object of social relations rather than to accept reform as truth producing and progressive. This entails a concern with the historical breaks and ruptures in schooling. The strategy of a social epistemology, though, is more than a conceptual method. Second, it is to construct a social philosophy and social theory that denies the intellectual an authoritative position in producing change. I gave attention to the ideas that intellectuals have of themselves. My discussion of social amelioration and popularist traditions highlighted the dangers of an epistemology of progress. The point is to challenge the common places and common senses of academics.

What is needed is a better understanding of the precarious qualities of the links of intellectuals in the world, while at the same time, a rejection of the philosophy that views theory (and the intellectual) as producing progress and intent. If we have learned anything from the scholarship of the past hundred years, it is to assume that progress is not built on rational knowledge alone. It is also to be skeptical of what we or others call progressive. Whether labeled progressive or not, calls for action and ongoing practices need to be scrutinized for their power relations. When we adopt a belief that scientific knowledge is about the future, we have left science and its relation to the empirical world to move into the realm of ideology and social regulation. The rituals of science become a rhetorical form intended to convince others that what is being done to them is in their own interests.

The autonomy of intellectuals that I speak of should not function so as to destroy commitment or exacerbate a disenchantment with the world. It should lead them to recognize that authority over social symbols is part of the battle in the production of the world. Educational research and its researchers are part of the political practices to be struggled over. Those who have authority to speak and what is authorized as speech are important elements in the construction and reconstructions of society.

> The essential political problem for the intellectual is not to criticize the ideological contents supposedly linked to science, or to ensure that his own scientific practice is accompanied by a correct ideology, but that of ascertaining the possibility of constituting a new politics of truth. The problem is not changing people's consciousness—or what's in their heads—but the political, economic, institutional regime of the production of truth. . . . The political question, to sum up, is not error, illusion, alienated consciousness or ideology; it is truth itself. (Foucault, quoted in Bové, 1989, p. 237)

Concerns about the intellectual are raised in relation to the reconstitution of social regulation occurring in contemporary school reform. In the preceding chapters, I argued there has been a narrowing of democracy. This narrowing has occurred even though the reform discourses express a rhetoric of professionalization and empowerment. The rhetoric of reform is intended to increase people's involvement in decisions at all layers of institutional life, but those decisions occur in a range of practices that are increasingly restricted. Participation is about technical solutions, efficiency, and functional approaches. This narrowing entails the positioning of intellectual practice as producing progress, be it from the tenets of social amelioration or of the popularist traditions.

The distinctions, visions, and categories of intellectuals are social practices that are part of the events that they portray.

NOTES
REFERENCES
INDEX
ABOUT THE AUTHOR

Notes

INTRODUCTION

1. There is an American misreading and selective appropriation of the work of Durkheim as positivist. See, for example, his school history (1938/1977) for the tradition that is the concern here. Also see Bourdieu (1977, 1984).

CHAPTER 1

1. This is contrary to the argument of Berger and Luckmann (1967), who separate primary and secondary institutions of socialization, defining school as the latter.

2. There are strands of educational sociology that have given priority to the historical location of educational thought. See Hamilton (1989), Goodson (1985), Williams (1965), Silver (1983), and Englund (1986).

3. All analysis contains presuppositions of structures, if only because it is based upon language and is to be communicative. Even the current interest in deconstruction has to be seen in relation to structures and as a historically constructed discourse. As Ortega y Gasset (1960) argued, it is only language that we have in the human sciences.

4. This point is developed within a Marxist position in relation to the debates about modernism and postmodernism. McLennan (1989), for example, calls his position a "pluralist marxism." He recognizes that epochal categorizations (such as capitalism and class analysis) have "enormous explanatory risk" (p. 261) and seeks to maintain a flexible approach that is sensitive to macrolevel (structural) theories in exploring the nuances and regional qualities of power. Without some notion of structure, McLennan argues, it would be difficult to gauge the significance of meso- and microphenomena.

5. In northern European countries, a similar pattern of structuring knowledge occurred under the influence of Lutherism.

6. For a critique of Giddens's position, see Archer, 1985; see also Held & Thompson (1989).

7. These theoretical concerns can be found in feminist theory, although focused there upon a particular social arena. See Nicholson (1986) and Weedon (1987).

8. The assumptions and implication of the changes are gleaned from a reading of a variety of sources, from Durkheim (1938/1977), LeGoff (1980) and Hamilton (1989), among others.

9. This subtly changed during the Reformation and Counter-Reformation; see Durkheim (1938/1977).

10. The collection of information about populations was not an invention of the 19th or 20th century. The Swedish "state" collected information in the 16th century, in order to collect taxes for the king and the church. The wars in 17th-century Europe would have been impossible without the military enrollment "board" and the farmers' payment to the soldiers.

11. In voting for the U.S. president, faith in the individual politician is perceived as more important than concrete political programs and past practices.

12. The discussion introduces the concept of the state as a problem of social management and governing into the patterns of socialization and upbringing (see Badie & Birnbaum, 1983; Block, 1977; Carnoy, 1984; Skocpol, 1980; Torres, 1989).

13. Different strands of pedagogy are discussed in Kliebard (1986).

CHAPTER 2

1. The particular manner in which a central administrative capacity developed in the United States is explored in Skowronek (1982). For a discussion of the state as a dynamic and relational concept, see Wittrock (1988) and Wittrock and Wagner (1988).

2. This conception of religion has been called a "civil religion" that contains a theme of collective and individual obligations to carry out God's will on earth. The activist and noncontemplative conception of fundamental religious obligation is historically associated with the Protestant position; it is not itself a particular Christian sect but Unitarian (Bellah, 1968; see also May, 1949).

3. The current reconstitution of a state bureaucracy in schooling is discussed in Chapter 4.

4. These forms of rationality also had a relation to a Protestant ethos.

5. Labaree (1988) argues, however, that we should not see the bureaucracy of the school as a "pure" ideal but as influenced by the market qualities of schooling.

6. According to Conway, the belief in the decline of the Christian family, which helped to legitimate the new role of the school, was in fact wrong, as the bourgeois family remained remarkably stable.

7. The experiment was introduced in New Harmony, Indiana, in 1824.

8. The individualization that appears in the 19th century as a technology of control can be seen in relation to the 16th-century effort of the Jesuits to

provide a form of education that countered the Reformation through discipline of the mind and body.

9. It is interesting to consider the pedagogy of Froebel in relation to the issue of the unification of the German states in which he was involved. His pedagogy stressed harmony and an acculturation that eliminated the evil traditions of the "old" world.

CHAPTER 3

1. I argue here against the separation found in Scheler (1980), who defines knowledge as related to the three different forms: salvation, power, and achievement. The argument is that all three functions of knowledge coexist within the discourse of social science.

2. This continues to the present. In a study that I did of an elementary reform program that was used in over 3,000 schools around the United States, it became clear that the organization of the school into units that combined three to five classes, or about 100 to 150 children, was the product of educational psychologists who needed a large enough sample to conduct their quasi-experimental designs (see Popkewitz et al., 1982).

3. This development needs to be seen in relation to the expansion of the state and emergence of civil associations, such as philanthropic foundations, in setting social agendas in the United States.

4. Bentham used the term *social science* in 1821, J. S. Mill in 1836 (Silver, 1983). Also see Veysey (1965) for a comprehensive but less political history of the American university.

5. The particular manner in which a central administrative capacity developed in the United States is explored in Skowronek (1982). For a discussion of the state as a dynamic and relational concept in the formation of the social sciences, see Wittrock (1988) and Wittrock and Wagner (1988).

6. There are distinctions among the British, French, and German universities, although American higher education was able to combine these three traditions into one that could interrelate character training with science and professional education.

7. The centrality of the university in relation to the social order is apparent in its role as a credentialing agency (see Collins, 1979).

8. It is important to understand that the bourgeois ideology about the home was itself a part of recent historical formation and "naturalized" in the 19th and 20th centuries (see Ariès, 1965). For discussion and critique, see Luke (1989).

9. See Popkewitz (1987c) for a discussion of the pedagogical issues that follow. Also see Franklin (1986), Kliebard (1986), and Durkheim (1938/1977) for social histories of pedagogy.

10. There is, though, literature that did reflect that tension, such as Marx (1964).

11. This has changed in the 1980s as organizational concerns of schooling have again become prominent (see Chapter 4).

12. While John Dewey's writings remain popular as citations in educational literature, the actual development of curriculum in teacher education and teaching maintains the legacy of behavioral psychology.

13. In fundamental ways, current educational reformers maintain these hopes but ignore past promises, practices, and their outcomes. See later chapters.

14. The obscuring of social interests was continually contested, and teachers did not always accept the reform technologies. See Franklin (1986) for discussion of the Minneapolis school district. Also see Mattingly (1975) for discussion of the formation of ideologies in teacher education that promoted notions of a classless profession.

CHAPTER 4

1. The use of a public discussion to build a consensus for prior social and economic changes is discussed in Dickson (1984), Westbury (1984), and the following chapters.

2. I am not arguing here that particular research results are actually used or that researchers have "power" in the society. Rather, my concern is with research as a practice that is part of institutional relations.

3. I wish to thank Tom Romberg for drawing my attention to this.

4. The federal government had previously made several attempts to influence schooling through legislation. The Morrill Act of 1862 required states to set aside land to be used to financially support agricultural and engineering schools, and the Smith-Hughes Act of 1917 supported vocational education. They provide a background to current initiatives, and also underscore the scope of current activity.

5. The demographic changes are also an element of Western and European domestic policy. Western European countries have had to reconsider social policy in light of "new" immigrants who alter their cultural homogeneity. Eastern, nonwhite populations of the Soviet Union have surpassed Western, Caucasian groups in their percentage of the total population.

6. I am indebted to Martin Lawn for this description.

7. Rationalization is used in its Weberian sense of flattening out social processes and its common sense of consistency of rules.

8. See Chance (1986) for an illustration of how foundations establish a discourse about reform that responds to political agendas.

9. While the cultural, economic, and political power of the large, midwestern land-grant universities is often associated with their knowledge producing/knowledge disseminating functions, the political economy is also related to the "presence" of the university in local and state affairs. A research university produces jobs and revenues from the large amounts of external grant money it

receives. The social life of a university is also a part of the political economy. The sports program, for example, has economic and social implications for the community as a whole. A School of Business study, reported in a recent local Madison newspaper article, computed that each University of Wisconsin home football game produces $29 million in economic activity for the city (Stamler, 1987).

10. This is not to impute the personal motivation of faculty but to direct attention to structural issues. New Jersey, for example, has legislation to enable teachers to develop their own teacher education programs. In actual practice, local school districts hire university faculty to run these programs, maintaining the same expert/client relations that previously existed.

CHAPTER 5

1. See, e.g., Boyer (1983), Twentieth Century Fund Task Force (1983), Adler (1982), College Board (1983), National Commission on Excellence on Education (1983), Task Force on Education for Economic Growth (1983), Holmes Group (1986), Carnegie Foundation for the Advancement of Teaching (1988), National Council of Teachers of Mathematics (1989), Shulman and Sykes (1986), U.S. Department of Education (1986, 1987), and National Association of State Boards of Education (1988). For an excellent listing of the multiple texts related to school reforms concerned with science, mathematics, and technology during the 1980s, see National Research Council (1989).

2. As we consider this discourse, we should be aware that the sensitivity of schooling practice to the social and cultural milieu in which it occurs is not a uniquely American phenomenon; although differing in their conceptions of individuality, other societies were experiencing social transformations in the 1960s that spawned similar calls for school change. Soviet reforms of that period produced content revisions and a reorientation in school instruction that reflected a new emphasis on science. Russian was the first foreign language into which Bruner's *The Process of Education* (1960) was translated. Zankov's late 1950s reforms of USSR elementary education stressed the cultural attitudes and orientations that are associated with scientific technological transformations of Soviet industry (see Popkewitz, 1984, Chapter 3).

CHAPTER 6

1. Even when focusing on this delimited research agenda, questions can be raised about whether cognition can be perceived as a matter of rational choice, that is, whether people do make clear rational assessment of situations to form their choices so as to maximize their interests. That view of linear decisions is questionable in pedagogical contexts (see Streibel, 1989). Further, the idea of relevance assumes a functional relation to existing social patterns;

relevance is socially constructed as certain types of distinctions and categories are given authority to define social experience. What is relevant or irrelevant is related to issues of power and who has authority to legitimately define social conduct.

2. See Shulman (1987, pp. 2–4) for a discussion of the notions of content that underlie the cognitive psychological studies of teaching.

3. I use the notion of misrecognize in its sociological rather than psychological sense, drawing on the work of Pierre Bourdieu (1977, 1984). It does not suggest an opposite to truth but the attention given to socially formed, objectively studied practices.

4. The discussion is based on a composite of a variety of lessons that occurred over time.

5. This is often a result of the adaptation of positivism into American experimental and cognitive psychology, see, e.g., Simon (1981). One might contrast the view of psychology with Vygotsky (1978); for a discussion of the relation of psychology and positivism, see L. Smith (1986).

CHAPTER 7

1. This chapter could not have been written without the prior collaboration with Marie Brennan on the study of changing certification rules in teacher education and Kathryn Lind on the assumptions and implications of the Wisconsin Teacher Incentive Program.

2. For a discussion of texts as power relations in education, see Cherryholmes (1988). The general issue is covered in Foucault (1980) and in Martin, Gutman, and Hutton, (1988).

3. Responses to the new certification requirements entail increases in mandated courses and expanded faculty hiring in testing, measurement, and counseling, among other subdisciplines.

4. In fact, they resulted in enormous costs for hiring of new faculty and creating of new courses.

5. In the current situation, the devaluing of teachers' work is related to the more general processes of labor that have been occurring in professional work. More and more of professional work has been incorporated into bureaucratic organizations rather than remaining autonomous. See Derber (1982) and Murphy (1988) for a distinction in the professionalization processes occurring.

CHAPTER 8

1. I use the notion of strategic knowledge as does Jürgen Habermas (1971).

2. The word *intellectual* is itself a recent historical innovation; appearing during the Dreyfus Affair in France.

3. As before, I use the Progressive Era and World War II as markers to indicate rates of change that involve multiple layers of institutional practices that move at uneven rates.

4. All structural categories need not be global and nonhistorical. For discussions of structuralism as dynamic and historical theories, see the work of Bourdieu and Foucault. I borrow this term from Foucault and think of it as within the historical tradition in which he worked (see Tiles, 1984).

5. The formulaic quality of a dissertation can be summarized as follows: A text that is scientific is organized by the statement of the problem, review of literature, methods and procedures, discussion of findings, and conclusions. The linear, additive, and discrete quality of knowledge is derived from behavioral and positivist assumptions.

6. At times, a researcher is called upon to write a tract about what ought to be in the world to underscore how the actual projects of research relate to underlying values. Once such a tract is written, the research can proceed with a science that is administratively to explore how that world can be brought about.

7. I focus on a generalized reading of literature that I call popularism. I do this to discuss the political significance of a genre but, at the same time, recognize there is diversity. Further, I distinguish popularism from that scholarship that directly focuses on the problem of praxis in pedagogical relations. The latter's semantic style, layers of phenomena for analysis, and claims for social action have a different form from that found in the popularist literature (see, e.g., Ellsworth, 1989).

8. I appreciate the comments of Ulf Lundgren in pointing me to this element of Comte's work.

9. This position is taken by Mark Ginsburg (1987), who asserts that a science is not critical unless its scientists leave the "'sidelines' and enter the 'field' as activists" (p. 111). While I disagree with this relation as posed by Ginsburg, he does, more than others in arguing this position, seek to explore the contradictory role of this stance.

10. Jim Ladwig's comments on an earlier draft helped in making this distinction about what he calls "the intellectual for the Oppressed," who focuses on the agent of practice, the teacher.

11. Wexler (1987) poses that popularists tend to be people of middle-class background who seek to define an academic space for themselves. That is an empirical question that Wexler raises but does not argue. He does point to the importance of considering the social field in which knowledge is produced.

12. In academic articles, popularists establish this stance in the last section.

13. A problem in the use of resistance is its lack of rigor in signifying what is resistance to structural factors and what is part of the diversity of people's involvement, detachment, and opposition to social events (see, e.g., Hargreaves, 1982).

14. The epistemic figure is a construction of positions of power and knowledge in particular sets of social relations. See Bourdieu (1988, especially Chapter 1).

15. There is an awkwardness in English as I use "these" and "this" to focus upon the strand of feminist literature explored here. I use these words to emphasize the particular branch that I refer to within the multiple traditions and political agendas of feminist writing.

16. The role of the intellectual in legitimating social movements for the New Right in the United States is part of the phenomenon of change that occurred during the 1980s. Conservative think tanks, for example, sponsored liberal intellectuals who wrote about choice in education as a way of producing legitimate visions through construction of texts.

17. This autonomy is tied to commitment and is never absolute. See below.

18. See, e.g., Berman (1989) for a discussion of the need to keep the commitments of modernism.

References

Abelson, R. (1981). Psychological status of the script concept. *American Psychologist, 36*(7), 715–729.

Abrams, P. (Ed.). (1968). *The origins of British sociology, 1834–1914*. Chicago: University of Chicago Press.

Adler, M. (1982). *The paideia proposal: An educational manifesto*. New York: Macmillan.

Alba, J., & Hasher, L. (1983). Is memory schematic? *Psychological Bulletin, 93*(2), 203–231.

Alcoff, L. (1988). Cultural feminism versus post-structuralism: The identity crisis in feminist theory. *Signs. Journal of Women in Culture and Society, 13*(4), 405–437.

Almond, G., Chodorow, M., & Pearce, R. (Eds.). (1982). *Progress and its discontents*. Berkeley: University of California Press.

Altbach, P., & Cohen, R. (1989). American student activism: The post-sixties transformation. In P. Altbach (Ed.), *Student political activism* (pp. 457–473). Westport, CT: Greenwood Press.

Apple, M. (1986). *Teachers and texts, a political economy of class and gender relations in education*. New York: Routledge & Kegan Paul.

Archer, M. S. (1985). Structuration versus morphogenesis. In S. N. Eisenstadt & H. J. Helle (Eds.), *Macro-sociological theory, perspectives on sociological theory* (Vol. 1) (pp. 58–89). London: Sage.

Ariès, P. (1965). *Centuries of childhood* (R. Baldick, Trans.). New York: Vintage.

Badie, B., & Birnbaum, P. (1983). *The sociology of the state* (A. Goldhammer, Trans.). Chicago: University of Chicago Press.

Ball, D. (1988). *Research on teaching mathematics: Making subject matter knowledge part of the equation* (Research Report 88-2). East Lansing, MI: The National Center for Research on Teacher Education.

Bazerman, C. (1987). Codifying the scientific style. In J. Nelson, A. Mogill, & D. McCloskey (Eds.), *The rhetoric of the human sciences* (pp. 125–144). Madison: University of Wisconsin Press.

Beechey, V., & Donald, J. (Eds.). (1985). *Subjectivity and social relations: A reader*. Philadelphia: Open University Press, Milton Keyes.

Bell, D. (1962). *The end of ideology: On the exhaustion of political ideas in the fifties*. New York: The Free Press.

Bellah, R. (1968). Civil religion in America. In W. McLoughlin & R. Bellah (Eds.), *Religion in America* (pp. 3–23). Boston: Houghton Mifflin.

Berger, P., Berger, B., & Kellner, H. (1973). *The homeless mind: Modernization and consciousness*. New York: Vintage.

Berger, P., & Luckmann, T. (1967). *The social construction of reality: A treatise in the sociology of knowledge*. Garden City, NY: Anchor.

Berman, E. (1990, November). *Philanthropy and the shaping of American education*. Paper presented at annual meeting of the History and Education Society, Decatur, GA.

Berman, M. (1989). Why modernism still matters. *Tikkun, 4*(1), 11–14; 81–86.

Berman, R., & McLaughlin, M. (1978). *Federal programs supporting educational changes: Vol. 8. Implementing and sustaining innovation*. Santa Monica, CA: Rand.

Bernstein, B. (1977). *Class, codes and control: Towards a theory of educational transmissions* (2nd ed.) (Vol. 3). London: Routledge & Kegan Paul.

Bestor, A. (1953). *The educational wasteland*. Champaign: University of Illinois Press.

Blau, P. M. (Ed.). (1976). *Approaches to the study of social structure*. London: Open Books.

Bledstein, B. (1976). *The culture of professionalism: The middle class and the development of higher education in America*. New York: Norton.

Bloch, M. (1963). *The historian's craft* (P. Putnam, Trans.). New York: Knopf.

Bloch, M. (1987). Becoming scientific and professional: An historical perspective on the aims and effects of early education. In T. Popkewitz (Ed.), *The formation of school subjects: The struggle for creating an American institution* (pp. 25–62). New York: Falmer.

Block, F. (1977). The ruling class does not rule: Notes on the Marxist theory of the state. *Socialist Revolution, 33*, 6–28.

Boli, J. (1989). *New citizens for a new society: The institutional origins of mass schooling in Sweden*. New York: Pergamon.

Bourdieu, P. (1977). *Outline of a theory of practice*. Cambridge, UK: Cambridge University Press.

Bourdieu, P. (1984). *Distinction: A social critique of the judgment of taste* (R. Nice, Trans.). Cambridge, MA: Harvard University Press.

Bourdieu, P. (1985). The social space and the genesis of groups. *Theory and Society, 14*, 723–744.

Bourdieu, P. (1988). *Homo academicus* (P. Collier, Trans.). Stanford, CA: Stanford University Press.

Bourdieu, P. (1989a). The corporatism of the universal: The role of the intellectuals in the modern world. *Telos, 81*, 99–110.

Bourdieu, P. (1989b). Social space and symbolic power. *Sociological Theory, 7*(1), 14–25.

Bové, P. (1989). *Intellectuals in power: A genealogy of critical humanism*. New York: Columbia University Press.

Boyer, E. (1983). *High school: A report on secondary education in America*. New York: Harper & Row.

Bransford, J., Sherwood, R., Hasselbring, T., Kinzer, C., & Williams, S. (no date). *Anchored instruction: Why we need it and how technology can help.* Learning Technology Center, George Peabody College of Vanderbilt University, Nashville, TN.

Braudel, F. (1980). *On history* (S. Matthews, Trans.). Chicago: University of Chicago Press.

Brewer, W., & Nakamura, G. (1984). The nature and functions of schemas. In R. Wyer & T. Srull (Eds.), *Handbook of social cognition* (Vol. 1) (pp. 119–160). Hillsdale, NJ: Erlbaum.

Britzman, D. P. (1989). Who has the floor? Curriculum, teaching, and the English student teacher's struggle for voice. *Curriculum Inquiry, 19*(2), 143–162.

Bruner, J. (1960). *The process of education.* Cambridge, MA: Harvard University Press.

Callahan, R. (1962). *Education and the culture of efficiency: A study of the social forces that have shaped the administration of public schools.* Chicago: University of Chicago Press.

Callinicos, A. (1989). *Against postmodernism, A Marxist critique.* Cambridge, UK: Polity Press.

Carnegie Forum on Education and the Economy. (1986). *A nation prepared: Teachers for the 21st century: The report of the task force on teaching as a profession.* New York: Carnegie Corporation.

Carnegie Foundation for the Advancement of Teaching. (1988). *Report card on school reform.* New York: Author.

Carnoy, M. (1984). *The state and political theory.* Princeton, NJ: Princeton University Press.

Chance, W. (1986). *The best of education: Reforming America's public schools in the 1980's.* Chicago, IL: Catherine T. MacArthur Foundation.

Cherryholmes, C. (1988). *Power and criticism: Post-structural investigations in education.* New York: Teachers College Press.

Cherryholmes, C. (1990). *Reading research.* Unpublished manuscript. Michigan State University, East Lansing.

Clark, C., & Peterson, P. (1986). Teachers' thought processes. In M. Wittrock (Ed.), *Handbook of research on teaching* (3rd ed.) (pp. 225–296). New York: Macmillan.

Clark, C., & Yinger, R. (1979). Teacher thinking. In P. Peterson & H. Walberg (Eds.), *Research on teaching: Concepts, findings and implications* (pp. 231–263). Berkeley: McCutchan.

Clifford, G. (1987). 'Lady teachers' and politics: The United States, 1850–1930. In M. Lawn & G. Grace (Eds.), *Teachers, the culture, and politics of work* (pp. 3–30). New York: Falmer.

Clifford, J. (1988). *The predicament of culture: Twentieth-century ethnography, literature and art.* Cambridge, MA: Harvard University Press.

Clune, W., & Witte, J. (1990a). *Choice and control in American education: Vol. 1. The theory of choice and control in education.* New York: Falmer.

Clune, W., & Witte, J. (1990b). *Choice and control in American education: Vol.*

2. *The practice of choice, decentralization and school restructuring.* New York: Falmer.

Cohen, M. (1990, April 17). Movement for potential school choice debated. *The Boston Globe*, p. 1.

College Board. (1983). *Academic preparation for college: What students need to know and be able to do.* New York: College Entrance Examination Board.

Collins, R. (1979). *The credential society, an historical sociology of education and stratification.* New York: Academic Press.

Connell, R., Ashenden, D., Kessler, S., & Powsett, G. (1982). *Making the difference: Schools, families and social division.* Sydney, Australia: George Allen & Unwin.

Conway, J. (1971). Women reformers and American culture, 1870–1930. *Journal of Social History, 5*(2), 164–177.

Conway, J. (1974). Perspectives on the history of women's education in the United States. *History of Education Quarterly, 14,* 1–11.

Cronin, J. M. (1983). State regulation of teacher preparation. In L. Shulman & G. Sykes, (Eds.), *Handbook on teaching and policy in education* (pp. 171–191). New York: Longman.

Cuban, L. (1984). *How teachers taught, constancy and change in American classrooms, 1890–1980.* New York: Longman.

Curti, M. (1959). *The social ideas of American educators.* Paterson, NJ: Pageant Books.

Curti, M., & Carstensen, V. (1949). *University of Wisconsin, a history, 1848–1925* (Vol. 1.). Madison: University of Wisconsin Press.

Curti, M., & Nash, R. (1965). *Philanthropy in the shaping of American higher education.* New Brunswick, NJ: Rutgers University Press.

Cushman, M. (1977). *The governance of teacher education.* Berkeley: McCutchan.

Cushman, P. (1990). Why the self is empty: Toward a historically situated psychology. *American Psychologist, 45*(5), 599–611.

Dahl, R. (1961). The behavioral approach in political science: Epitaph for a monument to a successful protest. *American Political Science Review, 55,* 763–772.

Danziger, K. (1987). Social contexts and investigative practice in early twentieth century psychology. In M. Ash & W. Woodward (Eds.), *Psychology in twentieth century thought and society* (pp. 13–31). New York: Cambridge University Press.

Davis, D. (Ed.). (1967). *Ante-bellum reform.* New York: Harper & Row.

DeGrazia, S. (1964). *Of time, work and leisure.* Garden City, NY: Anchor.

DeLone, R. (1979). *Small futures: Children, inequity, and the limits of liberal reform.* New York: Harcourt, Brace, Jovanovich.

Derber, C. (Ed.). (1982). *Professionals as workers: Mental labor in advanced capitalism.* Boston, MA: Hall.

Di Sibrio, R. A. (1973). *An analysis and comparison of certification requirements for elementary teachers in the United States.* Unpublished doctoral dissertation, Indiana University of Pennsylvania.

Dickson, D. (1984). *The new politics of science.* New York: Pantheon.

DiMaggio, P. (1987). Classification in art. *American Sociological Review, 52,* 440–455.

Dolbeare, K., & Dolbeare, P. (1973). *American ideologies: Competing political beliefs of the 1970s* (2nd ed.). Chicago: Markham.

Donovan, B. (1983). *Power and curriculum implementation: A case study of an innovatory mathematics program.* Unpublished doctoral dissertation, University of Wisconsin, Madison.

Donzelot, J. (1979). *The policing of the family.* New York: Pantheon.

Dreyfus, H., & Rabinow, P. (1983). *Michel Foucault: Beyond structuralism and hermeneutics,* Chicago: University of Chicago Press.

Durkheim, E. (1977). *The evolution of educational thought: Lectures on the formation and development of secondary education in France.* (P. Collins, Trans.). London: Routledge & Kegan Paul. (Original work published 1938)

Eagleton, T. (1983). *Literary theory: An introduction.* Minneapolis, MN: University of Minnesota Press.

Edelman, M. (1964). *The symbolic uses of politics.* Urbana: University of Illinois Press.

Educational Commission of the States (Task Force on Education for Economic Growth). (1983). *Action for excellence.* Denver, CO: Author.

Education Development Center, Social Studies Curriculum Program. (1968–76). *Man: A course of study* (curriculum package). Washington, DC: Curriculum Development Associates.

Edwards, T., Gewitz, S., & Whitty, G. (1990). *The state and private education: An evaluation of the assisted places scheme.* Lewes, UK: Falmer.

Ellsworth, E. (1989). Why doesn't this feel empowering? Working through repressive myths of critical pedagogy. *Harvard Educational Review, 59*(3), 297–324.

Elzinga, A. (1985). Research, bureaucracy and the draft of epistemic criteria. In B. Wittrock & A. Elzinga (Eds.), *The university research system: The public policies of the home of scientists* (pp. 191–220). Stockholm, Sweden: Almquist & Wiskell International.

Englund, T. (1986). *Curriculum as a political problem: Changing educational conceptions, with special reference to citizenship education.* Uppsala, Sweden: Student Litteratur, Chartwell-Bratt.

Fabian, J. (1983). *Time and the other, how anthropology makes its object.* New York: Columbia University Press.

Feyerabend, P. (1978). *Science in a free society.* London: New Left Books.

Fine, S. (1956). *Laissez faire and the general welfare state; a study of conflict in American thought.* Ann Arbor: University of Michigan Press.

Finkelstein, B. (1975). Pedagogy as intrusion: Teaching as values in popular primary schools in nineteenth-century America. *History of Childhood Quarterly, 2*(3), 349–378.

Finkelstein, B. (1989). *Governing the young: Teacher behavior in popular primary schools in 19th-century United States.* New York: Falmer.

Finn, C. (1988). Educational policy and the Reagan administration: A large but incomplete success. *Educational Policy, 2*(4), 343–360.

Fiske, E. (1990, February 26). Governors' group & Bush envision stronger schools; vast reforms proposed. *The New York Times*, p. 1.

Flint, A. (1990, April 18). Single curriculum for schools in U.S. prescribed by educator. *The Boston Globe*, p. 12.

Foucault, M. (1965). *Madness and civilization: A history of insanity in the age of reason* (R. Howard, Trans.). New York: Pantheon.

Foucault, M. (1973). *The order of things: An archaeology of the human sciences.* New York: Vintage.

Foucault, M. (1975). *The birth of the clinic; an archaeology at medical perception.* (A. Smith, Trans.). New York: Vintage.

Foucault, M. (1977). *Power/knowledge: Selected interviews and other writings, 1972–1977* (C. Gordon, Ed.). New York: Pantheon.

Foucault, M. (1978). Politics and the study of discourse. *Ideology and the study of discourse,* (3), 7–26.

Foucault, M. (1979a). *Discipline and punish: The birth of the prison.* (A. Sheridan, Trans.). New York: Vintage.

Foucault, M. (1979b). Governmentality. *Ideology and Consciousness, 6,* 5–22.

Foucault, M. (1980). *Power/knowledge: Selected interviews and other writings by Michel Foucault, 1972–1977* (C. Gordon, Ed.). New York: Pantheon.

Foucault, M. (1988). The political technology of individuals. In L. Martin, H. Gutman, & P. Huttan (Eds.), *Technologies of the self: A seminar with Michel Foucault* (pp. 145–162). Amherst: University of Massachusetts Press.

Franklin, B. (1986). *Building the American community: The school curriculum and the search for social control.* London: Falmer.

Franklin, B. (1987a). The first crusade for learning disabilities: The movement for the education of backward children. In T. Popkewitz (Ed.), *The formation of school subjects: The struggle for creating an American institution* (pp. 190–209). New York: Falmer.

Franklin, B. (Ed.). (1987b). *Learning disabilities: Dissenting essays.* New York: Falmer.

Fraser, N. (1989). *Unruly practices: Power, discourse and gender in contemporary social theory.* Minneapolis: University of Minnesota Press.

Freedman, K. (1987). Art education as social production: Culture, society and politics in the formation of the curriculum. In T. Popkewitz (Ed.), *The formation of school subjects: The struggle for creating an American institution* (pp. 63–84). London: Falmer.

Freedman, K. (1989a). Dilemmas of equity in art education: Ideologies of individualism and cultural capital. In W. G. Secada (Ed.), *Equity in education* (pp. 103–117). New York: Falmer.

Freedman, K. (1989b). The philanthropic vision: The Owatoma Art Education Project as an example of "private" interests in public schooling. *Studies in Art Education, 31*(1), 15–26.

Freedman, K., & Popkewitz, T. (1988). Art education and social interests in the development of schooling: Ideological origins of curriculum theory. *Journal of Curriculum Studies, 20*(5), 387–406.

Friedenberg, E. (1963). *Coming of age in America*. New York: Random House.

Fullan, M. (1982). *The meaning of educational change*. New York: Teachers College Press.

Furner, M. (1975). *Advocacy & objectivity: A crisis in the professionalization of American social science, 1865–1905*. Lexington: University of Kentucky.

Gardner, H. (1985). *The mind's new science: A history of the cognitive revolution*. New York: Basic Books.

Garland, S. (1987, August 10). Upgrading the schools: Business gets into the act, *Business Week*, p. 61.

Giddens, A. (1987). *Social theory and modern sociology*. Stanford, CA: Stanford University Press.

Gideonse, H. D. (1984). State education policy in transition: Teacher education. *Phi Delta Kappan 66*(3), 205–208.

Gilligan, C. (1982). *In a different voice: Psychological theory and women's development*. Cambridge, MA: Harvard University Press.

Ginsburg, M. (1987). Contradictions in the role of professor as actist. *Sociological Focus, 20*(2), 111–122.

Ginsburg, M. (1988). *Contradictions in teacher education and society, a critical analysis*. New York: Falmer.

Giroux, H. (1990). Rethinking the boundaries of educational discourse: Modernism, postmodernism, and feminism. *College Literature, 17*(2/3), 1–50.

Goodlad, J. I. (1984). *A place called school: Prospectus for the future*. New York: McGraw-Hill.

Goodman, P. (1966). *The urban school crisis: An anthology of essays*. New York: League for Industrial Democracy and United Federation of Teachers.

Goodson, I. (Ed.). (1985). *Social histories of the secondary curriculum, subjects for study*. New York: Falmer.

Gore, J. (1990). What we can do for you! What *can* "we" do for "you"?: Struggling over empowerment in critical and feminist pedagogy. *Educational Foundations, 4*(3), 5–26.

Gould, S. J. (1981). *The mismeasure of man*. New York: Norton.

Gramsci, A. (1971). *Selections from the prison notebooks of Antonio Gramsci* (Q. Hoare, Ed. and Trans.). New York: International Publishers.

Granheim, M., Kogan, M., & Lundgren, U. (1990). *Evaluation as policy making: Introducing evaluation into a national decentralized educational system*. London: Kingsley.

Greeley, A. M. (1985). *Unsecular man: The persistence of religion*. New York: Schocken.

Habermas, J. (1970). *Towards a rational society, student protest, science, and politics* (J. Sharipo, Trans.). Boston: Beacon.

Habermas, J. (1971). *Knowledge and human interest* (J. Shapiro, Trans.). Boston: Beacon.

Hall, G. S. (1923). *Life and confessions of a psychologist*. New York: Appleton.

Hall, G. (1969a). *Adolescence: Its psychology and its relation to physiology, anthropology, sociology, sex, crime, religion and education* (Vol. 1). New York: Arno Press and the New York Times. (Originally published 1905)

Hall, G. (1969b). *Adolescence: Its psychology and its relation to physiology, anthropology, sociology, sex, crime, religion and education* (Vol. 2). New York: Arno Press and the New York Times. (Originally published 1905)

Hamilton, D. (1980). Adam Smith and the moral economy of the classroom system. *Journal of Curriculum Studies, 12*(4), 781–798.

Hamilton, D. (1981). Robert Owen and education: A reassessment. In H. Patterson & W. Humes (Eds.), *Historical essays on Scottish education and culture* (pp. 9–24). Edinburgh, UK: John Donald.

Hamilton, D. (1989). *Towards a theory of schooling.* London: Falmer.

Hargreaves, A. (1982). Resistance and relative autonomy theories: Problems of distortion and incoherence in recent Marxist analyses of education. *British Journal of Sociology of Education, 3*(2), 107–125.

Haskell, T. (1977). *The emergence of professional social science: The American social science association and the nineteenth-century crisis of authority.* Urbana: University of Illinois Press.

Haskell, T. (1984). Professionalism versus capitalism: R. H. Towney, Emile Durkheim, and C. S. Pierce on the disinterestedness of professional communities. In T. Haskell (Ed.), *The authority of experts: Studies in history and theory* (pp. 180–225), Bloomington: Indiana University Press.

Held, D., & Thompson, J. B. (Eds.). (1989). *Social theory of modern societies: Anthony Giddens and his critics.* New York: Cambridge University Press.

Help wanted! America faces an era of worker scarcity that may last to the year 2000. (1987, August 10). *Business Week,* pp. 48–51.

Herbst, J. (1965). *The German historical school in American scholarship: A study in the transfer of culture.* Ithaca, NY: Cornell University Press.

Herbst, J. (1989). *And sadly teach: Teacher education and professionalization in American culture.* Madison: University of Wisconsin Press.

Hoeveler, J. (1976). The university and the social gospel: The intellectual origins of the Wisconsin idea. *Wisconsin Magazine of History, 59* (Summer), 282–298.

Hofstadter, R. (1955). *The age of reform, from Bryan to F.D.R.* New York: Vintage.

Hofstadter, R. (1962). *Anti-intellectualism in American life.* New York: Vintage.

Hofstadter, R., & Metzger, W. (1955). *The development of academic freedom in the United States.* New York: Columbia University Press.

Holmes Group. (1986). *Tomorrow's teachers.* East Lansing, MI: Author.

Holmes Group. (1990). *Tomorrow's schools.* East Lansing, MI: Author.

House, E. (1985). *Evaluation and social justice: Where are we?* Boulder: University of Colorado (mimeo).

Hunter, A. (1988). *Children in the service of conservativism: Parent/child relations in the New Right pro-family rhetoric.* Legal history working paper, Institute of Legal Studies, University of Wisconsin, Madison.

Illich, I. (1971). *Deschooling society.* London: Calder & Boyes.

James, T. (1986, April). *The social scientist and minority groups in crisis.* Paper presented at the annual meeting of the American Educational Research Association, San Francisco.

Jay, M. (1973). *The dialectical imagination: A history of the Frankfurt School and the Institute of Social Research, 1923–1950.* Boston, MA: Beacon.

Jay, M. (1984). *Marxism and totality; the adventures of a concept from Lukacs to Habermas*. Berkeley: University of California Press.

Johanningmeir, E. (1969). William Chandler Bagley's changing views on the relationship between psychology and education. *History of Education Quarterly*, Spring, 3–27.

Johnson, M. (1986). The stagnant South. *The New York Review of Books*, 33(8), 38–41.

Joncich, G. (1968). *The sane positivist, a bibliography of Edward Thorndike*. Middleton, CT: Wesleyan University Press.

Kaestle, C. (1983). *Pillars of the republic: Common schools and American society, 1780–1860*. New York: Hill & Wang.

Kaestle, C. (1985). The history of literacy and the history of readers. In E. Gordon (Ed.), *Review of research in education* (Vol. 12) (pp. 11–54). Washington, DC: American Education Research Association.

Kaestle, C., & Smith, M. (1982). The federal role in elementary and secondary education, 1940–1980. *Harvard Educational Review*, 53(4), 384–408.

Kalfayan, E. (Ed.). (1988). What makes teaching reform succeed or fail? . . . Rand looks at issues of quality, experience, licensing, and evaluation in the teaching reform movement of the 1980s. *Rand Checklist* (No. 371). Santa Monica, CA: The Rand Corporation.

Kantor, R. (1989). *When giants learn to dance: Mastering the challenge of strategy, management, and careers in the 1990s*. New York: Simon & Schuster.

Karier, C. (1967). *Man, society, and education. A history of American educational ideas*. New York: Scott, Foresman.

Karier, C. (1986). *Scientists of the mind: Intellectual founders of modern psychology*. Champaign: University of Illinois Press.

Karier, C., & Hogan, D. (1979). Schooling, education and the structure of social reality, *Educational Studies*, 10, 245–265.

Katznelson, I., & Weil, M. (1986). *Schooling for all: Class, race and the decline of the American ideal*. New York: Basic Books.

Kilpatrick, J. (in press). A history in mathematics education. In D. Grouws (Ed.), *Handbook on mathematics teaching and learning*, New York: Macmillan.

Kimball, B. (1988). The historical and cultural dimensions of the recent reports on undergraduate education. *American Journal of Education*, 96(3), 293–322.

Kirst, M. (1984). The vanishing myth of local control. *Phi Delta Kappan*, 66(3), 189–191.

Kliebard, H. (1986). *Struggle for the American curriculum*. London: Routledge & Kegan Paul.

Krasner, S. (1978). United States commercial and monetary policy: Unraveling the paradox of external strength and internal weakness. In P. J. Katzenstein (Ed.), *Between power and plenty, foreign economic policies of advanced industrial states*, (pp. 51–87). Madison: University of Wisconsin Press.

Krug, E. (1972). *The shaping of the American high school, 1920–1941*. Madison: University of Wisconsin Press.

Kuhn, T. (1970). *The structure of scientific revolutions* (2nd ed.). Chicago: University of Chicago Press.

Labaree, D. (1988). *The making of an American high school: The credentials market and the central high school of Philadelphia, 1838–1939.* New Haven: Yale University Press.

Labaree, D. (1990a). A kinder and gentler report: Turning points and the Carnegie tradition. *Journal of Educational Policy, 5,* 249–264.

Labaree, D. (1990b). *Power, knowledge, and the science of teaching: A genealogy of teacher professionalization.* Unpublished paper. School of Education, Michigan State University, East Lansing.

Lagemann, E. (1989). *The politics of knowledge: The Carnegie Corporation, philanthropy, and public policy.* Middleton, CT: Wesleyan University Press.

Landes, D. (1983). *Revolution in time: Clocks and the making of the modern world.* Cambridge, MA: Harvard University Press.

Lasch, C. (1977). *Haven in a heartless world: The family besieged.* New York: Basic Books.

Lasch, C. (1978). *The culture of narcissism: American life in an age of diminishing expectations.* New York: Norton.

Lather, P. (1990). Reinscribing otherwise: The play of values in the practices of the human sciences. In E. Guba (Ed.), *The paradigm dialog* (pp. 315–332). Newbury Park, CA: Sage.

Learned, W. (1927). *The quality of the educational process in the United States and in Europe.* The Carnegie Commission on Higher Education, Boston: P. B. Updike, The Merrymount Press.

Lears, J. (1981). *No place of grace, antimodernism and the transformation of American culture, 1880–1920.* New York: Pantheon.

Leary, D. (1987). Telling likely stories: The rhetoric of the new psychology, 1880–1920. *Journal of the History of the Behavioral Sciences, 23,* 315–331.

Lecourt, D. (1975). *Marxism and epistemology, Bachelard, Canguilhem, Foucault.* (B. Brewster, Trans.). London: New Left Books.

LeGoff, J. (1980). *Time, work and culture in the Middle Ages* (A. Goldhammer, Trans.). Chicago: University of Chicago.

Levy, F. (1986). *Dollars and dreams, the changing American income distribution.* New York: Russell Sage Foundation/Basic Books.

Lindblad, S. (1986). Teachers and social class orientation: An empirical note based on comparisons with different social classes in Sweden. *Scandinavian Journal of Education, 30,* 181–192.

Luke, C. (1989). *Pedagogy, printing, and Protestantism. The discourse on childhood.* Albany: State University of New York Press.

Lundgren, U. (1983). *Between hope and happening: Text and contexts in curriculum.* Geelong, Australia: Deakin University Press.

Lybarger, M. (1987). Need as ideology: A look at the early social studies. In T. Popkewitz (Ed.), *The formation of school subjects: The struggle for creating an American institution* (pp. 176–190). New York: Falmer.

Macpherson, C. (1962). *The political theory of possessive individualism: Hobbes to Locke.* New York: Oxford Press.

Manicas, P. (1987). *A history and philosophy of the social sciences.* Oxford, UK: Blackwell.

Mann, H. (1849). Massachusetts Board of Education 12th Annual Report, Boston, MA.

Manuel, F. (1974). *The religion of Isaac Newton*, London: Oxford University Press.

Manuel, F., & Manuel, F. (1979). *Utopian thought in the Western world*. Cambridge, MA: Harvard University Press.

Maraniss, E. (1990, May 9). Is the famous U.W.-state connection still special? *The Capital Times*, p. 1.

Maravall, J. (1986). *Culture of the Baroque: Analysis of historical structure*. (T. Cochran, Trans.). Minneapolis: University of Minnesota Press.

Martin, J. (1978). *The migrant presence, Australian responses 1947–1977*. Sydney, Australia: George Allan & Unwin.

Martin, L., Gutman, H., & Hutton, P. (1988). *Technologies of the self, a seminar with Michael Foucault*. Amherst: University of Massachusetts.

Marx, L. (1964). *The machine in the garden: Technology and the pastoral image in America*. New York: Oxford University Press.

Massey, D., Condran, G., & Denton, N. (1987). The effects of residential segregation on black social and economic well-being. *Social Forces, 66*(1), 29–56.

Massey, D., & Eggers, M. (1989). *The ecology of inequality: Minorities and the concentration of poverty 1970–1980* (Population Research Center Discussion Paper Series). Chicago: National Opinion Research Center/University of Chicago.

Mattingly, P. (1975). *The classless profession: American schoolmen in the nineteenth century*. New York: New York University Press.

Mattingly, P. (1981). Academia and professional school careers, 1840–1900. *Teachers College Record, 83*(2), 219–233.

Mattingly, P. (1987). Workplace autonomy and the reforming of teacher education. In T. Popkewitz (Ed.), *Critical studies in teacher education: Its folklore, theory and practice* (pp. 36–56). New York: Falmer.

May, H. (1949). *Protestant churches and industrial society*. New York: Harper.

McCarthy, C. (1912). *The Wisconsin idea*. New York: Macmillan.

McDiarmid, G., Ball, D., & Anderson, C. (1989). Why staying one-chapter ahead doesn't really work: Subject-specific pedagogy (Issue Paper 88-6). East Lansing, MI: National Center for Research on Teacher Education.

McLaren, P. (1986). *Schooling as a ritual performance*. Boston: Routledge & Kegan Paul.

McLennan, G. (1989). *Marxism, pluralism and beyond, classic debates and new departures*. Cambridge, UK: Polity Press.

Meyer, J. (1986). The politics of educational crisis in the United States. In W. Cummings, E. R. Beauchamp, S. Ichikawa, V. Kokayashi, and M. Ushiogi (Eds.), *Educational policies in crisis: Japanese and American perspectives* (pp. 44–58). New York: Praeger.

Meyer, J., & Rowan, B. (1977). Institutional organizations: Formal structure as myth and ceremony. *American Journal of Sociology, 83*(2), 340–363.

Miller, L. S. (1986, May 14). Nation-building and education, *Education Week*, p. 40.

Mills, C. W. (1959). *The sociological imagination.* New York: Oxford University Press.

Mirga, T. (1986, May 14). Here they come, ready or not? *Education Week, 5*(34), 13–37.

Montangero, J. (1985). *Genetic epistemology: Yesterday and today* (Helvetia Swiss Lecturship 3). New York: Graduate School and University Center, City University of New York.

Murphy, R. (1988, March). *Proletarization or bureaucratization? The deskilling thesis.* Paper presented at the Swedish Colloquium for Advanced Study in the Social Sciences, Uppsala, Sweden.

Napoli, D. (1981). *Architects of adjustment: The history of the psychological profession in the United States.* Port Washington, NY: Kennikat Press.

National Association of State Boards of Education [Task Force on Early Childhood Education]. (1988). *Right from the start.* Alexandria, VA: Author.

National Commission on Excellence in Education. (1983). *A nation at risk: The imperative for educational reform.* Washington, DC: U.S. Government Printing Office.

National Council of Teachers of Mathematics. (1989). *Curriculum and evaluation standards for school mathematics.* Reston, VA: Author.

National Research Council; Board on Mathematics Sciences [and] Mathematical Sciences Education Board. (1989). *Everybody counts: A report to the nation on the future of mathematics education.* Washington DC: National Academy of Sciences.

Newman, F. (1987). *Choosing quality, reducing conflict between the state and the university.* Denver, CO: Education Commission of the States.

Nicholson, L. (1986). *Gender and history, the limits of social theory in the age of the family.* New York: Columbia University Press.

Nisbet, R. (1969). *History and social change: Aspects of the Western theory of development.* New York: Oxford University Press.

Noble, D. (1970). *The progressive mind, 1890–1917.* Chicago: Rand McNally.

Noble, D. (1989). Cockpit cognition: Education, the military and cognitive engineering. *AI & Society, 3,* 271–296.

Noujain, E. (1987). History as genealogy: An exploration of Foucault's approach. In A. Griffiths, (Ed.), *Contemporary French philosophy.* (pp. 157–174). New York: Cambridge University Press.

O'Donnell, J. (1985). *The origins of behaviorism: American psychology, 1876–1920.* New York: University Press.

Offe, C. (1975). The theory of the capitalist state and the problem of policy formation. In L. Lindberg, R. Alford, C. Crach, & C. Offe (Eds.), *Stress and contradiction in modern capitalism, public policy and the theory of the state* (pp. 125–144), Lexington, MA: Lexington Books.

Offe, C. (1984). *Contradictions of the welfare state.* (J. Keane, Ed.). Cambridge, MA: MIT Press.

Omi, M., & Winant, H. (1986). *Racial formation in the United States, from the 1960s to the 1980s.* Boston: Routledge & Kegan Paul.

Orloff, A., & Skocpol, T. (1984). Why not equal protection? Spending in Britain,

1900–1911, and the United States, 1880s–1920. *The American Sociological Review, 49*, 726–750.

Ortega y Gasset, J. (1960). *The revolt of the masses.* New York: Norton.

Pateman, C. (1988). *The sexual contract.* Stanford, CA: Stanford University Press.

Peterson, P. (1985). *The politics of school reform, 1870–1940.* Chicago: University of Chicago Press.

Plank, D., & Turner, M. (1987). Changing patterns in black school politics: Atlanta: 1872–1973. *American Journal of Education, 95*, 559–590.

Popkewitz, T. (1976a). Reform as political discourse: A case study. *School Review, 84*, 43–69.

Popkewitz, T. (1976b). Myths of social science in curriculum. *Educational Forum, 60*, 317–328.

Popkewitz, T. (1977a). Community and craft as metaphor of social inquiry curriculum. *Educational Theory, 5*(1), 41–60.

Popkewitz, T. (1977b). Latent values of the discipline centered curriculum, *Theory and Research in Social Education, 5*, 41–60.

Popkewitz, T. (1978). Schools and the symbolic uses of community participation. In C. A. Grant (Ed.), *Community participation in education* (pp. 202–223). Boston: Allyn & Bacon.

Popkewitz, T. (1979). Educational reform and the problem of institutional life. *Educational Researcher, 8*(3), 3–8.

Popkewitz, T. (1981). Qualitative research: Some thoughts about the relation of methodology and social history. In T. Popkewitz & B. R. Tabachnick, *The study of schooling: Field based methodologies in educational research and evaluation* (pp. 155–180). New York: Praeger.

Popkewitz, T. (1982a). Whither, wither goes the curriculum field? *Contemporary Educational Review, 1*(1), 15–22.

Popkewitz, T. (1982b). Educational reform as the organization of ritual: Stability as change. *Journal of Education, 164*(1), 5–29.

Popkewitz, T. (1983a). The sociological basis for individual differences: The relationship of solitude to the crowd. In G. Fenstermacher & J. Goodlad (Eds.), *Individual differences and the common curriculum (82nd Yearbook)* (pp. 44–74). Chicago: National Society for the Study of Education.

Popkewitz, T. (Ed.). (1983b). *Change and stability in schooling, the dual quality of educational reform.* Geelong, Australia: Deakin University Press.

Popkewitz, T. (1984). *Paradigm and ideology in educational research: Social functions of the intellectual.* New York: Falmer.

Popkewitz, T. (Ed.). (1987a). *Critical studies in teacher education: Its folklore, theory and practice.* New York: Falmer.

Popkewitz, T. (Ed.). (1987b). The current reform reports on teaching and teacher education. *Social Education, 51*(7), 492–521.

Popkewitz, T. (Ed.). (1987c). *The formation of school subjects: The struggle for creating an American institution.* New York: Falmer.

Popkewitz, T. (1987d). Organization and power: Teacher education reforms. *Social Education, 51*(7), 496–500.

Popkewitz, T. (1988a). Culture, pedagogy, and power: Issues in the production of values and colonialization. *Journal of Education, 170*(2), 77–90.

Popkewitz, T. (1988b). Institutional issues in the study of school mathematics: Curriculum research. *Educational Studies in Mathematics, 19,* 221–249.

Popkewitz, T. (1990). Whose future? Whose past? Notes on critical theory and methodology. In E. G. Guba (Ed.), *The paradigm dialog* (pp. 46–66). Newbury Park, CA: Sage.

Popkewitz, T., & Freedman, K. (1985). Culture, art and consciousness: On social transformation and the production of myth in science and curriculum. *Contemporary Educational Review, 3*(1), 269–280.

Popkewitz, T., & Lind, K. (1989). Teacher incentives as reform: Implications for teachers' work and the changing control mechanism in education. *Teachers College Record, 90*(4), 575–594.

Popkewitz, T., & Pitman, A. (1986). The idea of progress and the legitimation of state agendas: American proposals for school reform, *Curriculum and Teaching, 1*(1–2), 11–24.

Popkewitz, T., Pitman, A., & Barry, A. (1986). Educational reform and its millennial quality: The 1980's. *Journal of Curriculum Studies, 18*(3), 267–284.

Popkewitz, T., & St. Maurice, H. (1991). Social studies education and theory: Science, knowledge, and history. In J. P. Shaver (Ed.), *Handbook for research in social studies education* (pp. 27–40). New York: Macmillan.

Popkewitz, T., Tabachnick, B., & Wehlage, G. (1982). *The myth of educational reform: A study of school responses to a program of change.* Madison: University of Wisconsin Press.

Poster, M. (1978). *Critical theory of the family.* London: Pluto Press.

Powell, A. (1980). *The uncertain profession. Harvard and the search for educational authority.* Cambridge, MA: Harvard University Press.

Prestine, N. (1989). The struggle for control of teacher education: A case study. *Educational Evaluation and Policy Analysis, 11*(3), 285–300.

Rajchman, J. (1985). *Michel Foucault. The freedom of philosophy.* New York: Columbia University Press.

Ramirez, F., & Boli, J. (1987). The political construction of mass schooling: European origins and worldwide institutionalization. *Sociology of Education, 60,* 2–17.

Reese, W. (1986). *Power and the promise of school reform: Grass roots movements during the Progressive Era.* Boston: Routledge & Kegan Paul.

Reiger, K. (1985). *The disenchantment of the home, modernizing the Australian family 1880–1940.* New York: Oxford University Press.

Rizvi, F. (1989a). Bureaucratic rationality and the promise of democratic schooling. In W. Carr (Ed.), *Quality in teaching: Arguments for a reflective profession* (pp. 55–78). New York: Falmer.

Rizvi, F. (1989b). *Pragmatics of explanation.* Unpublished manuscript. Geelong, Australia: Deakin University Press.

Romberg, T. A., & Stewart, D. M. (Eds.). (1985). *School mathematics: Options for the 1990s. Proceedings of the conference* (rev. ed.). Madison: Wisconsin Center for Education Research.

Romberg, T. A., & Stewart, D. M. (Eds.). (1987). *The monitoring of school mathematics: Background papers* (Vol. 1). Madison: Wisconsin Center for Education Research.

Rorty, R. (1979). *Philosophy and the mirror of nature.* Princeton, NJ: Princeton University Press.

Rorty, R. (1988, April 4). That old-time philosophy. *The New Republic,* pp. 28–33.

Rose, S. (1972). *The betrayal of the poor: The transformation of community action.* Cambridge, MA: Schenkmen.

Ross, D. (1984). American social science and the idea of progress. In T. Haskell (Ed.), *The authority of experts: Studies in history and theory* (pp. 157–179). Bloomington: Indiana University Press.

Roth, M. (1988). *Knowing and history; appropriations of Hegel in twentieth-century France.* Ithaca, NY: Cornell University Press.

Scheler, M. (1980). *Problems of a sociology of knowledge* (M. Frings, Trans.). Boston: Routledge & Kegan Paul. (Originally published 1924)

Schiesl, M. (1977). *The politics of efficiency, municipal administration and reform in America, 1880–1920.* Berkeley, CA: University of California Press.

Schneider, B. (1987). Tracing the provenance of teacher education. In T. Popkewitz (Ed.), *Critical studies in teacher education: Its folklore, theory and practice* (pp. 211–242). New York: Falmer.

Scott, A. (1988). The ever-widening circle: The diffusion of feminist values from the Troy Female Seminary, 1822–1872. In B. E. McClellan & W. J. Reese (Eds.), *The social history of American education* (pp. 137–164). Champaign: University of Illinois Press.

Sedlack, M., & Schlossman, S. (1987). Who will teach? Historical perspectives on the changing appeal of teaching as a profession. In E. Rothkopt (Ed.), *Review of Research in Education, 14* (pp. 93–131). Washington, DC: American Educational Research Association.

Sennett, R. (1978). *The fall of public man: On the social psychology of capitalism.* New York: Random House.

Shaver, J. (1979). The usefulness of educational research in curricular/instructional decision-making in social studies. *Theory and Research in Social Education, 7*(3), 21–46.

Sherman, J. A., & Beck, E. T. (Eds.). (1979). *The prism of sex: Essays in the sociology of knowledge: Proceedings of a symposium sponsored by WRI of Wisconsin, Inc.* Madison: University of Wisconsin Press.

Shor, I. (1986). *Culture wars, school and society in the conservative restoration, 1969–1984.* Boston: Routledge & Kegan Paul.

Shorter, E. (1975). *The making of the modern family.* New York: Basic Books.

Shulman, L. (1986). Those who understand: Knowledge growth in teaching. *Educational Researcher, 15*(2), 4–14.

Shulman, L. (1987). Knowledge and teaching: Foundations of the new reform. *Harvard Educational Review, 37*(1), 1–22.

Shulman, L., & Sykes, G. (1986). *A national board for teaching? In search of a bold standard.* New York: Carnegie Forum on Education and the Economy.

Silk, L. (1990, May 4). Can U.S. recover in electronics. *The New York Times*, p. C2.

Silva, E., & Slaughter, S. (1984). *Serving power: The making of the academic social science expert*. Westport, CT: Greenwood Press.

Silver, H. (1983). *Education as history: Interpreting nineteenth and twentieth century education*. London: Methuen.

Simon, H. (1981). *The science of the artificial*. Cambridge, MA: MIT Press.

Skocpol, T. (1980). Political response to capitalist crisis: Neo-Marxist theories of the state and the case of the New Deal. *Politics and Society, 10*(2), 155–202.

Skowronek, S. (1982). *Building a new American state: The expansion of national administrative capacities, 1877–1920*. New York: Cambridge University Press.

Sleeter, C. (1987). Why is there learning disabilities? A critical analysis of the birth of a field in its social context. In T. Popkewitz (Ed.), *The formation of the school subject matter: The struggle for creating an American institution* (pp. 210–238). New York: Falmer.

Smith, L. (1986). *Behaviorism and logical positivism: A reassessment of the alliance*. Stanford, CA: Stanford University Press.

Snow, C. (1962). *The two cultures and the scientific revolution* (Rede Lecture, 1959). New York: Cambridge University Press.

Soltis, J. (1968). *An introduction to the analysis of educational concepts*. Reading, MA: Addison-Wesley.

Spring, J. (1976). *The sorting machine: National educational policy since 1945*. New York: McKay.

Spring, J. (1984). Education and the Sony war. *Phi Delta Kappan, 65*(8), 534–537.

Spring, J. (1988). *Conflict of interests, the politics of American education*. New York: Longman.

Stamler, M. (1987, Sept. 12). Football nets city big bucks. *The Capital Times*, p. 1.

Stanic, G. (1987). Mathematics education in the United States at the beginning of the 20th century. In T. Popkewitz (Ed.), *The formation of school subjects: The struggle for creating an American institution* (pp. 145–175). New York: Falmer.

Stedman, L., & Smith, M. (1983). Recent reform proposals for American education, *Contemporary Education Review, 2*(2), 85–104.

Steinfels, P. (1989, March 19). Public schools put faith in religious studies. *Wisconsin State Journal*, p. 1.

Stephens, W. M. (1982). *Mathematical knowledge and school work: A case study of the teaching of developing mathematical processes*. Wisconsin Center for Education Research, Madison.

Stevens, W. (1988, March 22). Governors are emerging as a new political elite. *The New York Times*, p. 8.

St. Maurice, H. (1987). Clinical supervision and power: Regimes of instructional management. In T. Popkewitz (Ed.), *Critical studies in teacher education: Its folklore, theory and practice* (pp. 242–264). New York: Falmer.

Stoianovich, T. (1976). *French historical method, The* Annales *paradigm*. Ithaca: Cornell University Press.

Streibel, M. (1989). Instructional plans and situated learning: The challenge Suchman's theory of situated action for instructional designers and instructional systems. *Journal of Visual Literacy, 9*(2), 8–40.

Strober, M., & Tyack, D. (1980). Why do women teach and men manage? A report on research on schools. *Signs, 5*(3), 494–503.

Tabachnick, B. R., & Zeichner, K. M. (1991). *Issues and practices in inquiry-oriented teacher education*. New York: Falmer.

Task Force on Education for Economic Growth. (1983). *Action for excellence*. Denver, CO: Education Commission of the States.

Teach for America. (1990). *Teach for America*. New York: Author.

Thorndike, E. (1910). *Educational psychology* (2nd ed.). New York: Teachers College, Columbia University.

Tiles, M. (1984). *Bachelard: Science and objectivity*. Cambridge, UK: Cambridge University Press.

Time for results: The governors' 1991 report on education. (1986). Washington, DC: National Governors Association for Policy Research Analysis.

Tlusty, R. (1986). *Curriculum transformation as social history: Eau Claire High School 1890–1920*. Unpublished doctoral dissertation, University of Wisconsin, Madison.

Tom, A. (1984). *Teaching as a moral craft*. New York: Longman.

Torres, C. (1989). The capitalist state and public policy formation. Framework for a political sociology of educational policy making. *British Journal of Sociology of Education, 10*(1), 81–102.

Toulmin, S. (1988). The recovery of practical philosophy. *The American Scholar*, Summer, 337–352.

Trachtman, R. (1989). The new kid on the legislative block: The private sector and the politics of education. *Educational Horizons, 67*(Fall/Winter), 42–46.

Turner, M. (1989, April). *The politics of founding black high schools in the South: A case study of Atlanta and Augusta*. Paper presented at the annual meeting of the American Education Research Association Meeting, San Francisco.

Twentieth Century Fund Task Force on Federal Elementary and Secondary Education Policy. (1983). *Making the grade*. New York: Author.

Tyack, D. (1974). *The one best system. A history of American urban education*. Cambridge, MA: Harvard University Press.

Tyack, D., & Hansot, E. (1982). *Managers of virtue: Public school leadership in America, 1820–1980*. New York: Basic Books.

Urban, W. (1982). *Why teachers organized*. Detroit, MI: Wayne State University Press.

U.S. Department of Education. (1986). *What works: Research about teaching and learning*. Washington, DC: Author.

U.S. Department of Education. (1987). *What works: Schools that work, educating disadvantaged children*. Washington, DC: Author.

U.S. Department of Labor. (1986). Worklife estimates: *Effects of race and education*. Washington, DC: Author.

U.S. National Commission on Excellence in Education. (1983). *A nation at risk:*

The imperative of educational reform. Washington, DC: U.S. Government Printing Office.

Veysey, L. (1965). *The emergence of the American university*. Chicago: University of Chicago Press.

Vygotsky, L. S. (1978). *Mind in society: The development of higher psychological process* (M. Cole, V. John-Steiner, S. Scribner, & E. Souberman, Eds.). Cambridge, MA: Harvard University Press.

Walker, J. (1987). Democracy and pragmatism in curriculum development. *Educational Philosophy and Theory, 19*(2), 1–9.

Walters, R. (1978). *American reformers, 1815–1860*. New York: Hill & Wang.

Ward, L. (1915). *Pure sociology* (2nd ed.). New York: Macmillan.

Weber, M. (1958). *The Protestant ethic and the spirit of capitalism: The relationships between religion and the economic and social life in modern culture*. (T. Parsons, Trans.). New York: Scribner. (Original work published 1904–5)

Weedon, C. (1987). *Feminist practice and poststructural theory*. London: Blackwell.

Weick, K. (1976). Educational organizations as loosely coupled systems. *Administrative Science Quarterly, 21*, 1–19.

Weiler, H. (1989, May). *Decentralization in educational governance: An exercise in contradiction?* Paper presented at "EMIL"—A Norwegian Project on A National Evaluation and The Quality of Education convention; The Norwegian Research Council for Applied Social Science; Oslo, Norway.

Wells, A. (1989, Jan. 4). Backers of school change turn to sociologists. *The New York Times*, p. 17.

West, C. (1989). *The American evasion of philosophy, a genealogy of pragmatism*. Madison: University of Wisconsin Press.

Westbury, I. (1984). A nation at risk: An essay review. *Journal of Curriculum Studies, 16*, 431–445.

Westbury, I. (1990). Textbooks, textbooks publishers, and the quality of schooling. In D. Elliott & A. Woodward (Eds.), *Textbooks and schooling in the United States (89th yearbook)* (pp. 1–22). Chicago, IL: National Society for the Study of Education.

Wexler, P. (1987). *Social analysis of education; after the new sociology*. New York: Routledge & Kegan Paul.

Wheatley, S. (1988). *The politics of philanthropy: Abraham Flexner and medical education*. Madison: University of Wisconsin Press.

Whitty, G. (1985). *Sociology and school knowledge: Curriculum theory, research and politics*. London: Methuen.

Williams, R. (1965). *The long revolution*. Harmondsworth, UK: Penguin.

Wilson, S., & Wineburg, S. (1988). Peering at history through different lenses: The role of disciplinary perspectives in teaching history. *Teachers College Record, 89*(4), 525–541.

Wisconsin Department of Public Instruction. (1984, January) *Final report of the State Superintendents Task Force on Teaching and Teacher Education* (Bulletin No. 4250). Madison, WI: Author.

Wisconsin Department of Public Instruction. (1988). *Teacher education program approval rules and appeal procedures PI 4*. Madison, WI: Author.

Wisconsin Department of Public Instruction. (1990). *Proposal order of the state superintendent of public instruction creating/amending rules* (March 15, draft). Madison, WI: Author.

Wittgenstein, L. (1966). *The philosophical investigations: A collection of critical essays* (G. Pitcher, Ed.). Notre Dame, IN: University of Notre Dame Press. (Original work published 1953)

Wittrock, B. (1988). Rise and development of the modern state: Democracy in context. In D. Sainsbury (Ed.), *Democracy, state and justice* (pp. 113–126). Stockholm, Sweden: Almqvist & Wiksell International.

Wittrock, B., & Elzinga, A. (Eds.). (1985). *The university research system, the public policies of the home of scientists.* Stockholm, Sweden: Almquist & Wiksell International.

Wittrock, B., & Wagner, P. (1988). *Social science and state developments: The structuration of discourse in the social sciences.* Paper presented at the XIVth World Congress of the International Political Science Association, Washington, DC.

Woodward, A. (1987, April). *From professional teachers to activity managers: The changing role of the reading teachers' guide, 1930–1986.* Paper presented at the annual meeting of the American Educational Research Association, Washington, DC.

Wygant, F. (1983). *Art in American schools in the nineteenth century.* Cincinnati, OH: Interwood Press.

Young, M. (1971). *Knowledge and control.* London: Macmillan, Collier.

Zolberg, A. (1989, May). *Bounded states in a global market: From the vantage point of international migration.* Paper presented at Social Theory and Its Emerging Issues in a Changing Society symposium, University of Chicago.

Index

Abelson, R., 173
Abrams, P., 40
Accountability, 212–213
Adler, M., 149, 151, 152, 155, 156, 253*n*
Adolescence (Hall), 97
Advertising, 108
Alba, J., 173
Alcoff, L., 238
Alexander, L., 120
Almond, G., 34
Altbach, P., 234
American Behavioral Scientist, The, 139
American Economics Association, 88–90
American Federation of Teachers, 127
American Institute of Instruction, 71–72
American Journal of Education, The, 71
American Psychological Association (APA),
    97, 223–224
American Social Science Association (ASSA),
    70, 87–88
Anderson, C., 169
Annales, 5–7, 27–29
Anthropology, 201
Apperception, 72–73
Apple, M., 14
Archer, M. S., 249*n*
Ariès, P., 251*n*
Art education, 60–61
Ashenden, D., 26
At-risk students, 109, 129, 156, 196–198
Authority, attitudes to, in mass schooling,
    56–60
Autonomy, 241–243, 245

Bachelard, Gaston, 30
Bacon, Francis, 35, 40
Badie, B., 250*n*

Bagley, William Chandler, 98
Ball, D., 168, 169, 174, 184
Barnard, Frederick, 67, 68, 72
Baroque period, 28–29
Bartlett, F. C., 177
Bazerman, C., 223
Beck, E. T., 183
Beechey, V., 183
Begel, Simon, 140
Behaviorism, 95, 156, 170–172, 183, 220
Bell, Andrew, 58
Bell, Daniel, 138
Bellack, Arnold, 211
Bellah, R., 50, 250*n*
Berger, B., 19, 32
Berger, Peter, 9, 19, 32, 61, 94, 111, 249*n*
Berman, E., 126
Berman, M., 256*n*
Berman, R., 18
Bernstein, B., 180
Bestor, Arthur, 136, 140
Birnbaum, P., 250*n*
Blacks, 107, 181
    economic concerns of, 111
    mass schooling and, 51
Blau, P. M., 21
Bledstein, B., 46, 69, 82
Bloch, M., 27, 70, 99
Block, F., 250*n*
Boli, J., 42, 62
Borden Act (1946), 108
Bourdieu, Pierre, 5–7, 24, 26–27, 30, 40–41,
    112, 157, 190, 192, 201–202, 225, 227,
    234, 237–238, 241–242, 249*n*, 254*n*, 255*n*
Bové, P., 245
Boyer, E., 149–150, 153, 155, 253*n*
Bransford, J., 173

About the Author

Thomas S. Popkewitz is a professor of curriculum and instruction at the University of Wisconsin–Madison and a faculty associate at the Wisconsin Center for Education Research. His research concerning the problems and issues of school reform, teaching, and teacher education has appeared in scholarly journals in the United States, Australia, and Europe. He is co-author, with Robert Tabachnick and Gary Wehlage, of *The Myth of Educational Reform* (University of Wisconsin Press, 1982), a study of the impact of a national elementary school reform program, and has edited numerous books on historical, social, and methodological issues in the study of change. His book *Paradigm and Ideology in Educational Research* (Falmer, 1984), which focuses on the relation of social and philosophical assumptions in educational research, was cited by the American Educational Studies Association as "one of the outstanding books in education in recent years." This book and *Critical Studies in Teacher Education* (Falmer, 1987) have been translated into Spanish. He has also published articles in Hungary, Norway, and the Soviet Union. He has been a fellow at the Swedish Collegium for Advanced Studies in Social Science and received an honorary doctorate for his contribution to scholarship in studies of educational reform and research (Umeå Universitet, Sweden, 1989).

He has been project director and principal investigator in national evaluations of school reform and teacher education, including national studies of the impact of Teacher Corps intern programs, individually guided education, and the Ford Foundation's Urban Mathematics Collaborative. He has lectured on problems of studying educational reform in Europe, Asia, and Australia. Currently, he is studying alternative teacher educational programs in the United States and directing a project on the relation of educational research, educational researchers, and social movements in ten countries.